# SIGNATURE
# MORMON CLASSICS

Drawing on a rich literary heritage, Signature Books is pleased to make available a new series of classic Mormon works reprinted with specially commissioned introductions. Each book has left an indelible impression on the LDS Church and its members, while also having influenced non-Mormon perceptions of the Saints. The authors, whether inside or outside observers, occupy an important place in the development of LDS culture and identity. The re-issue of their works offers readers today an opportunity to better appreciate the origins and growth of a major religious and social movement.

SIGNATURE MORMON CLASSICS

# Robert N. Baskin

*Reminiscences of Early Utah*

with

*Reply to Certain Statements
by O. F. Whitney*

*foreword by*
Brigham D. Madsen

SIGNATURE BOOKS 🐾 SALT LAKE CITY 🐾 2006

## A NOTE ON THE TEXT

Except for the front matter and foreword, this Signature Mormon Classics edition is an exact reprint of *Reminiscences of Early Utah,* published in 1914 by the Tribune-Reporter Printer Company, Salt Lake City, Utah, and *Reply to Certain Statements by O. F. Whitney in His History of Utah,* published in 1916 by Lakeside Printing Company, Salt Lake City. Both works were authored by Robert Newton Baskin, who is noted on the title page to *Reminiscences* as being "an Ex-Chief Justice of the Supreme Court of Utah."

*Reminiscences of Early Utah,* ©R. N. Baskin 1914
*Reply to Certain Statements by O. F. Whitney,* ©R. N. Baskin, 1916

Signature Books Classics reprint edition with a foreword by Brigham D. Madsen, ©Signature Books, 2006. Signature Books is a registered trademark of Signature Books Publishing, LLC. All rights reserved.

www.signaturebooks.com


**Library of Congress Cataloging-in-Publication Data**
Baskin, R. N. (Robert Newton), b. 1835.
   Reminiscences of early Utah;. with, "Reply to certain statements by O. F. Whitney" / by Robert N. Baskin ; foreword by Brigham D. Madsen.
      p. cm. — (Signature Mormon classics)
   First work originally published: Salt Lake City : Tribune Reporter, 1914; 2nd work originally published: Salt Lake City : Lakeside Print. Co., 1916.
   Includes bibliographical references and index.
   ISBN 10: 1-56085-193-7 (pbk.)
   ISBN 13: 978-1-56085-193-6 (pbk.)
   1. Utah—History—19th century. 2. Mormons—Utah—History—19th century. 3. Frontier and pioneer life—Utah. 4. Whitney, Orson F. (Orson Ferguson), 1855-1931. Popular history of Utah. I. Madsen, Brigham D. II. Baskin, R. N. (Robert Newton), b. 1835. Reply to certain statements by O. F. Whitney. III. Title. IV. Title: Reply to certain statements by O. F. Whitney.

F826.B32 2006
979.02'02—dc22
                                           2006045811

# TABLE OF CONTENTS

v

TABLE OF CONTENTS

# FOREWORD

*Brigham D. Madsen*

On a glorious first of June 1901, Salt Lake City was awakened at dawn by a 100-gun salute, followed by a performance by the old Nauvoo Legion martial band. In the afternoon, church and government leaders gathered at the Saltair resort to honor the hundredth-year birthday of Brigham Young, the frontier dynamo who had dominated the American West for three decades. Three of his widows attended, including Amelia Folsom, his last "favorite wife," and one of his former slaves, Uncle Green Flake, as well as Governor Heber M. Wells and leaders of the Church of Jesus Christ of Latter-day Saints. Bishop Orson F. Whitney gave the opening prayer, followed by a xylophone solo from Professor Adelbert Beesley. Messrs. Clawson and Margetts entertained the throng with a comic duet. David McKenzie, who had served time in 1859 for counterfeiting warrants on the Young estate, was the master of ceremonies.[1]

Governor Wells spoke first, followed by Professor James E. Talmage and Apostle Heber J. Grant. However, the most remarkable speech came, not from one of the late LDS prophet's most devoted disciples, but instead from Utah Supreme Court Justice Robert N. Baskin, who Apostle George Q. Cannon had once denounced as "one of the worst enemies the people had." Baskin said the invitation showed how much conditions in Utah had changed and that "he was glad of it,"[2] that he had "no patience with those on both sides who were trying to stir up the prejudices of the people." According to the Mormon press, Baskin "thought it would be better for all to shut their eyes to the past and look forward to the future."[3]

Over the next dozen years, this era of good feeling between the state's majority and minority populations came to an end, the conflict between church and state re-igniting and intensifying.

Baskin himself found good reason to rethink his position in light
of the fact that Mormon historians asserted themselves with an extremely partisan approach to the state's history—a trend that
would persist for half a century. As Baskin explained in the preface
to *Reminiscences of Early Utah,* his book would expose the "glaringly false statements in [Orson F.] Whitney's *History of Utah"* and
defend federal officials in the territory who had been "besmirched
by him." To understand the highly charged atmosphere that existed between the strongly sectarian Whitney and "gentile" Baskin,
it is essential to examine their backgrounds and the motivations
that excited each man.[4]

Robert Newton Baskin was born on December 20, 1837, in
Hillsboro, Ohio. He attended Salem Academy, near Chillicothe,
Ohio, and then began his study of law with the firm of James H.
Thompson in Salem, Ohio. After two years, he left to pursue for-
mal legal education at Harvard University, from which he gradu-
ated and then returned home to begin a law partnership in Salem
with a Colonel Collins. In 1865, just after the Civil War, Baskin
left Ohio and, on his way to California, stopped in Salt Lake City.[5]

George A. Townsend, a reporter for the *Cincinnati Commercial,* wrote from the Mormon capital in 1871 that Baskin was rumored "to have shot somebody in Ohio."[6] Townsend's reports,
which were collected in a pamphlet titled *The Mormon Trials at
Salt Lake City,* had nothing good to say about any non-Mormons
in Utah but affectionately described Porter Rockwell, Brigham
Young's notorious bodyguard, as "a fat, curly-haired, good-natured
chap." Townsend dedicated his pamphlet to Young's son-in-law
William H. Hooper, territorial delegate to Congress, suggesting
the reporter probably benefitted from the tens of thousands of dollars the Mormon Church spent to buy favorable press between
1858 and 1896. Much of the most colorful information we have
about the young gentile attorney from Ohio comes from Townsend's unsympathetic reports.

The *Salt Lake Tribune's* later biographical sketch said nothing
about Baskin's alleged career as a gunslinger, noting merely that
after a few days in Salt Lake City he met Thomas Hearst, son of cel-

ebrated attorney William Hearst. With Hearst as his guide, Baskin visited the Little Cottonwood mining district, saw the possibility of making a fortune in minerals, and decided "to cast his lot in Utah." He established a law office in Salt Lake City and began the study of territorial statutes, which led to his role as a critic and denouncer of the economic and political control exercised by the LDS Church's leadership.[7] For the next thirty years, he held a prominent position with the area's non-Mormon population as they battled against polygamy and political and economic hegemony and for more equality for the minority population.

Townsend described Baskin (consistently misspelling his name as "Baskins") as "a lean, lank, rather dirty and frowsy, red-headed young man, but a lawyer of shrewdness and coolness, and inflamed against Mormonism." He added that the lawyer got "his redhot temper from his hair." Baskin did have a temper, as demonstrated in an altercation he had with the territorial Associate Justice, C. M. Hawley, in 1871. Townsend's description of the fracas deserves quoting. Hawley presented Baskin with a ruling that was not to the attorney's liking, and

> Baskins threw the paper on the floor, and ground it with his boot-heel into an inoffensive tobacco quid. The Judge, who is slender, conscious, and respects himself and his rulings, told Mr. Baskins he would fine him. "Go ahead with your fine," said Baskins, "you're of no account."
>
> The Judge fined Baskins one hundred dollars and sent him to Camp Douglas for ten days. Baskins twitched the order out of the Judge's hands and said that being an "old granny" the Judge should forthwith be kicked down stairs. At this Baskins threw open the door to expedite the descent of the venerable man, and rushed upon him, like Damon upon Lucullus. The Marshal interposed to save the author of so many learned and long opinions, and Baskins went to the Camp in custody. But as this notable Bench in Utah never consult together, [Associate Justice Obed F.] Strickland agreeing with [Chief Justice James B.] McKean in everything and Hawley in nothing, Judge McKean let Baskins out *habeas corpus* in four days, and Baskins disdained to pay his

fine. It is Baskins, therefore, who insists, as Prosecuting Attorney, that the laws of the United States and the Courts thereof must be respected in Utah.[8]

Baskin's contempt for plural marriage was so intense, he said in a speech before McKean's court, "If Joseph Smith had been a eunuch he would never have received the revelation on polygamy." The Mormon reply was that a man who had helped his wife obtain a divorce from her previous husband should not opine on other people's marital arrangements. Both sides engaged freely in this kind of *ad hominem* and plain language that was so typical of frontier society.[9] Much later, after agreeing to let bygones be bygones, the Mormon *Deseret News,* in its obituary of Baskin, commented that "he was not of the amiable, social temperament that makes friends everywhere" but that his better qualities "bound him to his intimate friends."[10] Journalist John Hanson Beadle added that he was the type who "did not know the word fail and would never give up beaten while there was a chance of success."[11]

Baskin was indeed, as Townsend charged, "inflamed against Mormonism," and even his political supporter, Colonel Joslyn, conceded that he was a "bitter man."[12] Baskin did have his reasons, as he asserted in his *Reminiscences.* For instance, when he represented a Dr. J. King Robinson, described as "an educated gentleman of courteous manners and affable disposition," in a dispute with the Salt Lake police, Robinson was suddenly brutally murdered at the corner of Main and Third in the middle of the night while on an errand of mercy. Looking at the mutilated body, Baskin resolved "to do all that I possibly could do to place in the hands of the federal authorities the power to punish the perpetrators of such heinous crimes." Mormon theocracy thereby acquired its most dedicated enemy.

Baskin fought his battles aggressively, with an extremism that led to his announcement in April 1877 that "unless the question [of Mormon control in Utah] is settled by appropriate legislation, it will be settled at the point of the bayonet and blood will flow." Mormons returned fire. The *Deseret News* said Baskin should rather repent of his sins and be baptized for their remission. On Joseph Smith's birthday in 1890, Abraham H. Cannon noted in his diary Apostle Joseph F. Smith's prayer "that Baskin should be made blind, deaf and dumb unless he would repent of his wickedness."[13] Baskin vented his anger in 1877 in an altercation with District Attorney Sumner Howard. "These two gentlemen being unable to see eye to eye and failing to convince each other by the peaceful means of logical reasoning, resorted to the knock down style of argument, fists and canes being the implements of war brought into requisition," the *Deseret News* reported. Both men survived without serious injury, although Howard's cane was broken by its "sudden and forcible contact with such an exceedingly hard substance as the *corpus* of his antagonist," the paper reported.[14]

In another typical insult, the *Deseret News* described Baskin as "overbearing and insolent," wholly ignorant of "correct deportment."[15] But again, Baskin provided the paper with plenty of fodder for its characterization of him. In an exchange with attorney Thomas Fitch, the latter said he was happy the guns at Fort Douglas were not trained on the city and that the military had not besieged city hall.

> *Mr. Baskin:* "That would have been my way to do it."
> *Mr. Fitch:* "I presume that Mr. Baskin would have knocked the City Hall and City Jail down."
> *Mr. Baskin:* "I would that."[16]

When speaking to more sympathetic audiences outside the city in mining communities, Baskin would often lay out his principal charges against the state's religious leaders, that they expected to be followed unquestioningly, thereby leading to "all manner of wickedness and abomination"; they refused to employ non-Mormons; and were generally un-American, which led him to think they should therefore not be allowed to hold office or vote.[17] Among the Latter-day Saints were some who were receptive to such themes and detected in these orations an inspirational note. Edward Tullidge reported that, among a number of speeches on one occasion in 1871, Baskin's had been "the ablest effort of the day."[18] It all depended on whose ox was being gored.

Where was Brigham Young during all this time? He was, in fact, prominently giving as well as he received, once calling Baskin a "pettifoger."[19] When the Cullom anti-polygamy bill was proposed, Young conceived the idea of organizing "female indignation meetings" and said he wished the government would give Baskin "some lick-spittle office here" so "our sisters [c]ould ... show him his walking-papers in the shape of a forest of broomsticks."[20] Even so, after the Woodruff Manifesto advised against polygamy in 1890, Baskin could claim he had agreed with Young about "everything but polygamy."[21]

This picture of a too-often pugnacious and angry man and bitter Mormon hater must be tempered with the acknowledgment that, when calm, Baskin could be judicious and even magnanimous. In 1870, when the gentiles of Corinne, Utah, proposed the annexation of northern Utah—everything north of the forty-first degree latitude—to Idaho Territory, Baskin testified to a Congressional committee that it was a hare-brained idea because it would break up the natural community formed by the Great Basin's geographic boundaries.[22] A reporter for the LDS *Young Woman's Journal* conceded that "while Mr. Baskin may be set in his ways and have opinions on certain subjects that nothing on earth could change, yet he is a good parliamentarian and his judgment on matters relating to law and judiciary is generally sound." The journalist was nonetheless critical of his tendency toward "flying machine oratory."[23] Mormon apostle John Henry Smith said he had always respected Baskin for his honesty despite the fact that Baskin had fought the Mormons "as viciously as any man ever did."[24]

Perhaps the best statement concerning Baskin's occasional calm judgment about Mormon practices came when he testified before the Committee on Territories in the U.S. House of Representatives: "I have been for five years past a resident of Utah. I must do the Mormons the justice to say that the question of religion does not enter into their courts in ordinary cases. I have never detected any bias on the part of jurors there in this respect, as I at first expected. I have appeared in cases where Mormons and Gentiles were opposing parties, and saw, much to my surprise, the jury do what was right." While quoting the above, the *Deseret News* could not avoid speculating that Baskin had probably perjured himself in this sworn statement.[25] Mormon antipathy to Baskin ran very deep.

Orson Ferguson Whitney, leading antagonist of Baskin and his circle, had come by his convictions from his Mormon parents who were descendants of the earliest church elite. Helen Mar Kimball Whitney, his mother, was a daughter of Heber C. Kimball and for a short time a polygamous wife of Joseph Smith. Orson's father, Horace K. Whitney, himself the son of early bishop Newel K. Whitney, was a leading citizen of Salt Lake City with a particular interest in drama and the arts.[26]

Orson was born in the Mormon capital on July 1, 1855, and spent his early years there. As a youth, he worked as a section hand on the Union Pacific railroad, a clerk in both a music store and mercantile establishment, and as a sewing machine salesman in southern Utah. He attended a few sessions at the University of Deseret but did not graduate, wanting instead to follow his real passion in the theater and perhaps a stage career in New York City. But he was called as a missionary to the eastern states in 1876, and during the seventeen months of his mission he acquired a new focus, including a lifelong interest in writing poetry. On his return home, he became bishop of the Salt Lake 18th Ward despite being only twenty-three years old and not yet married. He served in that capacity, as bishop, for twenty-eight years.[27]

He was soon named city editor of the *Deseret News*, which brought him some prominence and a connection to the church leadership. He further cemented his connection to the church when he married Zina Smoot, daughter of a prominent Mormon stake president, Abraham O. Smoot, and sister of the even more famous future U.S. Senator Reed Smoot. Whitney's public reputation was also enhanced through his poetry and public speeches, as well as by the fact that he periodically accepted roles in the theater.[28] When a *Tribune* reviewer criticized his thespian ability, the sensitive actor attributed this to an anti-Mormon bias.[29]

In 1881, Whitney was sent to England on a second mission to

edit the *Latter-day Saints' Millennial Star,* but the death of one of his children brought him back to Utah in 1883. Resuming his position at the *Deseret News,* he spent much of his energy during the next few years writing and speaking against the federal anti-polygamy Edmunds Act of 1882. This is what brought him into close conflict with the bill's chief supporter, Robert N. Baskin. In 1884, Whitney left his *Deseret News* job to become Salt Lake City treasurer and was honored by being appointed a regent of the University of Deseret, of which he became chancellor in March 1884.[30]

As the national anti-polygamy campaign gained momentum, Whitney emerged as the public voice of the LDS Church in the absence of Mormon leaders, who were away hiding on the "underground" to avoid federal authorities.[31] Whitney courted arrest himself by marrying a second wife. The details of this marriage are worth noting:

> If one of the unexpressed reasons for allowing Bishop Whitney to represent "the brethren" in public was the fact that he himself was a monogamist, that condition changed in 1888. It was on his birthday that year, July 1, that his wife Zina gave him an unusual birthday present. It was a Sunday morning. She entered his bedroom, awakened him, knelt by his bed, kissed him and gave her permission for him to take as a plural wife May Wells, daughter of President Daniel H. Wells of the First Presidency. Later Whitney went to the Tabernacle for a meeting. When he returned he discovered May Wells sitting in the parlor while Zina was preparing dinner. "I was more than surprised—I was amazed," Whitney later wrote, "for I knew how tender [Zina's] feelings were, and realized in part what this generous act must have involved. Never had I admired her so much. She looked more like an angel than a mortal. Tearfully I drew her to me, saying, "You never do things by halves, do you, Dear?" She answered sweetly: "When I asked you whom you wanted to dinner, you said, 'the members of my family.' They are here." Twenty-three days later Orson and May were married in Diaz, Mexico, with Zina present and repeating her consent.[32]

FOREWORD

Baskin would never understand the logic of such a marital union, nor would the majority of Mormons ever become entirely comfortable with it—even less so their gentile neighbors.

The financial problems associated with providing for two families became acute in 1890 when Whitney lost his job as city treasurer because the non-Mormon Liberal Party won the election. He found help from an unexpected source when the LDS church accepted an offer from Dr. John O. Williams to publish a multi-volume history of the territory by an author of the church's choosing. This was an era of commercial publishing ventures aimed at dollar profits and inoffensive content. In fact, a biographical volume was conceived to round out the offering, the assumption being that those whose lives were profiled would purchase copies for themselves and their friends. Whitney was hired at $200 per month, his second wife employed as his secretary at an additional $50 per month.[33]

In 1892 the first volume in this massive *History of Utah* appeared, followed the next year by a second volume, the third in 1898, and the final biographical tome in 1904. The narrative began with the early life of Joseph Smith and ended with the Woodruff Manifesto.[34] In 1941, Catholic historian Robert Joseph Dwyer wrote that "with all its faults and inaccuracies—and they are legion—that work has not yet been superseded."[35] Woodruff Thomson agreed eight years later that Whitney's work remained "the great storehouse of data on Utah history to 1890."[36] The explosion of research and writing about the history of Utah since World War II tempered that assessment, but Whitney's work still proves useful as a reference tool.

The series had five major deficiencies: (1) no footnotes indicating source material; (2) an absence of primary documentation; (3) a polemical slant in favor of Mormon interpretations; (4) an oratorical, almost emotional style; and (5) inaccuracies, which were quickly exposed by critics like Baskin.[37] Undaunted, Whitney produced an additional one-volume work in 1916 entitled *Popular History of Utah*, designed to reach the attention and pocketbooks of average citizens and serve as a textbook. It elicited an even more vitriolic attack from Baskin.[38] Nor was Baskin content to let his 1914 *Reminiscences* stand as an answer to Whitney's four volumes. In high indignation, the non-Mormon observer of Utah's development published a second work, this time more of a pamphlet, to destroy once and for all the Mormon writer's "duplicity and falsification of history, … [which] impels me to answer each of his groundless aspersions." Baskin entitled his twenty-nine-page essay *Reply to Certain Statements by O. F. Whitney*.[39]

Perhaps as he began his treatise, the various insults issued by Whitney, whose latest history was still fresh in Baskin's mind, provided grounds for the kind of anger and personal affront for which the non-Mormon jurist was known. Whitney had alluded to the author of *Reminiscences* as a "Bourbon of the dead past, who 'learns nothing' and 'forgets nothing.'" Whitney let out all the stops, writing that Baskin's reminiscences were:

> largely a rehash of stale anti-"Mormon" stories, based upon the testimony of apostates, jail-birds, and self confessed murders. He complains of inaccuracies in other writings, while his own book fairly bristles with them. It abounds in coarse abuse and venomous vituperation. Under pretense of correcting alleged mis[s]tatements of history, he vents his personal spleen, and pours the vitriol of his implacable hatred upon "Mormons" and "Mormonism" in general.[40]

Baskin could take comfort at least in having been excoriated in excellent prose. As will be seen, he would return the favor with equally impressive Harvard English.

Whitney's charge that Baskin's recollection bristled with errors was partly justified, but the inaccuracies were mostly trivial and probably reflected an aging memory. Baskin recalled United States Attorney Sumner Howard as William Howard; the "northern route" from Salt Lake did not connect to the California Trail "by way of Soda Springs" as he said, but rather at City of Rocks; Arkansas Senator James H. Berry's speech describing the return of the Mountain Meadows orphans to Carroll County was not in the *Congressional Record* of February 12, 1907; and Tecumseh Sherman sent the threatening telegram to Brigham Young before, not after, the murder of Dr. Robinson. A more serious failure was Baskin's lack of knowledge about Utah Indians. He attributed the human skeletons "exhumed in various parts of the city" to the Danites when, in fact, most probably came from Indian burials. More seriously, he vigorously exposed the slander of the victims of Mountain Meadows but not the absurdity and injustice of blaming the massacre on the Paiutes. As a man of his time, Baskin preferred to believe it was the Indians who murdered the women and children of the Fancher Party, but as Nephi Johnson finally confessed to an apostle, "white men did most of the killing."

Both in his *Reminiscences* and *Reply,* Baskin chose to criticize his opponent for his analysis of five historical topics: the Mormon Battalion, the causes of factional strife within the territory, the Mountain Meadows Massacre, anti-polygamy legislation and raids, and Danite death squads. His *Reply* was forceful and denunciatory, as his *Reminiscences* had been on these subjects.

He first undertook to prove that Brigham Young had sought government aid for the move west in 1846 and had relied on the Mormon Battalion payroll to help finance the trek to the mountains. There was no coercion in this; only later, during the emotional excitement of the Utah War, did the Mormon leader charge the government with trying to injure his people. In September 1857, Young lectured his followers in a speech in Salt Lake City: "There cannot be a more damnable, dastardly order than was issued by the [federal] administration to this people ... in 1846 ... while we were doing our best to leave their borders[,] [and] the poor, low, degraded cusses sent a requisition for five hundred of our men to go and fight their battles. That was President Polk, and he is now weltering in hell with old Zachariah Taylor."[41] Whitney perpetuated the myth of persecution by the federal government. As Baskin pointed out, Mormon historian Brigham H. Roberts had corrected the record in rather forceful language in a July 4 address in 1911, stating that the enrollment of the battalion had been what Brigham Young wanted. This was confirmed by diary entries from John Taylor and Wilford Woodruff.[42]

Incidentally, the recent splendid history of the Mormon Battalion by Norma Baldwin Rickets confirmed Baskin's position. She demonstrated definitively that Young solicited help from the government and urged Mormon men to enlist. She cites Young's written comments of April 5, 1848, that Mormon enlistment, "though looked upon with astonishment and some with fear, has proved a great blessing to this community. It was indeed the temporal salvation of our camp."[43] Baskin is thereby vindicated while Whitney remains, in this instance, somewhat reckless, whether deliberately or perhaps simply because of inadequate research.

The two antagonists agreed to disagree about the causes for the factional strife between Mormons and gentiles in Utah during the nineteenth century. Whitney pointed to the federal tendency, which he called "un-American," of "sending strangers to rule over communities with which they have little or nothing in common." Whitney's solution was to rely on local government to solve the problems faced by Utahns. Baskin's answer was a single "Pish!"[44] The pugnacious Baskin asserted that the causes for the turmoil were the domination of local affairs by the Mormon priesthood and attempts to drive from the territory "all who were not connected with them (the Mormon sect) in communion and sympathy." The final irritants in this regard were "the pernicious acts passed by the Mormon Legislature for the purpose of receiving immunity to polygamy and other heinous crimes."

To legitimize and strengthen these charges, Baskin quoted from the annual messages of U.S. Presidents Buchanan, Grant, Hayes, and Cleveland, all of whom had assailed the Mormons for making Brigham Young governor by "Divine Appointment"; for continuing to practice polygamy, "a remnant of barbarism repugnant to civilization"; by controlling grand and petit juries; and by making the Mormon kingdom of God superior to any earthly government, especially that of the United States. To remove what was the most obnoxious element of Mormonism, Baskin himself drafted the Cullom Bill, hoping to destroy polygamy for all time. This was an exercise that made him "very proud."[45]

Baskin took particular exception to Whitney's charge that he was one of the chief leaders of an "anti-Mormon Ring" operating from the "Wahsatch Club" in Salt Lake City. The Mormon historian cited the ubiquitous *Cincinnati Commercial* correspondent, George Townsend, who listed the following gentile leaders of an alleged cabal: Utah Chief Justice J. B. McKean; R. N. Baskin; George A. Maxwell, a former military officer from Michigan; U.S. Assessor J. P. Taggart; U.S. Collector O. J. Hollister; *Corinne Reporter* editor Dennis J. Toohy; *Salt Lake Review* publisher Frank Kenyon, "a paper which has superseded the *Salt Lake Tribune* in irritating the Mormons"; Utah Associate Justice C. M. Hawley; the judge's son, C. M. Hawley Jr.; Secretary of the Territory George A. Black; and Utah Governor George L. Woods, someone the reporter characterized as having "little mental 'heft.'"[46]

The derogatory jab at the *Salt Lake Tribune* reflected a long-term animosity between the Mormon *Deseret News* and the gentile *Tribune*, which lasted from 1871 until a truce was declared just before World War I. The editor of the *Deseret News* would have smiled at a blast delivered by another ally of the Mormon cause, the *Salt Lake Herald*:

> And so Baskin has a spark of self-respect left when he gets away from Utah and mixes with respectable people. Here in Utah Mr. Baskin recognizes our unesteemed morning [daily, the *Salt Lake Tribune*]; ... [H]e swears by the *Tribune,* he quotes it and upholds it financially and in its policy; but in Washington he understands how disreputable a thing his newspaper is, and he openly repudiates it, and begs not to be held in any way responsible for the slander it circulates.[47]

The *Deseret News* leveled similar criticism,[48] to which the *Tribune* responded in kind, defending Baskin as its leading protagonist.

During his early years in Utah, Baskin would have had difficulty persuading his Mormon neighbors that he was their friend as he became prominent in the anti-Mormon political group soon known as the Liberal Party. Even before the Liberals were formally organized, Baskin participated in a meeting of gentiles on January 30, 1867, to nominate a delegate to Congress. His longtime rival for recognition as a political organizer, retired Major General P. Edward Connor, was elected president of the convention. Nevertheless, Baskin took charge and called the meeting to order. Attorney William McGroarty was nominated at the meeting and received 105 votes in the general election, compared to the 15,068 received by the Mormon candidate, William H. Hooper.[49]

Three years later the Liberal Party was officially organized in the small railroad town of Corinne. Newspaper editor Dennis Toohy invited people to convene on "Patriots Day," July 4, 1870, and nominate a candidate for the office of Territorial Delegate. The initial meeting "broke up in a general row" over a split between uncompromising anti-Mormons and followers of Mormon apostate William S. Godbe who opposed "Brighamites" for political and economic reasons but wanted to retain their plural wives. A successful convention finally met on July 16 and nominated General George R. Maxwell as its delegate. General Connor presided as temporary chair and helped heal the breech between the two factions, aided by Baskin, who moved that Corinne and Box Elder County be allowed fifteen convention votes each instead of the ten votes first granted them. Ever since, Connor has been called the "father of the Liberal Party," but Baskin certainly competes for that honor.[50]

For the next two decades, the Liberal Party pursued its intent to destroy priesthood control of territorial politics and economics. Members of the party also belonged to a private group known as the Gentile League, later known as the Loyal League, whose adherents sent lobbyists to Washington, D.C., to agitate for antipolygamy legislation. Another objective was to help defeat proposals for statehood, which they believed would confirm the priesthood authority in controlling Utah politics.[51]

For the next twenty years, Baskin was involved in all these matters. He was nearly always chosen as a Liberal Party "stumper" for his oratorical skill at whipping up enthusiasm for party candidates. He was often promoted as a possibility for various state and municipal offices. For example, on January 14, 1874, he was one of four nominees for Salt Lake City alderman. According to one historian, "These nominees, with the possible exception of Robert N. Baskin, were quite highly esteemed by the Mormons and acceptable to them." In a Liberal Party speech on July 27, 1874, the *Salt Lake Herald* noted that Baskin "knew there were those in the assemblage who did not sympathize with the Liberal party, and he was glad of it, as he wanted to talk to the lost sheep." The *Herald* ridiculed him for offering to get a Congressional appropriation of $100,000 to plant trees in Utah if people would vote for him.[52] Baskin continued as a loyal supporter of the party until November 1893, when as a realist he left and joined the "Citizens Party," which elected him mayor of Salt Lake City. He served in that position through two terms.[53]

Throughout his years with the Liberals, Baskin was indefatigable, both with time and treasure, as an anti-polygamy lobbyist in Washington, D.C. He spent much of his own money for travel and living expenses, but Liberal committees also helped from time to time. The *Salt Lake Herald* reported on March 17, 1886, that "should the delegate's funds run short, the deputation sent from Salt Lake on the lead and silver questions are reckoned to be flush, and will doubtless not see the political department suffer. Mr. Baskin will leave immediately." During this particular appearance before the House Committee on Territories, Baskin was fair enough to contradict a report that half the Mormon males were polygamists. He averred that only about 2 percent were, which was a gross underestimate.[54]

Baskin traveled east often to oppose Utah statehood and speak in favor of the Edmunds Act to abolish polygamy, "exert[ing] all the influence he possesses for the injury of the 'Mormon' people, who have never wronged him in the least," according to the *Deseret News* of March 18, 1886. At various times Baskin contested the election of Mormon delegates to Congress and elaborated on how "the priesthood in Utah assume to direct every member where he shall live, where he shall go, what shall be his employment and for whom he shall vote." The *Deseret News* reported this in exaggerated disbelief, clarifying that these were Baskin's "exact words."[55] As a lobbyist, Baskin was energetic and determined, much to the dismay of his opponents. He became nearly apoplectic in talking about the "persecution complex" of the *Deseret News* editor and the "malicious falsehoods" spread by Orson Whitney in claiming acts of "terrorism" by federal agents hunting down "cohabs," the term for people living in polygamist cohabitation.

Whitney wrote of deputy marshals using paid informers, assuming the role of peddlers and tourists to catch Mormon polygamists, stopping children returning from school to interrogate them, prowling around people's houses at night, peeping through windows, and "thrust[ing] themselves into sick rooms and women's bed chambers, rousing the sleepers, by pulling the bed clothes from off them." He said they broke into houses and fired upon fugitives if they did not immediately surrender. Baskin demanded from Whitney specific names, dates, and details. When these were not forthcoming, Baskin concluded that Whitney's charges were "malicious falsehoods—framed in his own disordered brain to discredit the federal officers ... to make it appear, that at the time, the Mormons were being persecuted."[56]

Of all their differences of opinion, none assumed as much importance as the incident at Mountain Meadows, to which Baskin assigned a major portion of his *Reminiscences* and pursued again in his *Reply*. As a chief prosecutor at John D. Lee's first trial which began on July 13, 1875, Baskin was intimately involved in obtaining an accurate assessment of the historical facts in the case. With his interrogation of Lee and other witnesses as a basis for his position, he was able to refute the story Whitney told in his *History of Utah*.[57]

Whitney, both in his long history and his later 1916 version, asserted that the Fancher party of Arkansas emigrants, as they moved through Utah in 1857 on their way south, "conducted themselves in the most offensive manner." Specifically, they gave the "impression" they had been involved in the murder of Joseph Smith, acted like a "band of marauders," left poisoned beef so Native Americans along the way would eat it and be killed, poisoned springs, and were far from being the "white-souled saints that a certain writer would have the public believe."[58]

Baskin countered by quoting from the book, *Rocky Mountain Saints,* that the party of thirty families "were moral in language and conduct, and united regularly in morning prayers," even refusing to travel on Sundays. Historian Hubert Howe Bancroft in his *History of Utah* wrote that when the emigrants camped at Mountain Meadows on the Saturday evening before the massacre, they were preparing to rest on the Sabbath and conduct "divine service in a large tent." Baskin included remarks by U.S. Senator James H. Berry of Arkansas, who spoke during the U.S. Senate hearings on whether to seat Senator-elect Reed Smoot, that as a boy of seventeen he had witnessed the emigrants' departure from Carroll County. Berry said they "consisted of the best citizens of that country." Even Whitney himself had written that the "Arkansas emigrants were mainly made up of respectable people." In light of this, Baskin wrote, Whitney's continued characterization of the immigrants' alleged bad behavior was as "dishonorable as it is despicable."[59]

Baskin succinctly described the massacre in his *Reply*:

> At the first trial of John D. Lee and after it was shown that Lee had, by his treacherous promise of protection, induced the Arkansas emigrants to surrender and give up their arms, it was further shown by the evidence that a number of Indians were placed in concealment in a clump of cedars and oaks, near the road, several hundred yards from the emigrant corral. The wounded men and seventeen little children, too young to expose the awful crime, were placed in wagons. The women and other children were formed into a separate procession, the men were arranged in rank, and by the side of each was placed a Mormon assassin armed with a gun, ostensibly to protect the emigrants.
>
> The wagons containing the wounded men and young children, under order moved ahead, the women and other children followed at some distance behind the wagons, and the men with their ostensible guards followed at a distance of about one hundred yards in the rear. When the women and other children reached the ambuscade of the Indians, the signal agreed upon was given by Bishop Higbee, who was a major in the Utah Militia, and each fiendish Mormon guard shot or cut the throat of the defenseless victim he was pre-

tendedly guarding, and the Indians, not more merciless than the white skinned Mormons present, rushed from ambush and slaughtered the helpless women and innocent children, and the wounded men in the wagons were slain.[60]

Even the *Deseret News* gave a description of the massacre on August 5, 1875.[61] Whitney, by contrast, while agreeing that Colonel Isaac C. Haight had ordered the Mormon militia to march to the massacre site under command of Major John M. Higbee, wrote that it was only "on a mission of mercy to bury the dead and protect the survivors." Supposedly "others came upon the scene," lured to the meadows to bury the dead, "and some of these also took part" in the butchery that followed. Baskin commented that no sensible person could accept such a ridiculously absurd scenario.[62] He countered that besides Lee, those who had actually planned the massacre escaped punishment. Colonel William H. Dame, commander of the Iron County Brigade of the Nauvoo Legion, Haight, and Higbee all retained their militia commands, and Dame remained president of the LDS Parowan Stake until 1880. Higbee and Haight were excommunicated in 1870, together with Lee, but Brigham Young reinstated Haight in 1874. Haight, Higbee, Dame, and Bishop Philip Klingensmith were indicted with Lee, but all of them fled prosecution. Klingensmith eventually surrendered and turned state's evidence at Lee's first trial, but Haight died in exile, still protected by church leaders. Prosecutor Sumner Howard dropped the charges against Dame in 1876, apparently as part of the deal with LDS authorities allowing Howard to convict Lee. A local court dismissed the charges against Higbee after Utah achieved statehood. "None of the other fifty-two Mormon participants were ever disciplined by the church," Baskin observed.[63]

Baskin described how the perpetrators appropriated the property of the slaughtered emigrants, branded some of their cattle with the Mormon church brand, and sold most of the property at public auction in Cedar City. He thought the failure to use proceeds from the emigrant property to succor the surviving children was "secondary in perfidy to the Massacre itself." Whitney avoided any reference to the robbery of emigrant goods.[64]

The Harvard-trained attorney proved himself an able and fearsome cross-examiner as lead prosecutor in the first trial of John D. Lee. In questioning Klingensmith, Baskin attempted to prove that any male member of the church could be "put out of the way" if he did not obey his priesthood leaders. The bishop conceded he knew of one man who had been put out of the way, whereupon Baskin noted, "Then you acted upon that belief when you surrendered your manhood and took part in this transaction?" Klingensmith answered, "Yes, of course."[65]

The bishop was not the only one who wished to escape Baskin's ferocious questioning. John Hanson Beadle explained how Brigham Young escaped being on the witness stand by pleading ill health and filing a deposition before retreating to St. George. Beadle summed up his indictment of Young: "It was not age and ill-health, but the dread of Mr. Baskin's cross-examination that kept him out of the court-room."[66]

Baskin maintained it was "the cut throat sermons of Brigham Young and other high officials of the Mormon church" in the days and months before the massacre that had inspired the killings. He thought the unquestioned obedience to the priesthood and blood atonement doctrine, taught in the Mormon Endowment House, were the principal causes for the cowardly acts perpetrated at Mountain Meadows. Baskin quoted several sermons to substantiate his accusation, including the following excerpt from Young's rhetoric:

> I say, rather than that apostates should flourish here, I will unsheath my bowie knife, and conquer or die. (Great commotion in the congregation and a simultaneous burst of feeling, assenting to the declaration.) Now, you nasty apostates, clear out, or judgment will be put to the line, and righteousness to the plummet. (Voices, generally, 'go it, go it.') If you say it is right, raise your hands. (All hands up.) Let us call upon the Lord to assist us, and every good work.[67]

While many dismissed such high-flown emotional rhetoric as a way of venting frustrations and not to be taken literally, there were certainly those who accepted such denunciations as pronouncements of God's real intent. Action might well have followed by individuals who knew how to use bowie knives. There were tales of blood atonement and Danite killings in circulation throughout Utah Territory. It may be true that the Danites were more common when the Mormons resided in Missouri and Illinois, but the folklore surrounding them, if not the reality of some accounts, permeated the frontier Utah culture.

Recently more research has substantiated that it was Baskin's position that the "theocracy" was responsible for the massacre. In his speech to the jury at the first Lee trial, Baskin charged "that a part of the Mormon Religion is to kill—and a part and parcel of it—and a great part of it is to shed human blood for another.... There is no use to disguise it when counsel said that the Mormon Church was on trial.—I am willing to accept the gentleman's statement." He added: "I do hold Brigham Young responsible; I do hold the system which has carried out, which distinctly teaches and carries out in its preaching and practices the shedding of human blood to atone for real and imaginary offenses. I hold, I arraign this iniquitous system, and the leaders of the church."[68]

Long after Baskin delivered this indictment of church leadership and compiled his answers to Orson Whitney's histories, a highly competent and fearless historian wrote a volume that was hailed as the definitive history of the massacre. In 1950, Juanita Brooks, a native of southern Utah who had grown up surrounded by people whose ancestors had known of, or participated in, the incident, felt determined to get at the truth that had long been suppressed and ignored by church officials. She began a long period of research into documents that had been hidden from view for almost a hundred years. She pressed ahead despite knowing she was treading on dangerous ground and might bring censure on herself or even risk membership in the Mormon Church, to which she remained faithful.

In 1950 the first edition of her book, *Mountain Meadows Massacre,* appeared and elicited even more controversy than she had expected. I personally remember traveling with LDS Church Historian and president of the Council of the Twelve Apostles Joseph

Fielding Smith and asking what he thought of this recently published book. "Very bad! Very bad!" was his reply. It was perhaps a
particularly mild rebuke in the context of other more strident denunciations at the time. Yet, opinions began to change as Mormon
leaders and members alike came to appreciate the real service
Brooks had rendered and value in exploring the lessons to be
learned from such terrible episodes in our history. Brooks has deserved all the encomiums since given her as a result of her coura-
geous demonstration of scholarship.[69]

A puzzling question might be why Brooks included Baskin's
*Reminiscences* and *Reply* in her bibliography and yet referred to
them only once in her book. She repeated Baskin's statement that
Brigham Young had entered an agreement with U.S. Attorney
Sumner Howard, the prosecutor in the second Lee trial, which allowed Howard to impanel a Mormon jury and convict Lee on the
basis of affidavits provided in exchange for a predetermined out-
come—that Howard would "exonerate the authorities of the Mormon church of complicity in the massacre."[70] Why did Brooks not
acknowledge Baskin's remarkably accurate report of the incident
issued some thirty-six years before her book appeared? After all,
Baskin's two-paragraph summary closely resembled Brooks's own
conclusions, showing that Baskin had the major facts correct. It
turns out that Brooks learned of Baskin's work late in the process
and only from a colleague, Dale L. Morgan, who wrote to evaluate
her bibliography. At the time, the book was essentially complete.[71]
It may also be that Brooks was reluctant to rely too much on a
source so critical of Mormonism. In either case, it is unfortunate
that Baskin's brief but accurate account was ignored for so long.

Despite the opprobrium he suffered from Whitney and other
Mormons, Baskin always asserted his friendship with the Saints
and his position that having gotten rid of polygamy was to their
benefit. Two years before his death in 1918, he expostulated that
he was not the "inveterate Mormon hater" characterized by Whitney, not the "human mainspring of nearly every anti-Mormon
movement that Utah has known." He admitted to involvement

with the movements that challenged Mormonism and said he was proud he had "materially assisted in stopping the bitter conflict and brought about conditions different from the evil ones that existed in Utah Territory." At the end of his impassioned *Reply*, he reiterated that this did not mean he was a religious bigot. To the contrary, in a long contest to Americanize a theocratic stronghold and "stop the lamentable conflict and establish peace in the distracted Territory[,] [n]o one can be more highly gratified at the glorious results than I myself."[72] Like others approaching old age, Baskin wanted to be certain of his place in history, that it was told correctly and, naturally, from his point of view.

Prominent Latter-day Saints reacted positively to Baskin's olive leaf. "I never enjoyed a little speech more in all my life than that of Robert N. Baskin," future LDS President Heber J. Grant said of Baskin's birthday tribute to Brigham Young. Grant thought the judge was an "honest, straight-forward man who was once very much opposed to the Latter-day Saints, who today takes pleasure in bearing testimony as to the honor and integrity of the Mormon people."[73] Even the *Deseret News* eventually supported Baskin's campaigns for high public office and sang his praises: "He lived to see wonderful changes in the isolated country to which he came as a young man, and none will dispute the influential role he performed in affecting some of those changes, nor the prominence which he attained as a public character and a citizen."[74]

Given the ardor with which Baskin attacked Brigham Young in his memoirs, how could he in good conscience have saluted him on the occasion of the anniversary of his birth? "While he had differed with Brigham Young's policies in many particulars, as everybody well knew, he had still believed the Mormon leader to be a great man," read the newspaper summary of his remarks. Baskin observed that his old adversary "was not only a great leader, but a judge of men, and never made a mistake in selecting those who were to carry out his will."[75] The crowd might not have appreciated the subtle irony of this observation.

In judging the accuracy and impartiality of Baskin's works, it is important to remember that a reminiscence written long after the fact can suffer the hazards of convoluted memory and self-justification. Baskin's recollections contain some of that kind of baggage. But on the whole, his report of events he participated in reveal the trained mind of a competent attorney devoted to an accumulation and analysis of facts. That cannot be said of Whitney, whose manipulation of evidence in favor of his life-long religious allegiance comes through with a decided bias and pursuit of a personal vendetta against his non-Mormon antagonist. Baskin certainly was not free of animus toward Whitney either, but perhaps had better cause to vent in the face of some of Whitney's more outrageous falsifications. "Some of [Baskin's] points are well taken," two prominent Mormon historians, Davis Bitton and Leonard J. Arrington, confirmed in discussing Whitney's scholarly contributions. They concluded that "current scholarship on almost all if not all of the topics [Baskin] mentions would come closer to his interpretation than to Whitney's. But," they continued, "tempers were not cool enough in the 1890s—or in 1916—to make truly balanced history possible."[76] Let us hope that today such equilibrium is possible.

## Notes

1. "Utah Honors Brigham Young's Memory," *Salt Lake Herald,* June 2, 1901.

2. "Exercises at Saltair: Judge Baskin Pays a Tribute," *Daily Salt Lake Tribune,* June 2, 1901; George Q. Cannon to Brigham Young, March 23, 1876, Brigham Young Collection, archives, Historical Department, Church of Jesus Christ of Latter-day Saints, Salt Lake City, Utah.

3. "Utah Honors Brigham Young's Memory."

4. Robert N. Baskin, *Reminiscences of Early Utah* (Salt Lake City: Tribune-Reporter, 1914), 4.

5. *Salt Lake Tribune,* Aug. 27, 1918.

6. George A. Townsend, "Letters from Salt Lake City," *Cincinnati Commercial,* Oct. 20-27, 1871.

7. *Salt Lake Tribune,* Aug. 27, 1918.

8. Townsend, "Letters from Salt Lake City."

9. Ibid.

10. *Deseret News,* Aug. 27, 1918.

11. Orson F. Whitney, *History of Utah* (Salt Lake City: George Q. Cannon and Sons, 1893), 2:634.

12. Ronald Collett Jack, "Utah Territorial Politics: 1847-1876," Ph.D. diss., University of Utah, 1970, 333.

13. "Journal History of the Church of Jesus Christ of Latter-day Saints" vol. 14, daily entry for Apr. 18, 1877, LDS Archives; microfilm copy in Special Collections, J. Willard Marriott Library, University of Utah, Salt Lake City, Utah.

14. Ibid., Aug. 7, 1877.

15. Ibid., Feb. 13, 1889.

16. Whitney, *History of Utah,* 1:581.

17. "Journal History of the Church," Nov. 1, 1888.

18. Edward W. Tullidge, *History of Salt Lake City* (Salt Lake City: by the author, 1886), 526.

19. Stephan Cresswell, "The U.S. Department of Justice in Utah Territory, 1870-90," *Utah Historical Quarterly* 53 (Summer 1985): 219.

20. Brigham D. Madsen, *Corinne: The Gentile Capital of Utah* (Salt Lake City: Utah State Historical Society, 1980), 96.

21. Truman G. Madsen, *Defender of the Faith: The B. H. Roberts Story* (Salt Lake City: Bookcraft, 1980), 247.

22. Madsen, *Corinne,* 75.

23. William B. Dougall, "Utah Legislature of 1892," *Woman's Journal* 3 (Apr. 1892): 312.

24. Baskin, *Reminiscences,* 97.

25. "Journal History of the Church," May 13, 1886.

26. Davis Bitton and Leonard J. Arrington, *Mormons and Their Historians* (Salt Lake City: University of Utah Press, 1988), 56.

27. Woodruff C. Thomson, "Orson F. Whitney, Mormon Writer," M.A. thesis, University of Utah, 1949, 1-3.

28. Ibid., 3.

29. Bitton and Arrington, *Mormons and Their Historians,* 58.

30. Thomson, "Orson F. Whitney," 4-5.

31. Ibid.

32. Bitton and Arrington, *Mormons and Their Historians,* 59-60.

33. Ibid., 60-61.

34. Ibid., 62.

35. Robert Joseph Dwyer, *The Gentile Comes to Utah: A Study in Religious and Social Conflict* (Washington, D.C.: Catholic University Press, 1941), 253.

36. Thomson, "Orson F. Whitney," 120.

37. Ibid., 120-23; Bitton and Arrington, *Mormons and Their Historians,* 63-65.

38. Orson F. Whitney, *Popular History of Utah* (Salt Lake City: Deseret News, 1916), preface.

39. R. N. Baskin, *Reply to Certain Statements by O. F. Whitney in His History* (Salt Lake City: Lakeside Printing, 1916), 4.

40. Ibid., 3-4.

41. Ibid., 5-7; quoting *Journal of Discourses,* ed. George D. Watt, 26 vols. (Liverpool: Latter-day Saints Book Depot, 1854-86), 5:231.

42. Ibid., 6; B. H. Roberts, *Studies of the Book of Mormon,* ed. Brigham D. Madsen (Urbana: University of Illinois Press, 1985), 20.

43. Norma Baldwin Ricketts, *The Mormon Battalion* (Logan: Utah State University Press, 1996), 2-10.

44. Baskin, *Reply to Certain Statements,* 9, 14.

45. Ibid., 9-14, 29.

46. Townsend, "Letters"; Whitney, *History of Utah,* 2:624-25.

47. "Journal History of the Church," May 7, 1886, quoting the *Salt Lake Herald.*

48. Ibid., Feb. 13, 1889, quoting the *Deseret News.*

49. Brigham D. Madsen, *Glory Hunter: A Biography of Patrick Edward Connor* (Salt Lake City: University of Utah Press, 1990), 168.

50. Madsen, *Corinne,* 102-103; Jack, "Utah Territorial Politics," 159.

51. Edward Leo Lyman, *Political Deliverance: The Mormon Quest for Utah Statehood* (Urbana: University of Illinois Press, 1986), 14-15.

52. "Journal History of the Church," quoting the *Salt Lake Herald,* July 29, 1874.

53. Lyman, *Political Deliverance,* 212-13.

54. "Journal History of the Church," quoting the *Salt Lake Herald,* Mar. 17, 1886; quoting the *Deseret News,* Apr. 17, 1886.

55. Madsen, *Corinne,* 84; "Journal History of the Church," quoting the *Deseret News,* Mar. 18, 1886; Nov. 12, 1874; Jan. 26, 1889.

56. Baskin, *Reply to Certain Statements,* 23-24.

57. Baskin, *Reminiscences,* 83-149; Baskin, *Reply to Certain Statements,* 15-22.

58. Baskin, *Reply to Certain Statements,* 15-16, 21.

59. Ibid., 20-21.

60. Ibid., 16.

61. "Journal History of the Church," quoting the *Deseret News,* Aug. 5, 1875.

62. Baskin, *Reply to Certain Statements,* 17.

63. Ibid., 21, 22.

64. Ibid., 22.

65. Anna Jean Backus, *Mountain Meadows Witness: The Life and Times of Bishop Philip Klingensmith* (Spokane, WA, 1995), 120.

66. John H. Beadle, *Western Wilds, and the Men Who Redeem Them* (Cincinnati, 1878), 510.

67. *Journal of Discourses,* 1:83, transcript of address delivered in the Salt Lake Tabernacle, Mar. 27, 1853.

68. Leonard J. Arrington, ed., "Crusade against Theocracy: The Reminiscences of Judge Jacob Smith Boreman of Utah, 1872-1877," *Huntington Library Quarterly* 24 (Nov. 1960): 41n60.

69. Juanita Brooks, *Mountain Meadows Massacre* (Palo Alto, CA: Stanford University Press, 1950).

70. Ibid., 195, referring to Baskin, *Reminiscences,* 136.

71. Dale Morgan to Juanita Brooks, Sept. 2, 1948, Juanita Brooks Papers, MS 486, Special Collections, Marriott Library.

72. Baskin, *Reply to Certain Statements,* 29.

73. Heber J. Grant, *Conference Report,* Apr. 1902, 81.

74. "Judge Baskin," *Deseret Evening News,* Aug. 27, 1918.

75. "Exercises at Saltair."

76. Bitton and Arrington, *Mormons and Their Historians,* 65.

# Reminiscences of Early Utah

---

The following is an unaltered digital scan
of the first edition of *Reminiscences of Early Utah*,
published in 1914

---

BRIGHAM YOUNG.

# REMINISCENCES

## OF

# EARLY UTAH

*BY*

R. N. BASKIN

AN EX-CHIEF JUSTICE OF THE
SUPREME COURT OF UTAH

# CONTENTS

# LIST OF ILLUSTRATIONS

R. N. BASKIN

# PREFACE

The glaringly false statements in Whitney's History of Utah respecting the nature and effect of certain occurrences which have in great part gone to make up the history of the State, together with his malignment of the motives of myself and other Gentiles who in the past opposed the peculiar theocratic and anti-American system established and maintained in Utah while it was a Territory by the high priesthood of the Mormon church, are the reasons for the writing of these Reminiscences of my connection with the conflict waged for many years between Mormons and Gentiles. I can vouch for the accuracy of the statements of the facts here given; but whether my observations of the significance of these facts are warranted, the unbiased reader himself must judge.

After a careful scrutiny of Whitney's history, I deemed it due the men, many of whom were federal officials and few of whom are yet living, and who have been so wantonly besmirched by him, to correct, at least, some of his erroneous assertions and covert insinuations.

R. N. BASKIN.

Salt Lake City, Utah,
    June 1, 1914.

# CHAPTER I.

## The Conditions in Utah Which Caused the Opposition of the Gentiles.

A few days after my arrival in Salt Lake City, in the latter part of August, 1865, I became acquainted with Thomas Hearst of Philadelphia, the son of William Hearst, a distinguished lawyer of that city.

Young Hearst was the agent of James P. Bruner of Philadelphia, who owned the North Star mine situated in Little Cottonwood canyon. Near this property was the Emma mine, the richness of which, disclosed by development a few years afterwards, attracted to Utah a large number of prospectors and miners to whom is due the credit of developing the wonderful mineral resources of the State. Mr. Hearst, in urging me to accompany him to the mine, said he had the utmost confidence that in Utah, upon the completion of the Union Pacific railroad, there would be discovered many rich and extensive mines which would soon constitute one of the most important sources of the wealth of the Territory; and in view of that fact alone, Salt Lake City, prospectively, was a very desirable location for any attorney at law.

I accompanied him to the mine, and from the quantity of galena ore on the dump, the large boulders of the same material disclosed at the point of discovery, and the value of the ore as stated by Mr. Hearst, I was convinced that his confidence in the future of the city was probably well founded.

After this visit I changed my intention of going on to California, and concluded to settle in Salt Lake City. I secured an office and began to study the statutes of the Territory and inquire into its existent political and social conditions.

The provisions of the two following acts of the territorial legislature were the first to attract my attention.

"An Act for the Regulation of Attorneys. Sec. 2. No person or persons employing counsel, in any of the courts of this Territory, shall be compelled by any process of law to pay the counsel so employed for any service rendered as counsel, before, or after, or during the process of trial in the case."

"An Act in Relation to the Judiciary. Sec. 1. That all questions of law, meaning or writings other than law, and the admissibility of testimony shall be decided by the court; and no laws or parts of laws shall be read, argued, cited or adopted in any court during any trial, except those enacted by the Governor and Legislative Assembly of this Territory, and those passed by the Congress of the United States when applicable; and no report, decision or doings of any court shall be read, argued, cited or adopted as precedent in any trials."

In commenting on the foregoing acts, let me quote from recognized legal authority:

"The criminal law of England, both written and unwritten, in force at the date the colonies gained their independence, became common law in each colony, and remained in force in the states of the Union so far as it was adapted to the condition of the people and in harmony with the genius of their institutions, and so far as it was not changed by the constitution or laws of the particular state." (1 McLain's Crim. Law, Sec. 12).

"It is plain, both on principle and authority, that the common law must extend as well to criminal things as to civil." (Bishop's Crim. Law, Sec. 35).

Bigamy and polygamy are one and the same crime. Blackstone states that the latter term is "the better expression to designate that crime." At the date of our independence, under the laws of England, bigamy was a felony. Under the statute of James I, Sec. 11, bigamy was punishable by death; and under 9th George IV, any person counseling, aiding, or abetting the offender was equally guilty with him and subject to the same punishment.

All the states except Louisiana, and territories except Utah, had by statute adopted the common law so far as applicable to new conditions. That law was and is indispensably necessary for the proper government of any American community. It was, therefore, the imperative duty of the Utah legislature to adopt it at the first territorial session. Instead of doing so the foregoing absurd section of the judiciary act excluding it was passed. By adopting the common law under which polygamy is a felony, the legislature would have made the practice of the alleged divine polygamic

6

tenet of the Mormon church a crime. For that reason the legislature failed to perform its imperative duty and stultified itself by passing the section which excluded the common law, and all other laws except those passed by Congress and the territorial legislature.

By the provisions of the act of Congress organizing the Territory, the judicial power of the Territory was vested in a supreme court, district courts, probate courts and justices of the peace. By that act the supreme and district courts were given, respectively, chancery and common law jurisdiction, and the jurisdiction of the probate and justices' courts was to be as limited by law. By an act of the territorial legislature the probate courts were given civil and criminal jurisdiction in all cases except those arising under the acts of Congress. The act in relation to marshals and attorneys provided that there should be elected by a joint vote of both houses of the legislative assembly, a marshal and district attorney, and these officers were respectively made, by said act, the executive and prosecuting officers of the district courts in all cases arising under the laws of the Territory. Moreover, the act of Congress organizing the Territory had already provided for the appointment, by the President of the United States, of executive and prosecuting officers of the district courts.

Another subversion of legal procedure is disclosed in the act prescribing the mode of procuring grand and petit juries for the district courts. This act contained the following provisions:

"Sec. 2. The county court in each county shall at the first session in each year and at subsequent sessions, or other times as a neglect so to do at said first session and as other circumstances may require, make, from the assessment roll of the county, a list containing the names of at least fifty men, residents of the county eligible to serve as jurors."

The further provisions of said act required the names so selected to be placed in a box in the possession of the clerk of the county court, and that both the grand and petit juries were to be drawn from that box by the territorial marshal or sheriff, and the clerk of the county court. In case the names in the box during any session of the district courts became exhausted, under a provision of said act, talesmen

7

could not be summoned by the court, but the deficiency could only be met by the county court convening and selecting additional names. Until this was done, when the names in the box became exhausted, no case requiring a jury could be tried. To permit the summoning of talesmen—which is an ordinary method of filling the panel—might have resulted in forming a jury which was not subject to the will of the priesthood. Said act was evidently formed with a view of making it impossible to impanel any but a jury composed of Mormons. The acts containing the foregoing provisions were passed at the first session of the territorial legislature in 1852, and were approved by Brigham Young, then governor of the Territory.

As the offices of territorial marshal and the county courts were, under an act of the legislature, elective, none but members of the Mormon church were ever elected to any of said offices as long as the act relating to the selection of jurors remained in force. It remained in force for many years, and until superseded by an act of Congress. The evident intent of the provisions to which I have referred was to secure immunity to those practicing polygamy, and to enable Brigham Young, the President of the High Priesthood[1] of the Mormon church, and his successors, to control the execution of the laws by the district courts in all matters requiring trial by jury. That such was the purpose and effect of said provisions is apparent from the failure for so many years to execute the law of Congress respecting polygamy, and to indict and bring to trial the perpetrators of many horrible crimes hereinafter mentioned. And the sentiments expressed in numerous Mormon sermons of the period is practically conclusive evidence on this point.

Governor Harding, in a message to the legislature, said:

"I am aware that there is a prevailing opinion here that said act (the act of Congress on the subject of polygamy) is unconstitutional, and therefore it is recommended by those in high authority that no regard whatever should be paid to the same. I take this occasion to warn the people of this Territory against such dangerous and disloyal counsel."

That message was supplemented by Governor Harding, Chief Justice Waite, and Associate Justice Drake, sending to

---

[1]The High Priesthood consists of the president of the Mormon church and his two counselors.

8

Congress and recommending for passage, a bill providing that juries be selected by the United States marshal; that the governor be authorized to appoint militia officers, and that the powers of the probate courts be restricted to their proper functions. This so intensified the antagonism of Brigham Young that he issued a call for a meeting at the tabernacle, at which many vindictive and inflammatory speeches were made by the leading members of the Mormon church, and resolutions unanimously adopted condemning said message, and the action of the governor and judges. A committee was also appointed to wait on the governor and judges, and request these officers to resign. A petition to the President of the United States was also drawn up and signed requesting their removal. According to Whitney, the motive which inspired the territorial acts referred to is stated in the second volume of his history, page 551, as follows:

"Doubtless the fear, well-founded it seems, that judges would be sent to the Territory who would use the tribunals over which they presided as engines of oppression, was one of the reasons why the legislature clothed the probate courts— whose officers, instead of being sent from abroad, were elected by the people or their representatives—with unusual powers. A similar reason—the fear of conspiring United States attorneys and marshals using their functions to persecute, and not merely to prosecute—may have influenced in part the creation of the offices of territorial attorney general and marshal. A desire to maintain the principle of local self-government, was doubtless the ruling motive."

Yes, without doubt it was "fear" that inspired these disloyal acts—fear that the federal government would send judges and other officials here to execute impartially the law of the land—the same fear that today inspires the wrongdoer under the shadow of the law. What criminal would not prefer laws and decisions of his own making to those of legally constituted authority? Whitney is right here—if we read between the lines.

It may be well to instance a case in point. The incident following took place in the year 1867:

Isaac Potter, Charles Wilson and John Walker, residing at Coalville, were apostate Mormons. Walker was a boy about nineteen years of age. These three persons had previously been arrested for alleged thefts, and in every instance had been discharged by Judge Snyder, who at the time was probate judge of Summit county. In August of this year, they were again arrested on the charge of having stolen a cow. While they were under guard in the schoolhouse at Coalville, ten persons, armed, appeared about twelve o'clock at night at the building and ordered the prisoners to leave. Upon reaching the street they were placed in single file, a short distance apart, and in each intervening space two of the armed persons placed themselves. The others took positions at the front and rear of the procession thus formed. In this order they marched along the principal street of Coalville, through the mainly inhabited part of the town. Arriving at the outskirts, and their captors continuing to move on, Potter turned around and said to Walker: "John, they are going to murder us! Wouldn't you like to see your mother before you die?" Thereupon one of the armed men marching behind Potter thrust the muzzle of a shotgun against Potter's mouth. Potter in terror, shouted "murder!" Whereupon the armed man discharged the gun against the body of Potter at a range so close as to cause his instant death. At the discharge of the gun, both Wilson and Walker broke away and ran for their lives. Wilson was overtaken and killed at the edge of the Weber river. As Walker made his escape, a charge from a shotgun grazed his breast and lacerated his hand and wrist. He was wearing neither coat nor vest, and the charge set his shirt on fire and as he ran he extinguished the fire by the blood from his wounds. He was an athletic youth and soon distanced his pursuers. Although a number of shots were fired at him in the pursuit, he reached the river without further injury, swam across, and thereby escaped assassination. After numerous hardships he succeeded in reaching Camp Douglas, where the commanding officer, upon hearing what had taken place, gave him support and protection.

No steps having been taken by the authorities of Summit county to arrest any of the participants in the homicides mentioned, Judge Titus, whose judicial district included Summit county, upon the affidavit of Walker, issued a warrant for the arrest of the persons accused of the crime. They were arrested, and at the hearing before Judge Titus, at which I was present, what I have here stated respecting the murder of Potter and Wilson and the assault upon Walker, appeared

10

from the testimony of Walker, who was a witness. Several of the residents of Coalville testified that they were awakened by the shots fired, and rushed out to learn the cause of the disturbance; that they saw Potter dead upon the ground, with his throat cut from ear to ear. Walker, when on the witness stand, identified the prisoners severally, and stated what each had done up to the moment Potter was killed. Judge Titus committed the accused to the penitentiary to await the action of the grand jury. John T. D. McAllister, who under the territorial statute before quoted, was the executive officer of the district court, took charge of the prisoners and conducted them in wagons to the penitentiary. Upon arriving there, the prisoners gently lifted the marshal out of the wagon occupied by him and drove away. No effort was made to rearrest them, and a short time afterwards, over the signature of all of them except Arza Hinkley and John C. Livingstone, the following insolent letter appeared in the Salt Lake Daily Telegraph. This newspaper was owned and edited by one Stenhouse, then a zealous member of the Mormon church, but who afterwards apostatized and published a book, and in which he mentioned the murder of Potter and Wilson. The aforesaid letter reads:

"In the Pines, Elk Ranch District, Rocky Mountains,
September 7th, 1867.

"Editor of the Daily Telegraph, and to all whom it may concern:
"After arriving here we thought it due to judge, warden and marshal that they should know the reason for our refusing to accept the proposal of his honor, Judge Titus, to take up our abode in the penitentiary for the period of forty days to await the action of the grand jury then to be assembled.
"Firstly: On our arrival at that beautiful mansion in the delightful neighborhood of the Sugar House ward, we were astounded to learn that mine hosts' penitentiary larder was but sparsely supplied, and his stock on hand but limited, no appropriation having been made by nation, territory or county for the entertainment of guests whom the fates may send in that direction.
"Secondly: Not wishing to tax the warden's hospitality unnecessarily, and it generally being our custom to maintain ourselves by the sweat of our brow.

11

"Thirdly: The atmosphere of warden's boarding rooms was slightly impregnated with a bad influence arising from being occupied by individuals of the Potter, Wilson and Walker stamp, which is decidedly offensive to our olfactory nerves.

"Lastly: We concluded to sustain ourselves until the memorable fourteenth day of October, 1867, free of expense to the territory and county. On that day we will appear at the court house, G. S. L. City, individually and collectively. (His Honor may put that down)."

"Yours, etc.,

ALMA ELDREDGE,
JAMES MAHONEY,
EDMUND ELDREDGE,
MAHONRI CAHOON,
HYRUM ELDREDGE,
THOMAS DODSON,
JOSHUA WISEMAN,
JOHN STANLEY."

The only excuse ever claimed by any of the accused was that Potter, Wilson and Walker attempted to escape, and were shot while running away. In the light of the fact that Potter's throat was cut and his clothes scorched by the charge which killed him, and that Walker's shirt was set on fire by the shot which wounded him, such a claim is absurd. It was shown by the testimony that Arza Hinkley was in command of the participants in the affair and directed their movements. He was not a resident of Coalville at the time, his home being in Salt Lake City. He went to Coalville shortly after Potter, Wilson and Walker were arrested. After Potter and Wilson were killed he moved permanently to Coalville, was soon installed in the office of probate judge of Summit county in place of Judge Snyder, and served in that capacity for many years. Walker remained for some time at Fort Douglas after the accused parties were committed, but before the time set for the grand jury of the district court to convene he left the fort to visit his mother at Coalville. He did not visit his mother, but mysteriously disappeared, and has neither been seen nor heard of since that time. No doubt he was assassinated before reaching his home. His testimony was necessary to make a case against the accused, and his disappearance gave them perfect immunity.

The deportment of these men at the hearing, notwithstanding the evidence, showed beyond a reasonable doubt that they were guilty. What subsequently transpired at the penitentiary, and their insolent letter, convinced me that their crime was one of that class of homicides which like the Mountain Meadows massacre, the murders of Brown, Arnold, of Potter and Parish, of Hartley, Brassfield, Dr. Robinson and others, could be committed with perfect impunity under the conditions then existing, and that the accused were conscious of security from punishment.

Perhaps I should have first cited the cases of Dr. Robinson and Brassfield, since these precede the Coalville tragedy. My only object in reversing the order of events was simply to bring to the attention of the reader a more striking illustration of the subversion of legal procedure and justice than is afforded by the earlier cases.

\*    \*    \*    \*    \*    \*    \*    \*    \*    \*    \*    \*

Dr. Robinson was assassinated on October 22, 1866. At that time there were no public or private hospitals in Salt Lake City. He decided to build one, and began by erecting in the vicinity of the Warm Springs, upon unoccupied land situated a considerable distance beyond any habitation of the city, a small frame house to be used as a workshop in the construction of the hospital. Shortly after the workshop was finished a police force tore it down and warned the doctor that it would not be healthy for him to renew his operations there. The doctor subsequently came to my office, and after stating what had occurred, announced that he contemplated bringing suit to recover damages for the destruction of his property and enjoining further interference by the police. He also stated that another attorney whom he had consulted refused to institute a suit because he feared it would subject him, the attorney, to personal violence. Some of his friends had warned him that he would incur great personal hazard by bringing suit.

I replied that the attorney and his friends certainly must be very timid, for I did not believe it possible anywhere in the United States that a citizen would jeopardize his life by applying to the courts of his country for an adjudication of his rights in any case; that while in view of what he had stated I would not advise him to bring suit, if he decided to do so, I would not hesitate to act as his attorney. Shortly afterward he requested me to proceed in the matter, which I did.

A few weeks after the suit was instituted he was called from his bed at midnight by some unknown person, who stated that an acquaintance of the doctor had been severely injured by being thrown from a mule, and that his services were immediately required. Disregarding the dissuasion of his wife, he proceeded with the unknown person, and upon reaching a point near where the Walker dry goods store is now situated, at the corner of Main and Third South streets, he was brutally murdered. At the inquest held it appeared that seven persons were seen running from the place at the time the crime was committed. The suit instituted was never finally tried, and not having been revived, was abated by the death of the doctor.

Some circumstances antecedent to this murder are significant. A short time before, a crowd of men armed with axes broke the windows, doors, and fixtures of a building belonging to him, and destroyed a bowling alley situated therein. He procured a warrant for the arrest of the chief of police and other members of the police force on the charge of having maliciously destroyed his property, and they were bound over to answer to that charge. Two days before the doctor's assassination he called upon Mayor Wells, who was one of Brigham Young's counselors, and requested him to interpose and restrain the police force. In place of granting that natural and reasonable request, the mayor grossly insulted the doctor and ordered him out of the house.

Doctor Robinson was an educated gentleman of courteous manners and affable disposition. His deportment was in every respect exemplary. He was superintendent of the first Gentile Sunday school in Salt Lake City; was a skillful physician and surgeon; had an extensive practice, and it was generally known that his attendance could always be obtained by anyone, even when compensation was out of the question. He was charitable, and humane motives alone induced him to begin erecting a hospital. He was exceptionally popular, had no known enemy, nor quarrel with anyone except the city authorities. He had done nothing, so far as known, calculated to subject him to any hostility except that of occupying the land before mentioned, which was against the settled policy of Brigham

14

Young respecting the acquisition of property in Utah by Gentiles. That policy will be fully elucidated herein further on.

As at least seven persons were participants in the murder of Dr. Robinson, it is evident that they had previously met and deliberately agreed upon the manner in which it was to be accomplished. It is anomalous, in view of the circumstances disclosed, that seven or more persons living in a civilized community should conspire to murder such an estimable man as Doctor Robinson.

Following are quotations from an interview by a correspondent of the New York Evening Post, on November 7, 1867:

## TALK WITH BRIGHAM YOUNG.

"I have stated that the only explanation given by any of the Mormons of the murder of Dr. Robinson is that it was committed by Gentiles with the object of criminating the church. I called again today on President Young, notifying him that my object was to obtain some facts for the public eye, and in my long conversation with him he said that most of the Gentiles living here were bad enough to commit any act that would injure him and his people, and that he had no doubt that some wretch had been hired for about $10.00 to murder Dr. Robinson. He said that Dr. Robinson was one of the worst men he ever knew. 'He was saucy and impudent, and pushed himself right against us,' he said. He said he was sorry that the doctor had been killed, for he wanted him to live and die in the ditch like a dog, as he would have done if he had gone on. Still, he hoped the murderers would be discovered, though he had no idea the one-sided and prejudiced attorney conducting the case meant to discover them, for it would show the wickedness of their own clique, who had planned the deed, he thought. 'They selected Doctor Robinson,' he said, 'on account of having difficulty with the Mormon authorities, thereby intending that the blame should be thrown on them.' He lavished vigorous epithets on Governor Weller, the Gentile lawyer, and above all on Justice Titus. Referring to the latter gentleman, and some of his decisions, he said they were dictated occasionally by law, but generally by his personal feelings; that all of the United States judges were a set of prejudiced scoundrels, and he did not want any more of their decisions; that they had better be careful or they would have to go out of this place. 'Yes, I'll put them out myself pretty soon; send them home by a short cut.' [2] I

---

[2] In Whitney's History, Vol. II, page 325, it is stated that at a banquet in Salt Lake City, Senator Trumbull, of Illinois, related a conversation he had with President Young in which the latter, it was claimed, had said something to the effect that if the federal officials in Utah did not behave themselves, he would have them ridden out of the Territory.

referred to the destruction of Doctor Robinson's bowling alley, and other deeds of mob violence, to which Young said that in his opinion that band of men had done wrong; that instead of going by night to destroy the building, they should have gone through it in broad day. 'I'd have gutted it at noon, torn it down and destroyed it in the light of day, so that every man might see me.'"

\*     \*     \*     \*     \*     \*     \*     \*     \*     \*     \*     \*

Brassfield married a woman who had previously been the plural wife of a man named Hill, then on a mission in England. Hill and the woman had severed their relations and had not cohabitated for several years. Shortly after said marriage, Brassfield was brutally assassinated at twilight of an evening on one of the principal streets of Salt Lake City, at the time thronged with people. The assassin escaped and was never arrested.

Brigham Young, in a sermon reported in the Deseret News of April 12, 1866, referring to the event, said: "Whether he (Brassfield) was killed by someone whom he threatened to shoot, or by some relation or friend of Hill's family, or by someone who had made a catspaw of him in his ill-starred operations, or by some of his acquaintances to settle a grudge, thinking of course it would be laid upon the Mormons, is yet to be learned."

Such disgusting statements as the above, and those made respecting the murder of Doctor Robinson were characteristic of Brigham Young, as will appear more fully further on.

Brassfield was, beyond doubt, murdered because he married the former plural wife of Hill. There can be no doubt whatever that Brigham was aware of the facts of the crime, and that later he also knew why Doctor Robinson was murdered, and who murdered him.

Marriage between members of the Mormon church and Gentiles had been interdicted by the priesthood, and it was dangerous for any man not a member of the church to even become a suitor of a woman of Mormon predilections. I know of one instance in which a brilliant young man of good character was maltreated because he was a suitor of a daughter of a prominent Mormon. He had for a considerable time been paying his addresses to the young lady. While the father of the girl opposed, her mother favored his addresses. He and the young lady became engaged.  He had been warned several times by anonymous letters to cease paying further court to the young lady, but paid no heed to these warnings.  One night he and the young lady had attended the theatre, and having escorted her home, while returning to his home he was set upon by several masked men and dragged to one of the trees east of the temple block.  His coat and waistcoat were taken off, and while his arms were held around the tree, a policeman named Bill Hyde, whom the young man identified, most brutally lacerated his back with a blacksnake whip.

Under the conditions then existing, it would have been useless for the young man to institute criminal proceedings against Hyde: and to have killed him, as he intended, but from which he was dissuaded by me, would, beyond question, have cost him his life.

\*     \*     \*     \*     \*     \*     \*     \*     \*     \*     \*     \*

From my investigations I became thoroughly convinced that the high priesthood of the Mormon church were the actual rulers of Utah, and that the government established by the Organic Act had only a nominal existence; that the priesthood claimed to be divinely authorized to rule the members of the Mormon church in all matters, temporal and spiritual; that the adherents of that church constituting almost the entire population of the Territory, conceded the claim of the priesthood; that the legislative powers granted by the Organic Act, instead of being used as intended—namely, to pass laws necessary for the proper government of an American community, and thus to prepare the Territory for admission into the Union as a State, republican in spirit and in form, and with institutions in harmony with American civilization— were used only to sanction in legal form the will of the priesthood; to give immunity to the Asiatic system of polygamy which had been adopted as a tenet of the Mormon church, and to prevent the execution of any law except by agencies created and controlled by the priesthood.  In short, that there existed here an irrepressible conflict between the system established by the Mormons and the republican institutions of the United States which would preclude the admission of the Territory into the Union as long as that conflict continued, and that it could only be ended by destroying the temporal power of the priesthood. As to the reliability of my convictions on these matters the quotations following are in point.

As early as 1857 President Buchanan, in his message to Congress, said:

"Brigham Young has been both governor and superintendent of Indian affairs. * * He has been at the same time head of the church called the Latter-day Saints, and professes to govern its members by direct inspiration and authority from the Almighty. His power has been, therefore, absolute over both church and state."

President Garfield, in his inaugural address, said:

"The Mormon church not only offends the moral sense of manhood by sanctioning polygamy, but prevents the administration of justice through ordinary instrumentalities of law * * * nor can any ecclesiastical organization be safely permitted to usurp in the smallest degree the functions and powers of the national government."

Brigham Young, in the Journal of Discourses, Vol. IV, page 77, said:

"The Kingdom is established. It is upon the earth. The kingdom we are talking about, preaching about and trying to build up is the Kingdom of God on earth—not in the starry heavens, nor in the sun; we are trying to establish the Kingdom of God on the earth, to which really and properly everything pertaining to men, their feelings, their faith, their convictions, their desires, and every act of their lives belong, that they may be sealed by it spiritually and temporally. We are called upon to establish the Kingdom of God literally just as much as spiritually. There is no man on the earth who can receive the Kingdom of God in his heart and be governed according to the laws of that kingdom without being governed and controlled in all temporal matters."

In Vol. VI, page 23, of said Journal, he further said:

"The Kingdom of God circumscribes the municipal law of the people in their outward government."

In Vol. I, page 361, he said:

"Admit for the sake of the argument that the Mormon elders have more wives than one, yet our enemies have never proved it. If I have forty wives in the United States they do not know it and could not substantiate it. Neither did I ask any judge, lawyer or magistrate for them. I LIVE above the law, and so do this people."

In Vol. XI, pages 354 and 355, he said:

"Why do we believe save as we do on these points? Because God has spoken, and we believe him. We are aiming at something more than religious unity. We have a political existence none can ignore and destroy. They think they can; but they cannot. They cannot make us mingle with the confusion of Babylon no more than they can make oil and water coalesce. There is no affinity between us. They profess very little faith in God, and know nothing about him. While we profess faith in God, and we do know that he loves and speaks to his people. Hence unity between them and us is impossible."

Orson Pratt, one of the twelve apostles, and the most celebrated scholar of the Mormon church, published, in Liverpool, England, a series of essays from which the following is an extract:

## THE ONLY LEGAL GOVERNMENT.

"The Kingdom of God is an order of government established by divine authority. It is the only legal government that can exist in any part of the universe. All other governments are illegal and unauthorized. God, having made all beings and worlds, has the supreme right to govern them by His own laws and by officers of His own appointment. Any people attempting to govern themselves by laws of their own notion, and by officers of their own appointment are in direct rebellion against the Kingdom of God. * * * For seventeen hundred years the nations upon the Eastern hemisphere have been entirely destitute of the Kingdom of God—entirely destitute of a true legal government—entirely destitute of officers legally authorized to rule and govern. All emperors, kings, princes, presidents, lords, nobles and rulers have acted without authority * * *. Their authority is all assumed; it originated in man. Their laws are not from the great law giver, but are the production of their own false governments. Their very foundations were laid in rebellion, and the whole superstructure from first to last is a heterogeneous mass of discordant elements, in direct opposition to the Kingdom of God, which is the only true government which should be recognized on earth or in heaven."

The following is an extract from a sermon of John Taylor, one of the twelve apostles, and afterwards the successor of Brigham Young, found in the Journal of Discourses, Vol. V, page 149:

"Some people ask, What is priesthood? It is the legitimate rule of God, whether in Heaven or on the earth, and it is the only legitimate power that has a right to rule upon the earth. We came to serve God, to a place where we could more fully keep His commandments, where we could fulfil His behests upon the earth. This is why we came here. Well, then, if we are the only people whom God acknowledges as a nation, have we not a right to the privileges we enjoy? Who owns the gold and silver and the cattle on a thousand hills? God. Who then has a right to appoint rulers? None but Him or the man He appoints."

I could add a large number of other quotations of like import from Mormon sermons and publications, but it is unnecessary to do so. I will, however, add some enunciations from Gentiles of high standing, who have given the subject studious attention. The following is from the reply of Judge Rosborough, chairman of the Democratic central committee, to a communication from the chairman of the central committee of the People's party (church party) requesting him to participate in a constitutional convention called by the church party:

"Your party is the dominant church, and that church as a political organization constitutes your party; nothing contained in one is wanting in the other, and neither contains what is not tolerated in the other. They are one and the same in their membership, so that independent political action by an individual can never occur except with apostasy from the creed. The theory upon which our republican institutions are based is that all political power is derived from the people. On the contrary, the leaders of your party claim and teach, and their followers concede, that all rightful political power is derived from God, and is delegated to his chosen ministers, who have a divine commission to rule over the people whose first duty it is to obey counsel (i. e., submit to dictation) in temporal as well as spiritual concerns; and they further hold and teach as a political maxim as well as a dogma of a creed that this divine commission entitles them to the present right to and the near-future possession of sovereignty to be founded upon the ruins of all secular (man-made) governments. Such assumptions are utterly repugnant to American institutions, but at the same time these pretentions gauge the patriotism of these leaders and denote the intelligence and other qualifications of their followers for citizenship and statehood."

Judge McBride, committee chairman of the Republican party, in reply to a like communication, said:

"If Utah shall be clothed with the forms of a State, the result would be a theocratic State in which, as Mr. Cannon, one of your ablest and wisest oracles expressed it, 'the voice of God will be the voice of the people,' and this voice finds expression through his chosen mouthpiece—the head of the Mormon church. This political axiom of your People's party is announced by its recognized leaders, and is accepted with full faith and obedience. It reverses the entire theory upon which all republican governments are founded, and derives the authority to govern not from the people, but from those anointed, as you claim, by a divine commission to rule over them. These differences are too radical for accommodation, for our fundamental idea of all civil government is that it is derived from the people. In a State established under a theocratic idea, a free public sentiment finds no place. It extinguishes and annihilates all the fundamental beacons of the republican government around us, and remits us to the darkness of that superstition and fanticism which the world of intelligence and law has been struggling to escape. This element of your system—or faith, if you choose to call it such—renders it impossible for your people to live in harmony with any other communities in our land."

The supreme court of the Territory, in the case of the United States v. The Church (15 Pac. 467), uses this language in the opinion delivered by Chief Justice Zane:

"At the head of this corporate body (the church), according to the faith professed, is a seer and revelator who receives under revelation the law of the Infinite God concerning the duty of Man to himself and to his fellow beings, to society, to mankind and to God. In subordination to this head are a vast number of officers of various kinds and description comprising a most minute and complete organization. The people who comprise this organization claimed to be directed and led by inspiration that is above all human wisdom and subject to a power above all municipal government, above all man-made laws. These facts belong to history, therefore we have taken notice of them."

Governor West, in a message to the territorial legislature, said:

"These many voices of the past, replete with anguish, ask us why—of all the people in our land of nearly every nationality, of no religion, and all religions, with beliefs and creeds as various and numerous almost as the different nations of men—should this people stand singular and alone in its woeful history? Can anyone doubt who approaches with unprejudiced mind the consideration of the question that the cause is founded in the theocracy established and maintained here, in the education of the people to believe that God has chosen this people to take possession of the earth and dominate and control all other peoples? That through his priesthood God governs them immediately, not alone in faith and morals, but in all the affairs and relations of life, and that the council of the priesthood is the supreme voice of God, and must be obeyed without question."

"It necessarily follows that perfect and complete unity has and does exist among the Mormon people; an absolute oneness, without division and dissent. The unity in the State which comes from a fair discussing of public questions, securing by merit conviction of the mind and triumph of the right, is desirable and commendable. The unity that is obtained by recognizing the supremacy of one man, or set of men, the attributing to him or them a knowledge and power not granted to others—derived from a superhuman and supreme source, and therefore not to be questioned, but must be obeyed is the establishment of complete absolutism in those holding power, and the most abject and servile slavery on those submitting. The submission to a government by God through his priesthood, and the unity it enforces, brought this people to accept, sustain, and uphold polygamy whether practicing it or not, regardless of the sentiment of the Christian world, and in defiance to the laws of the land."

The Utah Commission, composed of G. Y. Godfrey, A. B. Williams and ex-Governor Arthur L. Thomas, in their report to the Secretary of the Interior, said:

"They (the Mormons) have established in the Territory a religious system with a political attachment, the two forming a strong, compact government, with the power of control centered in a few men who claim the right to speak by divine right, and whose advice, counsel and command is law unto the people."

In other connections, further facts in support of my statements will be set forth. The eradication of the intolerable conditions, the existence of which in the Territory I have shown, was the motive which inspired the outspoken opposition of the Gentiles. In Whitney's history these undesirables are variously designated as "conspirators," "crusaders," and "the ring." In view of these evil conditions which existed, the Gentiles would have shown themselves to be wretched miscreants if they had failed to organize and make a vigorous and united effort to end the iniquitous system. They organized the Liberal party for that purpose alone.

22

# CHAPTER II.

## The Organization of the Liberal Party.

In 1867 there were comparatively few Gentiles either in Salt Lake City, or the Territory.

After business hours certain Gentile business men of Salt Lake City were in the habit of meeting at the office of Abel Gilbert, a merchant, and a gentleman of infinite wit and social qualities. At these meetings the state of affairs in Utah was often discussed and condemned. At one of the meetings in 1867, at which William McGroarty, several other business men and myself were present, the approaching election of delegate to Congress having been mentioned by someone, I stated that if we intended to stay in the Territory we should organize and oppose the political control of the priesthood. As my suggestions were approved by all of the other persons present, I moved that we begin by nominating Mr. McGroarty as a candidate of the Gentiles for the office of delegate to Congress in opposition to Captain Hooper, the candidate of the church party for that office. McGroarty stroked his long beard and said: "Barkis is willing." Whereupon my motion was seconded, and passed unanimously. In a few days afterwards handbills announcing the candidacy of McGroarty were posted in the city, and sent to. the various parts of the Territory where there were any Gentiles. At the election McGroarty received 105 votes. McGroarty contested Hooper's seat, the main purpose of the contest being to direct the attention of Congress and the nation to existing conditions in Utah. That purpose was accomplished to some extent by a telling speech which McGroarty made in the House of Representatives in support of his contest.

Before the next election for delegate to Congress a convention of Gentiles convened at Corinne, organized more formally a political party and christened it the "Liberal party." That party continued to gain strength from its organization until the admission of the Territory as a State, when it was dissolved. Its sole motive was, as before stated, to correct the abuses prevalent in Utah, and to establish republican American rule in place of the usurped rule of the priesthood of the Mormon church. In 1876 I was nominated by that party as a candidate for the office of delegate to Congress.

John C. Young, a nephew of Brigham, who at the time of his death was postmaster of Portland, Oregon, and Zera Snow, the son of a prominent Mormon, who at present is one of the leading lawyers of Portland, accompanied me on a stumping tour from Salt Lake City to Logan, and we made the first political speeches delivered outside of Salt Lake City. To use a common expression, these young men "talked out in church." At Logan our meeting was almost broken up by Mormons evidently sent there for that purpose. It was very gratifying to me, and strengthened my faith that our party would ultimately succeed in accomplishing the praiseworthy purpose for which it was organized, to see such gifted young men of Mormon parentage as Young and Snow fearlessly face that threatening mob, and hear them defiantly assert their independence and right as free American citizens, to oppose the arbitrary dictation and political control of the priesthood of the Mormon church. I wrote a letter addressed to the chairman of the committee of the party accepting the nomination referred to, in which is stated what the Liberal party was striving to accomplish. Its context follows:

"Laws necessary to protect the ballot from corruption and fraud, and relieve electors from all fear and restraint in the exercise of the elective franchise, are vital to republican institutions. As the territorial legislature has not only failed to enact the customary laws to prevent corruption, fraud and intimidation in elections, but on the contrary, has passed laws which facilitate the commission of these wrongs, the Congress of the great Republic will certainly not much longer withhold relief from a minority which is struggling with an unscrupulous and anti-republican majority for that birthright of freemen—a fair chance at the polls. The political status of the Territory is anomalous. While the two great parties of the country are actively engaged in every State and other territories discussing the issue of the pending presidential campaign, in Utah the line which divides the great national parties is not drawn. Here an issue exists which has never arisen, and I pray may never arise, in national politics—an issue, the existence and settlement of which in other nations has caused more misery, opened wider the floodgates of evil passion, and caused the shedding of more human blood than all of the other causes of civil strife added together. This issue, in the form in which it presents itself in this Territory, is democratic-American principles against a union in the most obnoxious form of Church and State. Between these antagonistic principles there is an irrepressible conflict which will end only by the triumph of the former. The existence of such anomalous issues in the nineteenth century, within the jurisdiction of the greatest and freest republic on the face of the earth, is due to the failure of Congress in the exercise of its revisory legislative power over the territories, to disapprove the numerous laws which have remained in force on the statute books of the Territory for many years, and which were enacted by the ecclesiastical legislature of Utah for the purpose of fostering theocratic rule and defeating the execution of all laws which in any way interfere with such rule. Also to the failure of Congress to pass laws necessary to put into successful operation, in fact as well as in form, a republican form of government in the Territory, to establish the supremacy of law therein, and provide means for its faithful and efficient execution. Owing to the imperfections and want of legislation for the Territory, the federal government is powerless to efficiently execute the laws, and as a consequence the law of 1862, which prohibits the unlawful practices of the Mormon church, remains a dead-letter, and will so continue until Congress remedies the evil by proper legislation. It is vain to look to local legislation for any remedy, because local legislation has in the main contributed to create the evil. It is beyond the power of any man, ring, party, or church, to end this conflict between democracy and theocracy, except by establishing the supremacy of the former. My alien antagonist (George Q. Cannon) has stated to the Mormon community that I am their worst enemy. I assure the Mormon people that I am not their enemy, but their friend. I claim no rights or privileges for myself as an American citizen which I do not accord to my fellow-citizens. In common with the Liberal party I desire the establishment of the supremacy of law, freedom of thought, freedom of speech and freedom of action in Utah as it exists in other states and territories of the Union; the enactment of an election law which will insure honest elections and enable every man, however poor or dependent he may be, to go to the polls and freely deposit his ballot for whomsoever he may choose, without the fear of the infliction of ecclesiastical penalties; to establish a system under which every one may freely and fully exercise his own individuality, choose his own business, political and social relations, without the consent of any bigoted apostle, bishop, or teacher. A system under which every man will have an equal chance with every other man—an equal chance by personal worth or dint of honest effort to attain the highest social, political and business advancement without having to lay his manhood down at the foot of the priesthood, or kiss the great toe of some pretended prophet. A system under which the people, and not the church, may freely choose their own rulers, and religious bigotry cease to be an essential requisite to the attainment of office or business patronage. A system which will put an end to church business monopolies and church aristocracy, restore the natural laws of trade and social intercourse, and allow without question every man to manage his own affairs, hold the title to his own property,[1] and run the course of life without weight upon his shoulders. Such, and such only, are the ends which the Liberal party is striving to gain, and which it will finally accomplish. The present campaign is just as important as will be the one in which victory is eventually won by the Liberal party, because only by this and other similar campaigns can the temple of liberty be finally reached."

At the ensuing election I received about 5,000 votes, which was very encouraging, as it showed that since the candidacy of McGroarty the party had greatly increased and was beginning to present a formidable front to its antagonist. At the Salt Lake City election of 1889 the Liberal party elected George M. Scott as mayor, as well as the council and other city officers. Two years afterwards the party again carried the city, at which time I was elected mayor and held office for four years. When I was installed it became my duty to specially investigate existing affairs with a view of ascertaining what the necessities of the city required. By reason of the fact that but slight public improvements had been made before the Liberal party came into power, and the church party had failed to make such improvements during the many years of absolute control, gradually as the necessity imposed by growth arose, I found that it required several millions more money to make of Salt Lake City a modern city, than would have been requisite had the previously necessary improvements been made; that the waterworks and the sewer system were so inadequate that it was absolutely essential to build, almost entirely, new ones; that except Commercial street, and Main and State streets for two blocks each, which had been paved during Scott's term, the streets in the business center of the city were merely graveled, as were most of the sidewalks in that

---

[1]At that time, the "Order of Enoch" had been established by the priesthood, and members of the Mormon church were required to convey all of their property to that "Order," and in many instances such conveyances had been made.

center; that outside of the center the streets were on the native soil, as also the sidewalks, except for the limited distance where asphalt had been laid during Scott's term; that a woeful lack of sanitary conditions existed; that in most of the resident portions of the city the inhabitants were using water from wells, and that in their vicinity human excrement had for years been deposited in cesspools and privies, which had become a menace to public health by neglect; that in consequence, the city, instead of being among the healthiest as natural conditions warranted, was third in mortality in the United States, and that a general cleansing of the city was imperatively necessary.

Thus by the neglect of the former administration of the church party there was saddled upon the subsequent taxpayers an enormous burden. The public improvements necessary for the comfort and welfare of the inhabitants of the city were too great to be made during one or even a half dozen subsequent administrations, and to raise the money for immediate needs by taxation would have been too burdensome for the taxpayers. The Liberal administrations, therefore, to lighten this burden, issued long-time bonds of the city, so that future generations which would enjoy the benefits of the improvements would also have to defray part of the expense. During the administrations of the Liberal party, adequate waterworks and a sewer system were constructed, the streets in the business portion of the city were paved; many miles of sidewalks were laid; the city was thoroughly cleansed and made as healthful as any in the Rocky mountains; the water supply was increased; the Joint City and County Building—the pride of all beholders—was completed, and in all respects Salt Lake City was brought up to the standard of a city of the first class.

We are mainly indebted to the Liberal party for the new era in Utah. The organization of that party, contrary to what the masses of the Mormon people were taught to believe by their leaders, has not resulted in evil, but in great good to both Mormons and Gentiles. I will later refer to the beneficial results of that organization in another connection.

2

# CHAPTER III.

## Outline of the Cullom Bill.

By my investigations before referred to I became convinced that existing evils could only be corrected by adequate legislation of Congress, and therefore as I had mentally resolved while looking upon the mutilated body of my murdered client, Doctor Robinson, to do all that I possibly could do to place in the hands of the federal authorities the power to punish the perpetrators of such heinous crimes, I drafted the Cullom bill, which contained among others of less importance, the following provisions:

Sec. 2. Provides that the United States marshal and his deputies shall be the executive officers of the district courts.

Sec. 4. That the United States district attorney and his deputies shall be the prosecuting officers of said courts.

Sec. 7. Prescribes the method of procuring grand and petit juries.

Sec. 10. Provides that in all prosecutions for bigamy and the crimes specified in this act no person shall be competent to serve as grand or petit jurors who believes in, advocates, or practices bigamy, concubinage or polygamy, and upon that fact appearing by examination on voir dire or otherwise, such person shall not be permitted to serve as a juror.

Sec. 11. That in all prosecutions for bigamy, concubinage and adultery, the lawful wife of the accused shall be a competent witness to prove both the first and subsequent marriage or marriages of her husband, but for no other purpose.

Sec. 12. Be it further enacted, that whereas marriage in said Territory of Utah, rests solely on the contract of the parties followed by cohabitation, there being no form, manner or ceremony prescribed by the laws of said Territory for the solemnization of this important relation in society or requiring recordation certificate or publication of the same; that in all prosecutions for bigamy, concubinage, or adultery, it shall not be necessary to prove either the first or subsequent marriages by the registration or certificate thereof, or other recorded evidence thereof, but the same may be proved by such evidence as is admissible to prove a marriage in other cases, and proof of cohabitation by the accused with more than one woman no husband and wife, his declaration and admission that such women are his wives, his acts recognizing, acknowledging, introducing, treating or deporting himself towards them as such shall, unless rebutted, be sufficient to sustain the prosecution.

Sec. 13. That any man in said Territory who shall, after this act goes into effect, live or cohabit with one or more women other than his lawful wife as his wife or wives, shall be adjudged guilty of concubinage, and upon conviction thereof shall be punished by fine not exceeding one thousand dollars, and by imprisonment not exceeding five years at hard labor, and in all prosecutions for the violation of this section the adjudged concubines shall be competent witnesses to establish or disprove the charge, provided that no statement made by any such witness shall be used against, admitted, or allowed to affect them in any case whatever.

Sec. 14. That the statute of limitations shall not bar a prosecution for any of the crimes specified by this act, nor for the crime of bigamy, concubinage, or adultery hereafter committed.

Sec. 17. Provides in substance that in case the United States marshal, or any of his deputies, shall be resisted or threatened with resistance in executing any writ or process of any court, said marshal or either of his deputies may apply to the commander of any military camp or post of the United States in said Territory for a posse to aid such officers. Said commander is authorized upon such application to furnish such posse, and said marshal or any of his deputies were also authorized to make such application when necessary to suppress any mob, riot or disturbance of the peace.

Sec. 19. Provides that no alien living in or practicing bigamy, polygamy, or concubinage, shall be admitted to citizenship of the United States; nor shall any person living in or practicing bigamy, polygamy or concubinage, hold any office of trust or profit in said Territory, vote at any election therein or be entitled to the benefits of the homestead or pre-emption laws.

Sec. 23. Provides that no man, a resident of said Territory, shall marry his mother, his grandmother, daughter, granddaughter, stepmother, grandfather's wife, wife's granddaughter, wife's daughter, nor his sister, his half-sister, brother's daughters, father's sisters or mother's sisters.[1]

---

[1]At that time, and until the passage of the Edmunds Act of 1882, there was no law against incest. George D. Watt, who was connected with Brigham Young's office, and who reported most of the Mormon sermons contained in the Journal of Discourses, had married his half-sister and was cohabiting with her. There had been marriages between nephews and aunts, and numerous polygamists had plural wives who were sisters, and in some instances were a mother and her daughter.

The penalty for violating the foregoing section was imprisonment for not more than twenty years, and a fine of not more than one thousand dollars.

Sec. 24. Prohibits marking the ballots.

Sec. 25. Authorizes the probate courts to try and determine civil cases wherein the debt or damages claimed did not exceed five hundred dollars, and in criminal cases to act as committing magistrates.

Sec. 30. Provides a method by which polygamists could be compelled, when their plural wives and their children were in need, to support such wives and children.

By the provisions of said bill all acts and part of acts of the territorial legislature inconsistent with said bill were disapproved.

Every one of these provisions except those relating to the statute of limitations, the homestead and pre-emption laws, and a few others of minor importance which I have not referred to, were afterwards, in substance, incorporated by piecemeal in the Poland act of 1874, the Edmunds act of 1882, and the Edmunds-Tucker bill of 1887. The latter added several provisions which were more stringent than those of the Cullom bill. I presented a draft of the latter bill in 1869 at Washington city to Senator Cullom, who was chairman of the House Committee on Territories, and after explaining its bearing on the Mormon question, he introduced it and had it referred to his committee. Captain Hooper and myself discussed it before the committee, he opposing and I favoring its adoption. The committee reported it to the House and recommended its passage. That Senator Cullom understood what legislation was required to put an end to the evil system at which the provisions of the bill were aimed, the following extract of his speech in favor of its passage shows:

"All that is necessary in my judgment is to give the courts of the Territory power to enforce convictions for violations of law and break down the political power now wielded by the Mormon church, and show thereby that the government of the United States means business and intends to use all the necessary means to crush out this iniquity, and compel obedience to law. A persistent, straightforward determination to do this is all that is necessary; and if this course is pursued these people will submit to law as the people of other portions of the country do and are required to do. I am either for the repeal of the statute of 1862, making bigamy or polygamy a criminal offense, or I am for such legislation and such action on our part as will compel obedience to that law by the Mormon authorities and people.  *  *  * Are we to have any legislation that will effectually crush out this bold and defiant iniquity, or are we going on as we have been for over thirty years allowing this practice of polygamy and bigamy to flourish in violation of human and divine laws, cloaked by the title of Latter-day Saints, a pretended system of religion? Shall we continue to temporize any longer with it and allow its defenders and abettors to go unpunished? But if we are to have any legislation upon the subject, let us have such legislation as will reach the evil and put a stop to it."

The bill was passed in the House by a large majority. When it reached the Senate it was referred to the Committee on Territories, of which Senator Nye of Nevada was chairman. That committee, without opposition, directed the chairman to prepare a report in favor of the passage of the bill, and present it to the Senate.

Notwithstanding the fact that this session of Congress would end in thirty days, Nye, although I frequently urged him to do so, failed to prepare the report. Had the bill been reported as ordered, I do not think there is the least doubt that it would have been passed, for I had canvassed the Senate. What caused Nye's failure is a matter of conjecture. Undoubtedly the enactment of the Cullom bill in 1870 would at a much earlier day have caused the changed conditions in Utah which were gradually brought about by the various acts of Congress afterward, passed piecemeal during the lapse of twenty years.

# CHAPTER IV.

## The Englebrecht Case.

There is no better commentary on the social, political and religious history of a people than the certified record of its contemporaneous court decisions. For that reason I shall take the liberty to cite from time to time those cases which, I believe, are characteristic of the influences which dominated, and the spirit which actuated, the community life of Utah at this time.

Paul Englebrecht and Christian Rehemke, in 1870, were wholesale liquor dealers. They had in their establishment a stock of liquors which cost them before shipment from the east, according to the sellers invoices, $20,000. A dispute arose between them and the city license collector as to the amount which they were liable to pay. Jeter Clinton, the police magistrate of the city, without the institution of any suit, or giving them any notice, issued a warrant to the city marshal requiring him to destroy their stock of liquor. The city marshal and a number of the police force, on August 27, 1870, entered their establishment and rolled and carried on to the sidewalk, every barrel, keg, bottle and vessel containing liquor, and with axes and hammers broke all of them and poured the contents into the gutters. Likewise was destroyed every fixture and article used in their business.

As the attorney of Englebrecht and Rehemke, I instituted suit in the third district court to recover treble damages allowed by the provisions of a Utah statute for the malicious destruction of property. Judge McKean had recently been appointed by President Grant as chief justice of the Territory, but had not yet arrived. Associate Justice Strickland had been presiding over the third district court, and as the September term of that court was near, had issued an open venire to the United States marshal on which that officer had summoned a grand jury. Chief Justice Wilson was the predecessor of Judge McKean, and in the case of Orr v. McAllister had decided that Orr, who was United States marshal, was the proper executive officer of the district court, and that

McAllister, who was territorial marshal, was not. The question whether the United States attorney and marshal or the territorial district attorney and marshal were the proper prosecuting and executive officers of the district court, previous to 1870, had been a mooted one. The question hinged upon the character of the district courts. If they were United States courts, then the provisions of the judiciary act of 1789 applied to them, and the United States district attorney and marshal were the proper prosecuting and executive officers of those courts, and the mode of summoning said grand jury was correct. By the sixth section of that act the supreme court of the United States was authorized to "make rules of practice for the district and circuit courts of the United States." In pursuance of that authority, the following rule was made by the supreme court of the United States in 1864:

"In suits in equity for the foreclosure of mortgages in the courts of the United States, or in the courts of the territories having jurisdiction of the same, a decree may be rendered for any balance that may be found due to the complainant over and above the proceeds of the sale or sales, and execution may issue for the collection of the same."

Evidently the judges of the supreme court of the United States when that rule was made regarded the district courts in the territories as district courts of the United States. After the Territory of Florida was admitted into the Union, an act was passed by the State placing the records of the territorial court of appeals in the custody of a State officer. In the case of Hunt v. Palao et al, (4 How. 590), the question whether the United States or the State of Florida should control the records was involved, and Chief Justice Taney, in the opinion, said:

"The territorial court of appeals was a court of the United States, and the control of its records therefore belonged to the general government, and not to State authorities."

When Judge McKean opened the September term of the third district court in 1870, to which he had been assigned, he found in attendance a grand jury which had been impaneled on an open venire issued by his associate, Justice Strickland, summoned by the United States marshal. Jeter Clinton, and the police officers who had destroyed the stock of liquor mentioned, had been arrested on the charge of maliciously destroying said property, and were under bonds pending the action of the grand jury. Upon the opening of the court, their attorneys challenged the array of the grand jury. Major Hempstead, who was the United States attorney, and myself, made arguments in opposition to the challenge, and referred the court to the rule of the supreme court of the United States before mentioned, the decisions in Hunt v. Palao and of ex-Chief Justice Wilson in the case of Orr v. McAllister, and various acts of Congress bearing upon the question. The challenge was overruled. Respecting that ruling, the following comment is made in the second volume of Whitney's history, page 565:

"With the jurisdiction of the probate courts limited and curtailed as to throw most of the criminal and civil cases that might arise into the district courts, and those courts presided over and officered by men working all but confessedly in the anti-Mormon cause; with the power to select juries from which every Mormon was carefully excluded and none but non-Mormons chosen to find indictments or to render verdicts, the conspirators were jubilant and in high feather, and the rights and liberties of the people at large in imminent jeopardy. The revolution anticipated by the anti-Mormons was at hand. The Mormons were at the mercy of their enemies. The cause of 'the ring' was paramount."

Prior to this time I had never known of a Gentile, under the Mormon method, being selected to serve either as a grand or a petit juror. After the jury system was changed, and under the fifth section of the Edmunds law of 1882, any one "believing it right for a man to have more than one living and undivorced wife at the same time, or to live in the practice of cohabiting with more than one woman" was disqualified, and every member of the Mormon church for that reason was excluded from the juries in the numerous trials of persons charged with the crime of unlawful cohabitation which occurred after the passage of that law. No innocent person was ever indicted or convicted. I do not think that even Whitney, unscrupulous as his history shows him to be, will deny that fact. Nor do I think he really believed that the persons whom he called "crusaders" and "conspirators" had any other motive than to correct existing evils, and substitute in fact a republican system in place of an un-American, Asiatic system established and maintained in the Territory by the high priesthood of the Mormon church.

The Englebrecht case was tried before a jury summoned in the same way the grand jury had been. The plaintiff recovered judgment for treble damages. The supreme court of the United States reversed the judgment on the ground that the jury was not obtained in the manner prescribed by the territorial legislature. It was also held that the district courts of the Territory were not United States courts, and thereby that court not only reversed Judge McKean's decision on that point, but also one of its own, to wit, Hunt v. Palao. Judge McKean's decision was, however, approved by Congress, for afterwards its substance was included in the acts passed by that body. While the judicial proceedings in the Englebrecht case are truthfully stated by Whitney, his unjust deductions and insinuations regarding the case, as in many other matters, show his bigotry.

Judge McKean entered upon the discharge of his official duties a few days after his arrival in the Territory. Among the first questions submitted to him was the mooted one before mentioned. His decision of it accorded with the decisions of his predecessor, Chief Justice Wilson, and of his associate, Judge Strickland, and with the rule and decision of the supreme court of the United States before quoted, and was afterwards sustained by the supreme court of the Territory. A search of our supreme court reports will disclose the fact that numerous decisions of the lower court have been reversed, and that our supreme court has frequently reversed its own decisions. This has been done by every supreme court in the Union, as also by the supreme court of the United States; yet, notwithstanding this, and that Judge McKean's decision should have been the law—and was afterwards, in substance, made the law by the acts of Congress—his action in so deciding is bitterly decried in Whitney's history, as is the action of nearly everyone who has held a federal office in the Territory, and of nearly every individual who has actively opposed the control of governmental affairs by the priesthood. After the Englebrecht case was reversed, it was again tried and the plaintiff recovered a judgment. And as it was doubtful whether even the original cost of the liquor could be obtained on execution, the plaintiff accepted the offer of the defendant's attorney to pay the original cost of the property destroyed. That amount was paid by money taken from the city treasury.

## CHAPTER V.

**Bill Hickman's Confession; Conviction of Hawkins; the Law of Marital Relations Defined; the Uprise and Downfall of Tom Fitch; Vindication of Judge Zane.**

One evening in 1872, Samuel Gilson, who discovered the gilsonite deposits in eastern Utah, came to my office and informed me that the United States marshal held a warrant for the arrest of Bill Hickman, and that he was hiding to avoid arrest by the marshal and escape assassination by members of the Danite organization of which he had formerly been an active member. That having piloted General Connor's soldiers into Utah, and having severed his connection with that organization, his former Danite associates had become suspicious of him, and were seeking his life, and that he wanted to employ me as his attorney. I most positively refused to become Hickman's attorney. Mr. Gilson then stated that Hickman had expressed a desire to make a confession, and that even if I did not accept the offer of employment, that if I would agree to meet him he thought Hickman was in such a state of mind that he would tell me what he knew regarding the numerous murders which had been committed in the Territory. As I was desirous of ascertaining whether such an organization as the Danites or "Destroying Angels"— which was so much talked about and feared, especially by apostate Mormons—actually existed, and as Hickman—if it did exist—would know, I consented to meet him and instructed Mr. Gilson to inform him of that fact. In a short time afterward Mr. Gilson returned to my office and said that Hickman was ready to meet me if I would promise not to have him arrested. This I promised. Hickman, about eleven o'clock at night, in company with Mr. Gilson, came to my office. I had never seen Hickman before. After we had been formally introduced by Gilson, I stated to Hickman what Gilson had told me respecting his inclination to tell what he knew about the matters before mentioned. He hesitated, and I said to him that if, as generally asserted, he was or had been a member of such an organization, and had participated in the numerous murders which had been committed in the Territory, that the only atonement now within his power was to reveal the facts, as it might aid in preventing the commission of other like crimes. After deliberating for about a minute, he said that during his seclusion his mind had been greatly disturbed by the matter, and that he had finally concluded to reveal the facts to me, although in doing so he would acknowledge his own guilt. Procuring a pad and pencil I took down all that he said and also cross-examined him closely. We were together several hours. At that meeting he revealed most of the numerous crimes contained in his published confession, but in more minute detail. I told him that I wanted him to meet me again and repeat his statements. This he consented to do. Within two or three weeks thereafter I met him a second time and, as before, took down what he said and cross-examined him. My purpose in doing this was to test the truth of his confession, because if not true, his several statements would in all probability be inconsistent. At various times when I had leisure I critically examined and compared the statements, and while in the second one he mentioned two cases of murder which he had omitted in the first one, and in the second added some details which were not contained in the first, I failed to detect any contradictory statements. The statements of other persons made to me tended to corroborate his confessions. Having become satisfied that Hickman told me the truth, and at my request he having consented to go before the grand jury and tell what he had revealed to me, I placed the statements which I had so written in the hands of Major Hempstead, who was the United States district attorney, and informed him that Hickman was ready to go before the grand jury and testify to the matters therein set forth. In a few days afterwards I saw him, and, while talking the matter over, asked him if he intended to have Hickman appear before the grand jury. He replied that in view of the recent assassination of Doctor Robinson it would be hazardous to indict Brigham Young and the other persons implicated by Hickman. In reply, I said that in any other place than Utah such a confession would cause an investigation by the grand jury, and that I thought he would be derelict in the discharge of his duties if he failed to move in the matter. He returned the statements and nothing further passed between us on the subject.

A grand jury had, in accordance with the decision of Judge McKean, been summoned for the approaching term of the district court. Upon entering the courtroom on the morning that court was opened at that term, I was informed by the Judge that Major Hempstead had resigned as district attorney, and that his resignation had been accepted. He read from a statute of the United States a provision which authorized a district judge, in case of a vacancy in the office of district attorney or marshal, to appoint a person to exercise the duties of the vacant office until such vacancy should be filled, and said he intended to appoint me if I would accept the position. Notwithstanding I did not desire the appointment, I accepted without the least hesitation, because I could not with good grace decline a position in which it would become my duty to do what I had urged upon Major Hempstead, my most intimate and respected friend.

Upon entering upon the discharge of my duties I determined to procure indictments against the officers of the Mormon church for their violations of the law against polygamy, but I soon found that it could not be done because it was necessary to prove both the first and plural marriages. I was unable to prove the latter because they were entered into in the secret precincts of the "endowment house" of the Mormon church, and were not made public, but carefully concealed. As the legislature had passed no law whatever on the subject of marriage, it was almost impossible to procure evidence even of the first marriage in any criminal prosecution of a polygamist.

In 1852 the legislature had passed an act entitled, "An act in relation to crimes and punishments." Sections 31 and 32 are as follows:

"Sec. 31. Every person who commits the crime of adultery shall be punished by imprisonment not exceeding twenty years, and not less than three years, or by fine not exceeding one thousand dollars, and not less than three hundred dollars, or by both fine and imprisonment, at the discretion of the Court. And when the crime is committed between parties, any one of whom is married, both are guilty of adultery, and shall be punished accordingly. **No prosecution for adultery** can be commenced but on the complaint of the husband or wife.

"Sec. 32. If any man and woman, not being married to each other, lewdly and lasciviously associate and cohabit together * * * every such person so offending shall be punished by imprisonment not exceeding ten years, and not less than six months, and fined not more than one thousand and not less than one hundred dollars, or both, at the discretion of the court."

Shortly after my appointment, the wife of Thomas Hawkins came to my office, and made me the following statement: She said that she and her husband were married in England; that they joined the Mormon church and came to Salt Lake City; that for several years after their arrival they lived happily together; that they were poor and struggled hard to accumulate sufficient means to procure a comfortable home. That she did washing for outsiders; that when by rigid economy they had accumulated sufficient money, they bought a small piece of ground and built thereon a small comfortable dwelling house, and lived peacefully and happily in it for several years, until her husband against her will brought into the house another woman whom he claimed to have married as a second wife; that they were occupying a bedchamber next to her own with a dividing partition so light that she could hear all that transpired between them. As there was a grand jury in session, I said that her husband could be indicted and punished if she would go before the grand jury and testify to the facts as stated to me. This she very readily consented to do. Hawkins was indicted for adultery and convicted. Mrs. Hawkins was the principal witness for the prosecution. The defense objected to her testifying on the ground that being the defendant's wife she was disqualified as a witness against him, but that objection was overruled on the ground that under the provisions of the territorial enactments permitting the husband or wife to testify in a criminal proceeding for a crime committed by one against the other, and authorizing the wife to institute a criminal proceeding against her husband for committing adultery, Mrs. Hawkins was a competent witness. On examining her at the trial I was careful not to elicit any except the following facts: That she and her husband were married in

England; that they came to Salt Lake City and lived there in the residence which they built; and that her husband and the other woman slept together in the same bedchamber in said residence. Knowledge of none of these facts was gained by Mrs. Hawkins from any confidential communications of her husband.

In the case of The State v. Vollander (57 Minn., 255), it was held that upon a charge of adultery, the testimony of the injured husband or wife was competent to prove the offense. In the opinion, after stating that other courts had held otherwise on the ground of public policy, the Court said:

"In this State the matter of public policy is settled by the statute which provides that no prosecution for adultery shall be commenced except on the complaint of the husband or wife, save when insane. If it be consistent with public policy that the injured alone may institute the prosecution, it cannot be inconsistent with it that he or she may support it against the paramour by testifying to facts within his or her knowledge; and it would be strange if the party may make complaint, but may give no evidence in support of it."

Under a statute permitting the husband or wife to testify in a criminal proceeding for a crime committed by one against the other, the supreme court of Nebraska, in the case of Lord v. The State (Northwestern R. 507), held that, on the trial of a husband on an indictment for adultery, a wife was a competent witness against him.

The same doctrine as the above was held under the same statutory provisions as the foregoing in 31 Iowa, 24; 55 Iowa, 219; 59 Iowa, 165; 5 Texas Ct. App., 447 and 9 Texas Ct. App. 277. In the case in Texas, on the trial of a woman for adultery, it was held that her husband was a competent witness against her.

Section 5014 of the Revised Statutes of Utah, enacted by the territorial legislature in 1870 and in force at the time the Hawkins case was tried, contains the same provisions as those upon which the foregoing decisions were based.

In the case of the United States v. Bassett (5 Utah, 131), Chief Justice Zane delivered the opinion in which was held that under this section of the statute (5014, above referred to), in a prosecution for polygamy, the wife is a competent witness against her husband because polygamy is a crime

40

against the wife. The wife of Bassett, on the trial of that case, was permitted to testify over the objection of the defendant's attorneys. Judge Zane, after quoting from the cases above referred to, said, "Other supreme courts have held to the contrary, under similar statutes, but we are clearly of the opinion that upon principle and upon authority, the wife was a competent witness." Associate Justices Boreman and Henderson concurred in the opinion. But the judgment in the Bassett case, as in the Englebrecht case, was reversed by the supreme court of the United States.

A polygamist, if he cohabits with his plural wife is guilty of both polygamy and adultery, as will hereafter be shown, but Hawkins was only indicted for the latter crime, because the plural marriage could not be proved by Mrs. Hawkins. As Whitney has been a Mormon bishop, and has taken the oath of secrecy administered in the endowment house, he knows perfectly well that until the Edmunds law of 1882 was passed—which made unlawful cohabitation a crime—it was impossible to punish any one for practicing polygamy; and that the law of 1862 could not be enforced in the slightest degree at any time. No one, even today, if he were indicted for polygamy, can be convicted, because plural marriages at the present time are secretly performed and concealed, and cannot be proven. Brigham Young was a "foxy chap," and had procured such territorial legislation and such secrecy respecting plural marriage as to give polygamy immunity; and he exulted over the fact in a sermon before quoted, in which he said: "If I have forty wives in the United States, they (our enemies) do not know it, and could not substantiate it."

The difficulty of procuring either the indictment or conviction of a polygamist is illustrated by the case of Miles v. United States (103 U. S., 395). Miles was found guilty by the jury in the lower court, but the supreme court of the United States reversed the judgment. Special facts relative to that case are stated in another connection hereinafter. The following quotations are from the opinion in that case, delivered by Mr. Justice Woods:

"Upon the trial, evidence was given tending to show that a short time before the date laid in the indictment, Oct. 24, 1878, the plaintiff in error was in treaty for marrying, at or about the same time, three young women, namely, Emily Spencer, Caroline Owens, and Julia Spencer, and that there was a discussion between them on the question which should be the first wife; and that upon appeal to John Taylor, president of the Mormon church, the plaintiff in error and the three women being present, it was decided by him that Emily Spencer, being the eldest, should be the first wife; Caroline Owens, being the next younger, the second; and Julia Spencer, being the youngest, the third wife—that being according to the rules of the church.

"It appeared further that marriages of persons belonging to the Mormon church usually take place at what is called the endowment house; that the ceremony is performed in secret, and the person who officiates is under a sacred obligation not to disclose the names of the parties to it.

"It further appeared that on Oct. 24, 1878, the plaintiff in error was married to the said Caroline Owens, and that on the night of that day he gave a wedding supper at the house of one Cannon, at which were present Emily Spencer, Caroline Owens, and others. Evidence tending to establish these facts having been given to the jury, the court permitted to be given in evidence the declaration made by the plaintiff in error, on that night, in presence of the company assembled, and on subsequent occasions, to the effect that Emily Spencer was his first wife.   *   *   *   *   *   *   *   *

"The plaintiff in error lastly claims that the court erred in allowing Caroline Owens, the second wife, to give evidence against him touching his marriage with Emily Spencer, the alleged first wife; and in charging the jury that they might consider her testimony, if they found from all the evidence in the case that she was a second and plural wife.

"This assignment of error, we think, is well founded.

"The law of Utah declares that a husband shall not be a witness for or against his wife, nor a wife for or against her husband.

"The marriage of the plaintiff in error with Caroline Owens was charged in the indictment and admitted by him upon the trial. The fact of his previous marriage with Emily Spencer was, therefore, the only issue in the case, and that was contested to the end of the trial. Until the fact of the marriage of Emily Spencer with the plaintiff in error was established, Caroline Owens was prima facie his wife, and she could not be used as a witness against him.

"The ground upon which a second wife is admitted as a witness against her husband, in a prosecution for bigamy, is that she is known not to be a real wife by proof of the fact that the accused had previously married another wife, who was still living and still his lawful wife. It is only in cases

42

where the first marriage is not controverted, or has been duly established by other evidence, that the second wife is allowed to testify, and she can then be a witness to the second marriage, and not to the first.

"The testimony of the second wife to prove the only controverted issues in the case, namely, the first marriage, cannot be given to the jury on the pretext that its purpose is to establish her competency. As her competency depends on proof of the first marriage, and that is the issue upon which the case turns, that issue must be established by other witnesses before the second wife is competent for any purpose. Even then she is not competent to prove the first marriage, for she cannot be admitted to prove a fact to the jury which must be established before she can testify at all.

"Witnesses who are prima facie competent, but whose competency is disputed, are allowed to give evidence on their voire dire to the court upon some collateral issue, on which their competency depends, but the testimony of a witness who is prima facie incompetent cannot be given to the jury upon the very issue in the case, in order to establish his competency, and at the same time prove the issue.   *   *   *   *

"The result of the authorities is that, as long as the fact of the first marriage is contested, the second wife cannot be admitted to prove it. When the first marriage is duly established by other evidence, to the satisfaction of the court, she may be admitted to prove the second marriage, but not the first, and the jury should have been so instructed.

"In this case the injunction of the law of Utah, that the wife should not be a witness for or against her husband, was practically ignored by the court. After some evidence tending to show the marriage of plaintiff in error with Emily Spencer, but that fact being still in controversy, Caroline Owens, the second wife, was put upon the stand and allowed to testify to the first marriage, and the jury were, in effect, told by the court that if, from her evidence and that of other witnesses in the case, they were satisfied of the fact of the first marriage, then they might consider the evidence of Caroline Owens to prove the first marriage.

"In other words, the evidence of a witness, prima facie incompetent, and whose competency could only be shown by proof of a fact which was the one contested issue in the case, was allowed to go to the jury to prove that issue and at the same time to establish the competency of the witness.

"In this we think the court erred.

"It is made clear by the record that polygamous marriages are so celebrated in Utah as to make the proof of polygamy very difficult. They are conducted in secret, and the persons by whom they are solemnized are under such obligations of secrecy that it is almost impossible to extract

43

the facts from them when placed upon the witness stand. If both wives are excluded from testifying to the first marriage, as we think they should be under the existing rules of evidence, testimony sufficient to convict in a prosecution for polygamy in the Territory of Utah is hardly attainable. But this is not a consideration by which we can be influenced. We must administer the law as we find it. The remedy is with Congress, by enacting such a change in the law of evidence in the Territory of Utah as to make both wives witnesses on indictments for bigamy.

"For the error indicated, the judgment of the supreme court of the Territory of Utah must be reversed and the cause remanded to that court, to be by it remanded to the district court, with directions to set aside the verdict and judgment and award a venire facias de novo."

Notwithstanding Whitney's knowledge of the foregoing facts, in his history he upbraided Judge McKean and myself, because Hawkins was not indicted and tried for polygamy instead of adultery, in the following extract:

"The motive of the prosecuting attorney in proceeding under the laws of Utah, enacted by the Mormons themselves, instead of under polygamous cases, was probably this: That the laws of the territory against adultery and other sexual sins were much more severe than the act of Congress against the practice of polygamy. It is a recognized principle of jurisprudence that courts in interpreting a law, should be governed by the manifest intent of the lawmakers. The intent of the Utah legislature in this case was well known both to Judge McKean and to Prosecuting Attorney Baskin; and their deliberate attempt to wrest the law from its purpose and turn it in another direction to enable them to multiply indictments and inflict heavier penalties than Congress had authorized or justice would warrant, thus wreaking partisan spite upon their religious and political opponents arraigned as prisoners at the bar, was as dishonest as it was despicable." (Whitney, Vol. II, pp. 590-592.)

It is true that a statute must be enforced by the court in accordance with the intention of the legislature. When, however, the intention is expressed by unambiguous language, the intention so expressed must prevail, and cannot be changed by extrinsic matters. It would be dangerous in the extreme to infer from extrinsic circumstances that a case for which the words of the statute expressly provides shall be exempt from its operation.

"The intention of the legislature being plainly expressed so that the act, read by itself or in connection with other statutes pertaining to the same subject, is clear, certain and unambiguous, the courts have only the simple and obvious duty of enforcing the law according to its terms." (Sutherland, State Const., 237.)

Sections 31 and 32, heretofore quoted, are plain and unambiguous. A man who has sexual intercourse with a woman other than his wife commits adultery, and is guilty of polygamy when, having a wife living, he marries another. Cohabitation is not an element of the latter crime; nor does the second marriage make the woman he marries his wife, because such marriage is void, and therefore produces no effect whatever.

In the case of the United States v. West, (7 Utah), the defendant was indicted in separate counts for polygamy and adultery. He was tried before Judge Anderson, convicted and sentenced on both counts of the indictment. On an appeal by him to the supreme court, the judgment was affirmed, and Judge Blackburn, in delivering the opinion in which Justice Miner concurred, said:

"The bigamy was completed when the defendant, having a wife, married another * * * The crime of polygamy being completed, any sexual intercourse the defendant afterwards had with the woman, (the plural wife) constituted the crime of adultery, because the marriage was void, and they were to each other as if no marriage ceremony had been performed."

The West case, the Reynolds case and the Miles case are the only ones that I know of in which a polygamist in Utah was convicted.

In Swancoat v. State (4 Tex. App., 105), it was held that bigamy and adultery are not the same offense, nor maintenable by the same evidence, and therefore a former acquittal of bigamy constitutes no defense against the charge of adultery.

In Owens and Bealy v. State, (94 Ala., 97), it was held:

"The offense of adultery is not necessarily involved in bigamy, and there may be a prosecution and conviction for living in adultery, the parties claiming to have been married, on proof showing that one of them was guilty of bigamy in contracting that marriage. * * * Bigamy and adultery are distinct offenses, and a person may be convicted and punished for each under the same state of facts." (4 American and English Encyclopedia of Law, 35.)

In Vol. II, page 618, Whitney further vents his spleen in the following diatribe:

"The miracle—unforeseen by Judge McKean—which rescued Thomas Hawkins from the consequence of the crimes of his persecutors, was the Englebrecht case, in which the amount at issue being in excess of one thousand dollars, was sufficient to allow an appeal to the supreme court of the United States. Had it not been for this, there is no telling to what lengths the Utah Jeffreys and his fellow violators of law and justice might have caused in their merciless crusade against the Mormons."

The following libelous matter is also contained in Whitney's history:

"That 'something of the kind' (the overthrow of the Mormons) was desired by Judge McKean, who was a religious enthusiast, may be believed. A man who could say and feel as he did, that God had given him a mission in Utah as high above his office of federal judge as Heaven is above the earth, and that whenever the laws of the United States conflicted with his ideas of duty he would unhesitatingly trample them under his feet, was just the one to cherish such a design, and if possible to put it into execution."

That any judge of intelligence or rectitude would utter the disgraceful, discrediting and absurd language attributed to Judge McKean in the foregoing quotation is too extraordinary and improbable to admit of belief, especially on the uncorroborated statement of a historian as unscrupulous as Whitney has shown himself to be. Nor will any unbiased person who reads Whitney's own estimation of Judge McKean's general character, expressed in the following quotation, believe that Judge McKean was guilty of an impropriety so gross and foolish as the utterance of such language by him would have been:

"In society few could be more courteous, pleasant and winning than Judge McKean. These qualities, added to his intelligence, made him many friends, who were warmly attached to him. He was an accomplished scholar and could write good newspaper or magazine articles, and, withal, he was a brave man and a determined one, and but for the element of fanaticism in his nature so manifest in his dealings with the Mormons, a proneness to prejudice, which blinded his judgment, biased his official conduct, and trailed like a serpent among flowers over all of the noble traits of his character, would have been 'a man picked out of ten thousand' for most of the qualities that go to make up a sound and complete manhood. * * * No one questioned his sincerity, his patriotism, his earnestness in the discharge of what he deemed his duty; and it does not mend matters to say that Judge McKean believed himself to be an upright Judge, a merciful magistrate; so, too, no doubt, did Jeffreys, England's judicial infamy, and likewise the Spanish inquisitor, Forquemada."

The following is a quotation from a speech delivered by Tom Fitch at the constitutional convention of Utah in 1872:

"James B. McKean is morally and hopelessly deaf to the common demands of the opponents of his policy, and in any case where a Mormon, or a Mormon sympathizer, or conservative Gentile was concerned, there may be found rulings unparalleled in the jurisprudence of England or America. Such a man you have among you—a central sun. What of his satellites? The mineral deposits of Utah have attracted here a large number of active, restless, adventurous men, and with them have come many who are unscrupulous, many who are reckless—the hereditary foes of industry, order and law. This class, finding the courts and federal officers arrayed against the Mormons, have with pleased alacrity placed themselves on the side of courts and officers. Elements ordinarily discordant blend together in the same seething cauldron. The officers of justice find allies in those men who, differently surrounded, would be their foes; the bagnios and the hells shout hosannas to the courts; the altars of religion are invested with the paraphernalia and the presence of vice; the drunkard espouses the cause of the apostle of temperance; the champion of harlots preaches the beauties of virtue and continence. All believe that license will be granted by the leaders in order to advance their sacred cause, and the result is an immense support for those friends of immorality and architects of disorder who care nothing for the cause, but everything for the license. Judge McKean and others are doubtless pursuing a purpose which they believe in the main to be wise and just, but their following is of a different class. There is a nucleus of reformers and a mass of ruffians; a center of zealots and circumference of plunderers. The dramshop interests hope to escape the Mormon tax of $300 per month by sustaining a judge who will enjoin a collection of the tax, and the prostitutes persuade their patrons to support judges who will interfere by habeas corpus with any practical enforcement of municipal ordinances.
"Every interest of industry is disastrously affected by this unholy alliance; every right of the citizen is threatened,

if not assailed, by the existence of this combination. Your magistrates are successfully defied, your local laws are disregarded, your municipal ordinances are trampled into the mire. Theft and murder walk through your streets without detection; drunkards howl their orgies in the shadow of your altars. The glare and turmoil of drinking saloons, the glitter of gambling hells, and the painted flaunt of the bawd plying her trade, now vex the repose of the streets which beforetime heard no sound to disturb their quiet save the busy hum of industry, the clatter of trade and the musical tinkle of mountain streams."

The foregoing is an infamous slander, and yet Whitney has given it currency by quoting it with approval in his history. The motive of Tom Fitch in making that outrageous speech is explained by antecedent occurrences given hereunder. At the time the Cullom bill was pending in Congress, Fitch was a representative from Nevada, and made a speech against it in which he lauded the Mormons and from which the following are extracts:

"I am impelled to the conviction that this bill, if enforced as law, would provoke consequences most prolific of misfortune, and entail results altogether unapprehended. The Mormons would regard the passage of this bill as a declaration of war, and, panoplied by a purpose only less dear to them than life itself, they will hasten to fortify and provision and arm themselves. They will promptly proceed to cut off all means of communication with the outside world. With their facilities for organization, they could destroy hundreds of miles of the great overland railroad in a week. They could maintain a contest for months, perhaps for years. Of course we could finally conquer them because we could exterminate them. But it would cost us millions upon millions of treasure; it would cost us the interruption of that travel which is permanently growing in importance, and which promises, if undisturbed, to fulfill the dream of Columbus, and make America a new highway to the Indies. * * * The truth is that our system of government is unfit to deal with a problem such as the Mormon question presents. Our government rests upon the virtue and intelligence of the people, and laws unsustained by opinion are apt to remain unenforced. Every State and Territory is to some extent self governed, and independent. If the people of any country tacitly agree that a particular crime shall not be considered a crime if committed within that country, what is to be done about it? If grand juries persistently refuse to find indictments, or petit juries regularly return verdicts of 'not guilty'

48

for that particular crime, there is no way to reach the matter or punish the offender through the ordinary processes and means permitted under a republican form of government.

"There is no power vested in the executive or judge to take offenders beyond the limits of their State for trial. Cases of this character can be reached only by finding evidence of such an armed and general conspiracy to resist the laws as to authorize the suspension of civil authority within the infected district and the interposition of military rule. That remedy is expensive and its frequent use most dangerous and should never be resorted to except in extreme and desperate cases. I do not believe the present is such a one. If we deliberately elect to precipitate this Mormon war, right or wrong, let us reckon the requirements. We must select our bravest men and put them in the front. Men who will fight for the lust of blood, for the inspirations of patriotism, of national faith or even of political liberty—all are wanting. This bill is as inoperative as ill-considered; as worthless for all practical purposes in detail as it is generally unwise and premature. * * * I do not intend that my position upon this matter shall be misrepresented to my constituents or the country. I regard polygamy as an evil to discourage, and a violation of law which should be, if possible, prevented.

"I simply doubt the wisdom of the means selected to achieve that result. For the coercions, misrepresentations and fraud with which the Mormons have sometimes sought to carry out their purposes there will come a day of reckoning and repentance. For the murderers of Mountain Meadow the God of Justice holds in his hand some terrible retribution But because of crimes some of that people may have committed in the past, nor yet because of their refusal to obey the laws we have made for them alone, I am not willing to plunge headlong into war. If there be those upon this floor who desire to confiscate the property of these outcasts—who consent to give their men to the sword and their women to the bagnio, and are ready to meet the just reproaches of a tax-burdened and humane people, they must proceed without my help. I am not willing to look upon the ruin of the great road which forms the keystone of the arch of the highway around the world. I am not willing to destroy the channels through which my people hope to receive the life-currents of empire. I count the cost and I count the result, and I am not willing to pay the price of reaching the result. I will not vote for this bill which will add millions to the debt and thousands to the muster roll of the nation's dead and in the name of a people who have burdens enough to bear and kindred enough to mourn, I protest against the passage of this most unwise and ill-considered bill!"

That bill was passed in the House by a large majority, but was not voted upon in the Senate because Senator Nye of Nevada, chairman of the Senate Committee on Territories, failed as directed by his committee to report to the Senate a resolution favoring its passage.

All of the provisions of the Cullom bill, except a few minor ones, were afterwards enacted by Congress and enforced in Utah. Instead of causing war, their enforcement materially contributed to the betterment of the evil conditions in Utah, to correct which those provisions were enacted by Congress.

While by that speech Fitch gained great eclat and popularity among the Mormons in Utah, it ruined him in Nevada. When, as a candidate of the Republican party, he stood for re-election to Congress at the ensuing election, he was badly defeated, nowithstanding a large majority of the electors at that time in Nevada were members of his party.

Persons who resided in Nevada and took part in that election have told me that Fitch while speaking in various places in the State in support of his re-election was often interrupted by the question, "Tom, tell us how much Brigham paid you for making that speech against the Cullom bill?"

After his humiliating defeat for re-election, Fitch came to Utah and started the movement for Utah statehood, in pursuance of which the constitutional convention was convened, at which he made the speech in which he uttered the infamous slander before quoted. He was a crafty and adventurous aspirant for the office of United States senator. That speech was not an expression of conscientious conviction. He expected that its delivery would add to the popularity he had already gained by opposing the Cullom bill and procure the support of the priesthood which would insure his election as United States senator, when, as he confidently expected, admission of Utah as a State would be gained under the movement started by him.

The constitutional convention, which convened on February 19, 1872, provided in the constitution adopted by it that an election of state officers should be held on March 18th of that year, and previous to the anticipated admission of the Territory into the Union. Tom Fitch was elected United States senator at that election. He succeeded by his methods, before referred to in gaining the support of the Mormons; but soon after his election the failure of the movement for statehood thwarted his scheme of preferment and he soon afterward left Utah and remained away until after the enabling act for the admission of Utah was passed in July, 1894. Soon after that event he again settled in Salt Lake City, and announced his candidacy for United States senator.

It is evident that he returned to Utah with the expectation of being elected United States senator as a reward for his former services in behalf of the Utah hierarchy. He knew that but few Gentiles would be elected to the new State legislature, and that he had no chance whatever of receiving any of their votes. He expected, however, that the reputation he had previously gained would secure for him the support of the Mormon members of the legislature. But a salutary change in Utah conditions had occurred during his long absence from the Territory, and such services as he had rendered, and for which he looked to be rewarded, had ceased to be appreciated. In the balloting for United States senators by the legislature he failed to receive a single vote. Soon afterward, the hierarchy having failed to requite him for supporting its cause, as it has generally done respecting other jack-Mormons when their support, like Fitch's, ceased to be useful, he again "shook the dust of Zion from his feet." While Tom Fitch by his well-known record had won the sobriquet of "Silver Tongued Orator," he has not gained by it a reputation for probity.

\*  \*  \*  \*  \*  \*  \*  \*  \*  \*  \*  \*

The reversal of the Englebrecht case rendered the execution of the laws in Utah impossible except through Mormon instrumentalities, and rendered effective the acts of the territorial legislature passed for the purpose, as before shown, of preventing the execution of certain laws by the federal authorities. That reversal, instead of injuring, strengthened the Liberal cause. It directed the attention of the nation to the necessity of additional legislation by Congress and brought about the enactment of the rulings of the lower courts in the Englebrecht and Barrett cases.

Whitney, like Hawkins, having been guilty of the crime of polygamy, the acts of Congress made necessary by the reversal of the Englebrecht decision naturally caused him to become spleeny and apprehensive. He could no longer practice polygamy with impunity, and in his history he displayed his venom by casting wholesale aspersions on faithful federal officers and members of the Liberal party who had been active in bringing about the betterment of the social status in Utah.

Tom Fitch's infamous slander and Whitney's despicable calumnies have been disseminated by quotations in a base "take-in" entitled "History of the Bench and Bar of Utah," recently published, and in which currency is given to the following insinuations:

"Judge Zane's Decisions—Kenner tells us that from this point on the campaign against polygamic offenses waxed warm and active, the Judge lending all that his position was capable of to it. In point of effectiveness and results, Judge Zane made Judge McKean's record look like a thing of threads and patches. 'Abandon hope all ye who enter here,' was not written over the entrance to the courtroom, and would not have been appropriate anyway, because if the defendant happened to be accused of anything else than unlawful cohabitation or polygamy he stood as good a chance to get away as though it were any other court."

Judge McKean was both upright and intelligent, and has been derided by Whitney and other fanatical polygamists because, under his decisions in the Englebrecht and Hawkins cases, they could no longer violate with impunity the law of Congress against polygamy. The overruling of the former decision, as before stated, led to enactments by Congress under which polygamists could be punished, notwithstanding the means devised by the priesthood and the acts of the territorial legislature which for so many years had rendered impossible the enforcement of the law of 1862 against polygamy in Utah.

Judge Zane, having been appointed chief justice, arrived in Salt Lake City August 23, 1884, and has since resided there. He is too well known, and his uprightness both as a judge and as a citizen is too well established to be impaired by such an atrocious slur as the foregoing. A more conscientious, impartial and humane judge than he never sat upon the bench. During his administration as chief justice a large number of Mormons were convicted of unlawful cohabitation under the Edmunds law of 1882, in the third district court over which he presided. Neither Whitney nor anyone

52

else has the audacity to assert that any of the persons so convicted were innocent, or that any of them had not been granted a fair and impartial trial.

William H. Dickson as United States district attorney, and his deputy, Charles S. Varian, were the prosecuting officers of the court during these trials, and they, like Judge Zane, have since resided in Salt Lake City. Their reputations for ability, official integrity and fair treatment of their fellowmen are well established; and every intelligent unbiased person who is cognizant of the record and character of Judge Zane and those prosecuting officers knows that if any of those cases, or in any case, the evidence had failed to justify a verdict of guilty, further prosecution would have been abandoned and the jury instructed to acquit the accused.

# CHAPTER VI.

## Indictment of Brigham Young and Others.

The grand jury that indicted Thomas Hawkins also indicted Brigham Young and other high officials among the privileged Mormon ranks. They were charged with having violated Section 32 of the statute against lewd and lascivious cohabitation, quoted in the previous chapter, and by virtue of the confession of Bill Hickman, Brigham Young and those implicated by Hickman were also indicted for murder.

"Lewd" and "lascivious" are synonymous. The crime of lascivious cohabitation is defined in Bouvier's law dictionary to be "the act or state of man or woman not married, who dwell together in the same house, behaving themselves as man and wife." I had no doubt that cohabitation with almost the score of plural wives sealed to Brigham would place him among the violators of the provisions of the statute against lewd and lascivious cohabitation.

The two sections of the statute before set out were no doubt passed to punish Gentiles only. The procedure in the trial of the Hawkins case, and the indictment of Brigham Young and others for "lewd and lascivious cohabitation," greatly enlightened the members of the priesthood on that subject. For when it was discovered that those sections applied to their own unlawful practices—that their plural marriages followed by cohabitation was not only the commission of the crime of polygamy, but also of adultery and lewd and lascivious cohabitation—that they were liable to indictment and punishment for either or all these crimes in the same action, the legislature thereupon repealed both sections. Governor Emery stultified himself by approving the act repealing them, and from the time he did so until the passage of the Edmunds law of 1882, neither of the latter crimes was punishable in Utah.

I knew that the indictment of Brigham and others would cause great excitement, especially among the polygamic element of the Mormon church, and if a collision occurred it it would be at the time Brigham was arrested on the charge of murder. To meet such a contingency the United States marshal had appointed about one hundred deputies, most of whom had been soldiers in the Civil war, and General de Trobrian, commander of Camp Douglas, had been ordered to furnish upon the request of the governor a posse of soldiers to aid the marshal. I knew that the arrest of anyone except Brigham would not be resisted. I therefore had Hawkins arrested and tried before taking any steps in the other cases. During that trial the street in front of the courtroom was daily crowded by hundreds of men, many of whom were armed and whose demeanor was most threatening towards the court. I knew that the mob which daily assembled in front of the court house, and which seemed to be in charge of Lot Smith (leader of the squad in 1857 that captured and burnt one of Gen. Albert Sidney Johnston's army trains), in time would become tired and disperse, if nothing more was done than to arrest and place under bonds the persons indicted who were less conspicuous than the high priests of the Mormon church. From time to time, for a period of two weeks, I had such persons arrested. The mob in the meantime had dispersed, and the general excitement had been greatly allayed. Brigham was then arrested on the charge of lewd and lascivious cohabitation, and brought into court. He gave bonds, just as others were required to do. No special demonstration was made upon that occasion. In a few days later I had a warrant issued for his arrest on the murder charge. On Saturday evening I placed the warrant in the hands of the marshal and instructed him to make the arrest on Monday morning, before the court convened, and to inform his deputies to be ready to lend assistance if it became necessary. Evidently some of the marshal's deputies betrayed him, as Brigham learned of his intended arrest. On Sunday afternoon a meeting of a large number of Mormons was held at Jeter Clinton's ranch, which was situated about a mile beyond Garfield Beach. Brigham and other officials of the Mormon church were present. The meeting was convened to decide whether or not the arrest of Brigham should be resisted by armed force. Many present favored resistance, but others opposed resorting to force. Brigham finally decided that instead of resisting he would make a journey to "the south" for his health. Consequently that Sunday night he started south, but he did not, as was his usual custom, travel in state, nor was he met, as usual, by a large delegation at each town through which he passed. His journey from Salt Lake City to Kanab was secretly made. In the height of the excitement, and when the armed mob was menacing the court, a number of prominent Gentiles called upon me and stated that they had reliable information that, unless the prosecutions were stopped, the prominent Gentiles who had taken an active part in opposing the Mormon "system" would be assassinated; that they had been appointed a committee to advise me of the fact and request me to dismiss the cases. I told the spokesman he would make a splendid angel, and as I did not intend to grant the request, he had better prepare to go to Abraham's bosom. He replied that the matter was "too serious to treat facetiously."

I then said: "Gentlemen, speaking seriously, I think I know Brigham Young better than you do. He has assumed the role of a lion, and, if by roaring he can scare me as he has you, and thereby put an end to the prosecutions, it will strengthen the belief of his credulous followers that, as claimed by him, he is under the guidance and protection of a divine power greater than that of the United States; that as a lion he is not of much consequence, and when he fails, as he will, to accomplish his purpose in the role of a lion, he will assume that of the fox, in which he is very formidable." This was not the only time I had been subjected to a fire from the rear by men who should have encouraged instead of opposed me.

When I was in Washington urging the passage of the Cullom bill, which would have brought about much sooner the change which occurred more than twenty years afterwards, a number of men who should have aided, became frightened at the threats made by the leading Mormons in a meeting convened by Brigham, and having met in the Masonic hall in Salt Lake City, adopted resolutions protesting against the passage of that bill and forwarded the same to the Mormon delegate, to be used by him to defeat it.

In November, 1872, before any of the indicted parties except Hawkins were tried, George Caesar Bates, who had been appointed to fill the vacancy in the office of United States attorney, arrived in the Territory. At his request, I explained the status of the cases I had commenced, placed in his hands the written statements I had made of Hickman's confession, and gave to him the names of the other persons who had made statements tending to corroborate Hickman. Subsequently I had frequent consultations with him about the cases. He expressed a desire to bring the cases to trial at the next term of court and requested me to assist him, to which request I assented. He afterwards received a letter from Attorney General Akerman, dated December 20th, which was in answer to one sent to him by Bates, in which the attorney general said: "I have answered by telegraph that you are at liberty to employ Mr. Baskin, and I herewith enclose a commission for him." He delivered the commission to me, and we went along harmoniously for several weeks, but soon he began to make objections. He said that there was no money available to defray the expenses of the prosecution; that upon further investigation he was averse to bringing the cases to trial. At our frequent conversations regarding the matter he habitually made objections. I finally lost my patience, and said to him that it was evident to me that for some unaccountable reason he had changed his former intention of trying the cases, and did not intend to do so; that I had not been employed to discuss with him why the cases should not be tried, but to assist him in the trial; that I would no longer act in the matter and would return my commission to the attorney general with a statement of my reasons for doing so—and this I did.

Later, the judgment in the Englebrecht case was reversed by the supreme court of the United States, and as the grand jury which had found the indictments against Brigham and others was held by that court to be invalid, the criminal cases in question were dismissed. I regret that those cases were not tried, because their trial would have exposed, as did the first trial of Bishop John D. Lee, the deplorable conditions which then existed in the Territory; and the examination of Hickman, in my opinion, would have convinced the public that his confession was true, especially if he had been subjected to a rigid cross-examination.

Bates having been requested to resign, refused to do so, but was removed by the President, and William Cary appointed in his place. Respecting Bates' removal, Whitney, on page 371, Vol. II of his history, says: "Mr. Bates had not shown a sufficiently antagonistic spirit towards the Mormons to suit the President's advisers in Utah affairs. William Carey, however, assumed the role of a 'crusader.'"

Mr. Cary was incorruptible, and faithfully discharged the duties of his office, which caused Whitney to denounce him as he has every other incorruptible and faithful federal officer of the Territory. George Caesar Bates, soon after his removal, became attorney for the church and was employed later by Brigham Young to defend John D. Lee.

At the first trial of Lee on the charge of having participated in the Mountain Meadows massacre, Bates appeared as his attorney and took an active part in the trial. The animus of Bates is shown by the following extract of an article written by him, and contained in Whitney's history:

"Chief Justice McKean and his co-conspirators had their plans apparently well laid, but 'man proposes, God disposes.' Chief Justice Chase and his associates, inspired by the God of Justice, stepped in at the last moment, overwhelmed the enemies of the Mormons, and scattered to the winds their unrighteous machinations. Before we present the proofs, however, from the records of this most remarkable interposition to arrest the hands of those would-be judicial murderers, we will give an analysis of the laws bearing upon the case. * * * Under this state of things the conspirators deemed it necessary at the outset to get rid of the territorial marshal and attorney general, and vest their duties in the United States marshal and district attorney. They also wished to nullify the statutes of Utah providing for the drawing and impaneling of grand and petit jurors, as they could not otherwise use the courts as instrumentalities for the destruction of the Mormons."

# CHAPTER VII.

## The Case of Ferris v. Higley, in Which it Was Decided That the Probate Courts of the Territory Did Not Have Civil or Criminal Jurisdiction.

Previous to the time the case of Ferris v. Higley was commenecd in the probate court of Salt Lake County, I had in several cases put in issue the jurisdiction of that court. But in all of those cases the question of jurisdiction was avoided, and decided in favor of my clients on other grounds. When employed by the defendant in the Ferris case I determined to test the jurisdiction of the court, and with that purpose in view filed a plea to the jurisdiction. Upon its being overruled I rested the case and appealed to the district court from the judgment rendered. That court reversed the judgment of the probate court and sustained the plea. The plaintiff appealed to the supreme court of the Territory, and the district court was sustained. The case was carried by writ of error to the supreme court of the United States. The decision of the court is reported in 20 Wall., 375, and what was decided is shown by the following syllabus of the case.

'The act of the territorial legislature conferring on the probate courts a general jurisdiction in civil and criminal cases, both at chancery and at common law, is inconsistent with the organic act, and is therefore void."

The only courts having general civil and criminal jurisdiction in equity and at common law were the district and supreme courts of the Territory. Yet from the time that the first legislature passed the void act referred to, the probate courts continued to exercise illegally general, civil and criminal jurisdiction, until the final decision of the case of Ferris v. Higley. During that time practically all the legal business, except a few cases in which the United States was a party, was transacted in the probate courts of the Territory.

In several instances individuals were convicted of capital crimes and executed. Of course, all the judgments and decrees rendered in said courts were void. The granting of such unwarranted jurisdiction to the probate courts was inexcusable, and its purpose was to transfer the legal business in local matters, rightfully belonging to the district courts, to courts chosen by and under the control of the hierarchy which existed here.

# CHAPTER VIII.

## The Reynolds Case, in Which the Validity of the Act of 1862 Against Polygamy was Sustained by the Supreme Court of the United States.

In Whitney's History, Vol. III, pages 46 and 47, this statement is made:

"In the summer of 1874, negotiations were opened between the Mormon authorities and United States Attorney, Mr. Carey, and it was arranged that a case should be provided. Mr. Carey and his assistant were preparing at this very time to launch a series of prosecutions for polygamy against prominent Mormons, who, though it was known that they could not be legally convicted—their polygamous relations being of longer standing than the law under which it was proposed to prosecute them—had nevertheless been singled out as a target for a vain, though vigorous onslaught.

"The district attorney agreed that if a test case were furnished, these proceedings should be dropped. This circumstance no doubt expedited the subsequent arrangement. It was stipulated that the defendant in the case should produce the evidence for his own indictment and conviction, and it was generally understood that the infliction of punishment in this instance would be waived. Only the first half of the arrangement was realized. The defendant in the test case, George Reynolds, supplied the evidence upon which he was convicted, but his action did not shield him from punishment, though it doubtless had the effect of mitigating the same. Messrs. Carey and Baskin prosecuted."

Reynolds was convicted of polygamy and sentenced to be imprisoned at hard labor for the term of two years, and to pay a fine of $500. The foregoing statement of Mr. Whitney is absolutely untruthful, as are many of the statements relating to the Mormon question contained in his History of Utah. In his comments he not only misstates the motives of the federal officers of the Territory, but also the motives of the Gentile inhabitants who opposed the despotic hierarchy. If such an agreement had been entered into, and Reynolds in pursuance thereof, as alleged, had furnished the evidence upon which he was convicted, his heavy sentence was a glaring outrage. Mr. Cary, the able attorneys who defended

Reynolds, and myself were present when he was sentenced, and no objection whatever was made to the sentence imposed. If any such "arrangement" had been made, for Mr. Cary or myself (if I had, as alleged, been his assistant in the trial), to have remained silent and failed to interpose an objection to the sentence, would have been dishonorable in the extreme. Moreover, it is irrational to suppose that Reynolds' attorneys being present, would have failed to object. If they had done so and stated the alleged arrangement, the court on its own motion would have either granted a new trial, or imposed the lightest sentence possible. Whitney's statement is flagrantly untrue. In the trial the case was contested from start to finish. Every tangible exception was taken by the able attorneys for the defense, and afterwards urged in the appellate courts. If any arrangement had been made, the long and hotly contested trial was wholly unnecessary. All that was required in the case, if it were intended for a test one, was a demurrer to the indictment on the ground that the anti-polygamy law of 1862 was unconstitutional, and upon its being overruled, an entry of a plea of guilty. Furnishing evidence by the accused was wholly unnecessary, and, in fact, was not done. The facts regarding the securement of the witness whose testimony convicted Reynolds are as follows:

I was not an assistant to Mr. Cary. At the time of the trial General Cowan, who was assistant Secretary of the Interior, was in the city, having been sent here by President Grant to investigate affairs in Utah. He expressed to me a desire to go to the court house where the trial of Reynolds was in progress. I accompanied him there. Daniel H. Wells and other witnesses by whom Cary expected to prove the second marriage, testified that they knew nothing respecting the alleged plural marriage of Reynolds. While Mr. Wells was being examined, and had positively denied all knowledge of such a marriage, General Maxwell, who was United States marshal, stated to me that Cary had failed to prove the second marriage; that there were no other witnesses in attendance, and that the court would have to instruct the jury to acquit the accused. I asked the marshal if the plural wife had been subpoenaed, and he said that she had not. I then secured a subpoena for the plural wife as

DANIEL H. WELLS.

otated in the letter of General Cowan, hereinafter set out, and it was placed in the hands of Arthur Pratt, a deputy marshal, with instructions to procure a buggy and bring the witness to the court house as soon as possible. In about twenty minutes Pratt appeared in the courtroom with the witness, and she was immediately sworn. In her examination she frankly stated that she and Reynolds were married, and that Brother Daniel H. Wells had performed the ceremony. The first marriage having before been shown, the testimony of his plural wife completed the chain of evidence which proved Reynolds' guilt beyond reasonable doubt. Had not the plural wife's attendance been procured in the manner it was accomplished, Reynolds would have been acquitted; and yet that saintly historian has given currency to a patent falsehood, which by implication charges both Mr. Cary and myself with having been guilty of infamous conduct towards George Reynolds, with the evident intention of placing the federal authorities in a false light before the public. For, what could be more disgraceful than the sentence of Reynolds if Whitney's statements are true? The statements were also intended apparently to make it appear that the leaders of the Mormon church had such implicit faith in the unconstitutionality of the law of 1862 that they were anxious to "make a case" for the purpose of testing its validity.

The grand jury which found the indictment against Reynolds was composed of twenty-three members, and among the numerous exceptions taken by the defense was one attacking the validity of the grand jury. On an appeal by the defendant the judgment against Reynolds was reversed by the supreme court of the Territory, which held that the legal grand jury under the law of the Territory consisted of fifteen members, and that the indictment against Reynolds, having been found by a grand jury composed of twenty-three members, was illegal. The indictment was therefore quashed. (See 1 Utah, 226.)

Reynolds was afterwards indicted and convicted for the same offense. He was defended by attorneys, of whom P. L. Williams, the distinguished and able attorney for the Oregon Short Line railroad company, was the chief.

Mr. Williams recently assured me that he and his assistants did their best to secure the acquittal of Reynolds, and took every available exception. At the second trial Amelia Jane Scofield, the plural wife of Reynolds, whose testimony at the former trial convicted him, could not be found, but upon a showing that she had been spirited away by the defendant to prevent the marshal from subpoenaing her to attend as a witness at the second trial, her former testimony was introduced over the objection of the defense and again convicted Reynolds. The judgment on final appeal to the supreme court of the United States was affirmed, and the validity of the anti-polygamy law sustained.

The decision of the case in the supreme court of the United States is reported in 98 U. S., 145. The following extract from the opinion, which was delivered by Chief Justice Waite, shows the number of exceptions urged by the counsel of Reynolds at the hearing of the case on appeal in that court:

"The assignments of error when grouped present the following questions:

"First: Was the indictment bad because found by a grand jury of less than sixteen persons?

"Second: Were the challenges of certain petit jurors by the accused improperly overruled?

"Third: Were the challenges of certain other jurors by the government improperly sustained?

"Fourth: Was the testimony of Amelia Jane Scofield given at a former trial for the same offense, but under another indictment, improperly admitted in evidence?

"Fifth: Should the accused have been acquitted, if he married a second time, because he believed it to be his religious duty?

"Sixth: Did the court err in that part of the charge which directed the attention of the jury to the consequences of polygamy?"

General Cowan, after the final decision of the Reynolds case, wrote a letter to the Cincinnati Commercial, which was published in that paper, and in which he said:

"George Reynolds had been a clerk in the endowment house in Salt Lake City, a position which threw him into immediate communication with the most prominent officials of the Mormon church. He was also well known in the city, and the fact of his polygamous marriage was notorious in the community. The jury, which had been selected in the usual way, was composed of eight or nine Mormons and three or four Gentiles. They were men of fair average intelligence, and to judge from their appearance, would compare favorably with the average jury in the States. The courtroom was filled with a crowd composed largely of Mormons, who were evidently very much interested in the result of the trial. The Gentiles present were most bitterly hostile to the whole Mormon system, and to the polygamous features of it, especially. The case excited additional interest from the fact that it was understood that it would be a test case, and therefore, that the result would settle definitely the question of polygamy in the Territory for the future. The first marriage of Reynolds was proven without difficulty, and the next and only point to prove was the second, or polygamous marriage. To do this the prosecution relied on the following witnesses:

"First: Daniel H. Wells, one of the very highest dignitaries of the church, and the one who had solemnized the marriage. He was at the time mayor of the city and commander-in-chief of the Nauvoo Legion.

"Second: Orson Pratt, a well-known leader and high official of the Mormon church, a witness of the marriage, and one whose duty it seems to have been to keep the records of marriage.

"Third: A bashful young man, whose name is forgotten, who was married at the same time and place, and under the same ceremony as Reynolds.

"Fourth: A sister of Reynolds, who resided with her brother and his second wife.

"One would suppose with such a quartette of witnesses, it would be the easiest thing in the world to prove the second marriage of Reynolds. Yet such a supposition shows an entire ignorance of the true inwardness of Mormon influence over the acts and words of the true-believers, inasmuch as the prosecution was a failure so far as these four witnesses were concerned. Bear in mind that the marriage had taken place but a few months before the trial, probably in August of the preceding year. General Wells swore positively and without hesitation that he had no recollection of performing the marriage ceremony, although the defendant had been in his employ at the time of the marriage and ever since. Orson Pratt had never heard of such a marriage, and did not remember whether he had ever made a record of it or not. The bashful young man, who had kept step with Reynolds while they marched through the mysteries of the endowment house under the matrimonial yoke, had not the faintest recollection of what Reynolds was doing there on that interesting occasion. Miss Reynolds did know that the second wife was living at her brother's house, but did not know in what capacity she was there, showing a lack of curiosity as rare as it was curious. At this point the prosecution had exhausted its resources, and had utterly failed to make out a case. The district attorney could not conceal his chagrin and disgust over his discomfiture, while the Mormons in the courtroom were jubilant, and leaned over the railing to congratulate the exultant defendant over his easy victory. The Gentile spectators were utterly disheartened at the turn of the testimony, as it seemed to them the whole fabric of the prosecution had melted away before the unblushing perjury of the witnesses. At this critical moment, Mr. Baskin, a well-known lawyer of Salt Lake City, formerly of Hillsbourough, in this State, twice the Liberal candidate for delegate to Congress from Utah—a gentleman who is probably as bitterly hated by the Mormons as any other man in Utah— passed to the writer a card on which was written, 'Tell him to call the second wife.' This card was passed to the district attorney, who read it and sprang to his feet as if aroused by an electric shock, and asked the indulgence of the court for a short time. Marshal Maxwell left the court room, and in ten minutes brought in the second wife by a side-door, from which she could be seen by the entire audience. As the marshal stepped aside from the door and revealed the person of Mrs. Reynolds No. 2 framed in the doorway, the consternation in the Mormon crowd was startling. The ghost of Joe Smith would scarcely have produced a more profound sensation. Reynolds settled himself low in his seat with a look of hopeless terror, while the general look of dismay spread through the entire Mormon auditory. Intuitively all seemed to think that here was a witness who was bound to tell the truth. Not expecting that she would be called as a witness, and knowing positively that she had not been subpoenaed, no effort was made to compel her to perjure herself; and such effort, if made, must have failed, as she must either have sworn herself the lawful wife of George Reynolds, or tacitly confessed to being his concubine. The polygamous wife took the oath and advanced to the witness stand in a very quiet and unassuming manner, when the following facts were elicited: 'My name is —— Reynolds (I have forgotten her christian name). I was married to George Reynolds in the endowment house in this city in August last by General Wells. Mr. Orson Pratt was present, and also Mr. ——(naming the bashful young man with the poor memory, referred to above). I spoke to Mr. Wells a few days ago about the case, when he told me that I need not be uneasy about it; that I would not be called as a witness, and that

66

they could not convict George. I have lived with George Reynolds ever since our marriage.'

"And that was all. Now, here was a predicament. Everyone who heard and saw Mrs. Reynolds knew that she was telling the truth, but the truth convicted General Wells, Orson Pratt, and the other two witnesses of perjury, and convicted Reynolds of polygamy. It made a clean sweep, and utterly confounded the whole Mormon outfit there present. But a moment's reflection showed that their reserves were intact, and the district attorney, albeit naturally elated at the temporary triumph, remembered that he had yet some eight or nine apparently insurmountable obstacles between him and a verdict of guilty, in the persons of the many hard-headed Mormons in the jury-box. He was evidently at a loss what move to make next. He had won a victory, but how to secure its fruits—this was the dilemma. He looked around in a helpless sort of a way, as if for counsel. Again Mr. Baskin came to the rescue with another card which was handed to the writer, who read it hastily and handed it to the district attorney. He had written, 'Do not give the case to the jury tonight, but dismiss them to their homes until morning.' Relying upon the sagacity of the advice, the court adjourned after gravely cautioning the jury to have no conversation with anyone with regard to the trial. Mr. Baskin then gave the reasons for his advice, which in substance were: 'The Mormon jurors had advice from Brigham Young to return a verdict of **not guilty**, which he probably thought would be justified under the failure of the prosecution. These instructions would have been followed at any hazard, the result of which would have been a hung jury. Now, Brigham Young and the Mormons generally believe there is a gentleman here present (alluding to the writer) who represents the federal government, and who will report the details of this trial. The evidence of the last witness was so conclusive that a verdict of acquittal would have been an outrage which might justify the government in instituting more vigorous steps for the suppression of **polygamy.** The jury being dismissed, the Mormon members of it will get a new set of instructions, and tomorrow will join in a verdict of guilty, while Brigham will depend on the law's delay, and on uncertainties of the courts, to carry his point.'

"A few minutes later, in a conversation with the judge who presided at the trial, he advanced the same theory, and complimented the district attorney on his tact. Whether the theory was correct or not, the result of the trial fully indicated his sagacity. The cause was submitted without argument the next morning, and in a very short time the jury returned with a verdict of guilty. To Mr. Baskin is due the credit of the conviction of Reynolds in the district court, although he had no direct connection with the case, and the writer trusts he will pardon the mention of his name in connection with the trial. It cannot injure him with the Mormons, as their hatred of him cannot be intesified by any means whatever. Mr. B's instrumentalities in the conviction of Reynolds were not generally known in Salt Lake City, but the recent decision of the supreme court in the case will revive interest and cause all the details of the trial to be read by those who enjoy the study of causes celebres. The trial of Reynolds developed a peculiar trait of the witnesses to protect their peculiar institutions at all hazards, and the unanimity with which they perjured themselves compels the conclusion that there was somewhere a power controlling and directing the current of events in the trial. While the theory with regard to the jury was simply conjecture, yet the conduct of the witnesses in the case certainly justified the belief that the juries, guided by the same mysterious power, would scarcely be expected to prove more virtuous when brought face to face with perjury than the witnesses had been. Polygamy is bad enough in all conscience, but it is simply an incident, a feature of a grand whole, which constitutes one of the most absolute tyrannies under the guise of religion that the sun shines on. It is a disgrace to the government that a colony, the leaders of which ordered and planned the Mountain Meadow massacre, and who have committed hundreds, if not thousands, of as cowardly murders since within the jurisdiction of the federal laws, should be allowed to maintain its organization and flaunt its treason to the world."

If the alleged agreement between the district attorney and the Mormon authorities had been made, as the latter parties have always claimed, and, as they have taught that the constitution of the United States is an inspired instrument, they would have thereby impliedly promised to yield obedience to the law against polygamy in case its validity should be sustained by the supreme court of the United States. After the constitutionality of that law was sustained, the Mormon authorities and their adherents still continued to advocate and practice polygamy. When Reynolds returned to Salt Lake City after serving in the penitentiary the term for which he was sentenced, he was met by church officials, not as a criminal who had been convicted and imprisoned for defiantly committing a felony, but in company with those officials, at the head of a large procession of school children and prominent Mormons, was, as a heroic victim of persecution, escorted to his polygamous home.

Statements similar to those contained in Whitney's history respecting Reynolds were made throughout the Territory by church officials soon after his conviction. The Mormon masses and many Gentiles today are ignorant of the fact that those statements are false. Evidently George Sutherland, a United States senator from Utah is ignorant of that fact, for in his speech in defense of his associate, Reed Smoot, reported in the Congressional Record of January 23, 1907, he said:

"There never was a prosecution at all under the law (against polygamy) until fourteen years after it was passed. In 1876 a prosecution was commenced against one George Reynolds. Mr. Reynolds himself furnished the testimony necessary to bring about his own conviction, contenting himself by depending upon the sole ground that the law was invalid and unconstitutional, and as being an interference with his mode of religious worship."

The officials of the Mormon church knew that General Cowan was in the city for the purpose of investigating the Mormon question. The following is an extract from my speech before the Judiciary Committee of the House in support of the Edmunds-Tucker bill:

"If the law of 1862 had been faithfully executed, much of the hardships that must now follow the solution of this question might have been avoided. The Mormons simply paid no attention to that law. And why? Because they knew it was impossible to enforce any penalties; because the jury system at that time was entirely in the hands of the Church Theocracy, and it was impossible to select a jury in that country to find indictments. It was impossible to take the first step in any prosecution. Their position in relation to this law was that it was unconstitutional and that the amendment to the constitution of the United States gave them the right to practice polygamy as a religious rite. That question has been settled. The law of 1862 was passed on in the Reynolds case, so that it is not now an open question, and I simply call attention to it to show the absurdity or insincerity of the claim of these gentlemen. At the passage of the amendment to the constitution on the subject of religious toleration, every State in the Union had laws against polygamy. It was punished by the laws of England from which we derive our common law. Every State in the Union, from the date of the adoption of this amendment, up to the present time, has had laws against it, and every Territory except Utah. These gentlemen say that that amendment was understood and was intended to give them the constitutional right to practice this anti-American, Asiatic system in our republic. Is it not absurd to suppose that this amendment was intended to give immunity to a practice which was criminal under the statutes of every State by which said amendment was adopted? Just think what that implies. If polygamy is protected by the constitution of Utah, it is also in every State in the Union, and it follows that every man who has been convicted under State laws has been convicted in violation of the constitution of the United States. Looking at the claim of these gentlemen, saying nothing about the vice involved in their system, in view of the circumstances existing when that amendment of the constitution was passed, I cannot give them credit of sincerity. [1]It is simply a subterfuge. They state that they made the case of Reynolds to test the constitutionality of the act of 1862. That statement is untrue. They say in that connection 'We believe the constitution of the United States is an inspired instrument.' Do not these gentlemen know that in that instrument the manner is laid down in which all disputes may be determined? The clause that all cases arising under that constitution shall be submitted to the supreme court, and its decision shall be final upon the question, is as much inspired as any other clause. They say that they made a case to test the constitutionality of this law. Does not that imply an intention to yield the point if the decision should be against them? The decision was against them, but they still insist that the law is unconstitutional, and have continued to treat it as void. Our monogamic system of marriage is just as much a part and parcel of our institutions as any other.

These men have, under pretext of religious toleration, attempted to engraft on these institutions the Asiatic system of polygamy. I ask, Is it remarkable that the American people should object to that? There is just one of two ways to treat the question, that is either to acknowledge their claim that they have a right to practice polygamy and repeal all laws against it, or to meet and overturn it. The bill known as the Poland bill was passed in 1874, which established the present jury system in the territory. These gentlemen at once raised the question of the validity of that act. Afterwards, what is known as the Edmunds bill was passed. None of these meas-

[1]On December, 8, 1788, after the passage of the act establishing religious freedom, and after the convention of Virginia had recommended as an amendment to the constitution of the United States the declaration of the Bill of Rights that "all men have an equal, natural, and unalienable right to the free exercise of religion, according to the dictates of conscience," the legislature of that State substantially enacted the statute of James I, including the death penalty, for the commission of polygamy. (12 Hening's Stat. 691.)

ures settled the matter. As fast as these laws were passed these gentlemen raised the constitutional objection. They carry their cases to the courts, and as often as these are decided against them they insist that the laws are unconstitutional; that they are being persecuted, and that their rights have been invaded; that through prejudice on the part of the country, they are being injured, and that the Gentile population in their midst are seeking to rob and ruin them. In answer to all these things I say that there is not a word of truth in these allegations. In the brief filed on their behalf they arraign everybody who has had anything to do in any shape or form with the execution of the law against polygamy. They even impute improper motives to the supreme court of the United States. They state that the decision of the supreme court on the subject of the Edmunds bill was the result of popular prejudice to which the court yielded. They question the integrity of the legal courts and of every person connected with the execution of the law, however high their standing. They are simply attempting to create sympathy by crying persecution. I undertake to say that there is no desire on the part of the persons intrusted with the execution of these laws to punish innocent men."

In a sermon by Brigham Young reported in the Journal of Discourses, Vol. IV, page 77, he said:

"I have many a time on this stand dared the world to produce as mean devils as we can. We can beat them at anything. We have the greatest and smoothest liars in the world; the cunningest and most adroit thieves, and any other shade of character you can mention. We can pick out elders in Israel right here who can beat the world at gambling, who can handle cards, cut and shuffle them with the smartest rogues on the face of God's footstool. I can produce elders here who can shave the smartest shavers, and take their money from them. We can beat the world at any game. We can beat them because we have men here that live in the light of the Lord, that have the holy priesthood, and hold the keys of the Kingdom of God. But you may go through the sectarian world, and you cannot find a man capable of opening the door of the Kingdom of God to admit others in. We can do that. We can pray the best, preach the best, and sing the best. We are the best looking and finest set of people on the face of the earth; and they may begin any game they please, and we are on hand and can beat them at anything they have a mind to begin. They may make sharp their two-edged swords, and I will turn out the Elders of Israel with greased feathers and whip them to death."

Brigham's assertions are verified in at least two particulars in Whitney's history. Whitney's untruthful statement of the Reynolds case, and his unjust characterization of the action of Judge McKean and myself in the Hawkins case, "was as dishonest as it was despicable."

# CHAPTER IX.

## Marked Ballots and the Absurd Election Law.

The act of the territorial legislature, which was approved January 3, 1853, and remained in force nearly thirty years, contained the following sections:

"Sec. 3. The senior justice of the peace shall be judge of elections in his precinct, and shall appoint one clerk, and furnish the necessary stationery and a ballot box; and in the absence of a justice of the peace, the electors first assembled on the day of election to the number of six, may appoint some suitable person to act as judge of that election."    *    *    *    *

Sec. 5. Each elector shall provide himself with a vote containing the names of the persons he wishes elected, and the offices he would have them fill, and present it neatly folded to the judge of election, who shall number and deposit it in the ballot box; the clerk shall then write the name of the elector, and opposite it the number of his vote."

There was no provision respecting the manner of conducting the election at the polls, but the matter was left entirely to the discretion of a single judge. Non-taxpayers were disqualified from voting or holding office. The Liberal party, as time progressed, continued to increase rapidly in membership, and it was evident that in a few years it would have a majority in Salt Lake City. It was also evident that under the existing election law the Liberal party could not elect its ticket after it acquired a majority. A number of Liberal Mormons, especially among the younger members, from time to time expressed to me a desire to vote the Liberal ticket, but refrained from doing so because their marked ballots would disclose the fact and subject them to discipline or expulsion from the Mormon church, and injure their business in a way they could not afford. It was useless in my opinion to expect the territorial legislature to change the absurd election law, and in view of the fact that it was necessary to have it changed, in connection with Senator Christiancy, who was formerly chief justice of the supreme court of Michigan, I drew up an election bill. He introduced it in Congress and had it referred to the Senate Committee on Territories, of which he was chairman. The bill never became a law, but its most vital provisions were incorporated into other acts passed by Congress. George Q. Cannon and myself discussed the bill before the committee and inasmuch as my speech will show its scope and purpose, and my motives, I make the following extracts from it:

"Gentlemen: The immunity which this crime (polygamy) has so long enjoyed has made it bold and aggressive, as was apparent from the remarks of Mr. Cannon, and unless its progress be soon arrested by wise and adequate legislation by Congress, its evil at no distant day will culminate in calamity of great magnitude to the nation. It strikes at the very foundation of society by destroying the harmony, and contaminating the pure and important relations of husband and wife, parent and child. Mr. Cannon objects to the last section of the bill because it disqualifies polygamists from voting or holding office. He asserts that polygamy is part of the Mormon religion and that the law of 1862 providing for its punishment is in violation of the constitution, and until its constitutionality is declared by the supreme court of the United States, the Mormons have a right to disregard and violate its provisions. The absurdity of such a proposition is surpassed only by its audacity. The application of such a doctrine would totally destroy society, because the thief, the burglar and the murderer would, with as much reason and propriety, make the same claim.

"At the date of the formation of the constitution, polygamy was recognized as a crime throughout the civilized Christian world. Every State at that time and at the time of the adoption of the amendment of the constitution guaranteeing religious freedom, had statutes punishing polygamy, and every Territory, except Utah, has such statutes. It is also a crime both at the common and civil law. Is it not therefore the height of absurdity to claim that the constitution in guaranteeing religious freedom gives immunity to a crime which is universally recognized and punished as such in every Christian nation? Suppose some religious monomaniac should in his delusion imagine that he had received a revelation that the custom of wearing clothes is a perversion of nature, and that it is the will of God that men should go naked, and that in obedience to such a revelation a sect should spring up and insist upon appearing and openly mingling in society in a nude condition—Would the constitution protect such a practice? No, indeed, and why not? Simply because it would outrage the general moral sense of the community. Such a practice would not be much less repugnant to the moral sense of civilized and Christian people than is polygamy. The protection of religion by the constitution ends where license begins.

"The shedding of human blood for the remission of certain sins is a doctrine of the Mormon church as plainly taught and as well understood as polygamy, in proof of which the following quotations will fully show. The Mountain Meadows butcher, John D. Lee, in his confession said:

"For the past seventeen years—in fact, since the commission of the crime—I have given this subject much thought and reflection. I have made an effort to bear my confinement with fortitude and resignation, well knowing that most of those engaged in this unfortunate affair were led on by religious influence, commonly called fanaticism. And nothing but devotion to God and their duty to him, as taught to them by their religion and their church leaders, would ever have induced them to commit the outrageous and unnatural acts—believing that all who participated in the lamentable transaction, or most of them, were acting under orders which they considered it their duty to their religion to obey."

"The following are quotations from the sermons of Brigham Young, contained in the Journal of Discourses, an official publication by the Mormon church. In speaking of the words of Jesus, 'Love thy neighbor as thyself,' he says:

"All mankind loves themselves; let those principles be known by an individual and he would be glad to have his blood shed. This would be loving ourselves even unto eternal exaltation. * * * Will you love your brother and sister likewise when they have a sin that cannot be atoned for without shedding their blood? This is what Jesus Christ meant. * * * Any of you who understand the principles of eternity, if you have sinned a sin requiring the shedding of blood except the sin unto death, should not be satisfied or rest until your blood should be spilled, that you might gain the salvation you desire. That is the way to love mankind. * * * I have known a great many men who have left the church for whom there is no chance whatever for exaltation, but if their blood had been spilled it would have been better for them." (Journal of Discourses, Vol. VI, pp. 219-220.)

"There are sins that cannot be atoned for by an offering upon the altar, as in ancient days; and these are sins that the blood of a lamb, or calf, or of turtle doves cannot remit, but they must be atoned for by the blood of the man." (Idem, Vol. IV, p. 54.)

"When the time comes that we have need to shed blood, then it will be necessary we should do it, and it will be just as innocent as to go and kill an ox when we are hungry, or in time of famine." (Ibid., Vol. VI, p. 59.)

"Many similar quotations could be added from the Journal of Discourses, as also from the Deseret News, a church paper of which Mr. Cannon was formerly the editor, but time will not permit.

"Is that portion of the Mormon creed also protected by the constitution? Polygamy at the formation of the constitution was as well recognized as a crime as that of homicide, the difference being only one of grade.

"The gentleman said that 'there has been only one conviction for polygamy since the passage of the law of 1862.' This is true, and I do not believe that it will be possible to procure another one until by some means jurors can be selected who recognize the supremacy of municipal law, and yield to the obligation of an oath administered by a civil magistrate. The Mormon people do not recognize the supremacy of that law. On this subject Brigham Young, in another sermon said, 'I live above the law, and so do this people.' Because persons guilty of open crime have not been and cannot be punished is no reason why they should continue to enjoy immunity, but is the very best reason in favor of the provisions of this bill.

"Suffrage is not a right, but a privilege, and it rests with the law-making power to fix the limit, and regulate its enjoyment. The laws on this subject are various. Persons who have engaged in a duel, either as principals or seconds, are disqualified by the constitutions of many states, and by the statutes of others, as also by the statutes of Colorado and other territories from voting or holding office. In some instances conviction is required, in others it is not. Persons are likewise, before conviction, frequently disqualified from voting at any election who have bet or are interested in any wager upon the result thereof. By the statute which this bill is intended to supersede, persons who are not taxpayers are disqualified from holding office, voting, or serving on a jury. The provisions of the bill under consideration apply the principles of these precedents to a class of persons, not as the legislature of Utah has done, because they are poor, but because they are guilty of a crime alike revolting to Christianity as it is destructive of the well-being of society.

"Objection is also made because the disqualification does not depend upon conviction. The gentleman well knows that under a system of law which allows criminals to be placed upon juries to indict and try each other there can be no convictions. He has stated that there has been but one conviction of polygamy in fourteen years, and that was aided by the Mormons for the purpose of testing the constitutionality of the law. The latter part of that statement is not true; but, even if it were, it is a pregnant circumstance that while the gentleman was speaking in this connection, he omitted the only thing which could give it any point, namely, he was careful not to pledge either himself or the Mormon people to yield submission to the law in case it should be pronounced valid. The testing of the constitutionality of that law was a safe experiment, even if any such purpose existed, because if such an improbable result should occur as holding the law void, much would be gained by the Mormons; otherwise nothing would be lost, but they could still go on and violate the law with impunity, as they always have done.

"The gentleman complained because adultery and fornication are not also made disqualifying causes. There is a great difference between the cases. Adultery and fornication are not continuing in their nature, while polygamy is. Besides, the polygamic legislature of Utah has passed the most stringent laws to suppress and punish all illicit intercourse between the sexes, which are most harshly and rigidly enforced against all classes outside of the Mormon church, while members of that church are not molested in the indulgence of unbridled lust. Adultery and fornication even in Utah are hid from the light of day, and are only carried on behind bolted doors, and in hidden, dark streets, while polygamy, which in its constituent elements embraces both adultery and lewd and lascivious cohabitation, boldly and shamelessly invades the sacred precincts of the home, and its adherents there revel in debauchery and lust in the home of the lawful wife, and in the presence of her family. Even the sacred ties of consanguinity are disregarded in its invasions, and it unblushingly stalks abroad in open day spreading moral contagion. Adultery and fornication are not so shameless as to claim constitutional protection, while polygamy, with an effrontery which is amazing, makes such a claim and asserts for itself the sanctity and purity of holy religion. Adultery and fornication are not frequent nor general, while polygamy is of daily occurrence.

"The only other objection worthy of notice made by the gentleman, was to that portion of the twenty-fifth section, which makes it penal for any person to threaten, vote for, or in any way take part in the excommunication of any person from any church, or organization called a church, on account of having voted for or failed to vote for any particular persons or person. While the bill renders it impossible to detect how anyone votes by reason of the manner in which the election under it is conducted, it will be very easy in the absence of this provision for the Mormon church, absolute as it has made itself, to force a member by threats of excommunication to disclose how he voted. The gentleman complained that this provision interferes with the church in fixing the rules of fellowship. That is exactly what is intended to the extent specified in the bill and for the best of reasons. No church has any right to exercise such power, because in its exercise the freedom and independence of the ballot box might be entirely destroyed, and in Utah, it most certainly would be. Excommunication from the Mormon church in Utah means, if the party excommunicated be a laboring man, no more employment from his former brethren. If he has a family, in many instances it means to deprive his children of their daily bread. If he be a merchant or a business man, it means bankruptcy and financial ruin. To all persons excommunicated, it means an unfriendly neighborhood, which as General Sherman said of war, 'is hell.' Yea, more, it may mean personal violence or assassination. Let one of Brigham Young's sermons and the bloody history of the Territory say what it means. I quote from Brigham's sermon published in the Journal of Discourses, Vol. I, page 83:

"Now, you Gladdenites, keep your tongues still, lest sudden destruction come upon you! * * * I say, rather than apostates should flourish here, I will unsheath my bowie-knife, and conquer or die ! [Great commotion in the congregation and simultaneous burst of feeling assenting to the declaration.] Now, you nasty apostates, clear out, or judgment will be laid to the line, and righteousness to the plummet! [Voices generally, Go it! Go it!] If you say it is right—raise your hands. [All hands up.] Let us call upon the Lord to assist us in this and every good work."

"Strike out this clause of the bill and the excommunication of a few persons from the Mormon church for voting against the church ticket would do as much, yea, more to affect the freedom of the ballot at the succeeding elections as any threat could possibly accomplish at or before such time. If, as the gentleman asserts, there is no possibility that anyone will be excommunicated from the Mormon church for the causes specified in the bill, then the provision is certainly harmless; otherwise it is very necessary.

"The hackneyed cry of persecution which the gentleman makes is not germane to the question, and I have only this to say in reply: that mere general assertions will fail to convince anyone who is at all familiar with the toleration and liberality which has always characterized American communities on the frontier, especially in matters pertaining to religion, that the Mormons were ever harshly treated without some enormous provocation on their part. Polygamy had not been publicly promulgated or openly practiced when the Mormons emigrated from the States. Polygamy, therefore, could not have been the cause of the disturbance referred to by the gentleman.

"In referring to the settlement of the Territory, he omitted to state the fact that, notwithstanding the hostility of the heads of the Mormon church, an industry has sprung up which produces the principal articles of exportation of any importance in the Territory. The product of silver last year was between six and seven million dollars, and the yield of the present year, is expected to amount to ten or twelve millions. There is also a large production of lead and considerable gold. This important and growing industry is almost exclusively carried on by the class whom the church leaders in their tabernacle harangues denounce as 'nasty Gentiles.' The development and increasing wealth of the Territory are not reasons, however, why the ordinary safeguards should not be thrown around the ballot-box. On the contrary, they furnish the very best of reasons why this should be done. Neither does the settlement of Salt Lake valley by Mormons justify combinations to defeat the execution of the law or constitute a valid reason why democratic principles should not be established and protected there by legislation of Congress, the territorial legislature having failed to do so. Hundreds of other communities in this country have been instrumental in redeeming the soil from the blight of dense wilderness and building up prosperous, progressive cities, yet have fair election laws.

"Gentlemen, Mormonism, according to Brigham Young, is at war with republican institutions, and is today a blight, as it has always been, upon one of the richest territories in the country.

"The gentleman thought proper to designate the advocates of this bill as 'a ring.' Yet its advocates include the entire Gentile population, and thousands of the Mormon rank and file. Both the Republican and Democratic parties in the Territory have passed resolutions in favor of it. What will be the effect of this bill? First, it excludes a class of persons from the exercise of a privilege who have forfeited all claim to enjoy the same; second, it inflicts upon polygamists the only punishment which is practicable by reason of the fact that the polygamist theocracy has rendered the enforcement of the law of 1862 by the courts impossible; third, it will destroy polygamy without violating either precedent or principle, by rendering available an opposition majority which at no distant day is as sure to be the case as that the sun shines in the heavens. The only immediate effect, however, on theocratic rule will be (as after disqualifying polygamists the Mormons have still several thousand majority over the opposition) to transfer the offices now almost universally held by polygamists to Mormons not living in violation of the law.

"Without such provisions of law as this bill contains the Mormon church can keep itself in power long after it ceases to be a majority, because it can poll or return whatever number of votes may be necessary to overcome the opposition. As the passage of this bill will be the death knell of polygamy, I suggest that the word 'cohabits' be substituted in place of 'has cohabited' so that the bill will then itself restore persons to civil rights who are disqualified as soon as they cease to be polygamists in practice. This change will give them the opportunity of choosing between enfranchisement and the practice of a pernicious crime. Does this display improper animus? Is this persecution?"

\* \* \* \* \* \* \* \* \* \* \* \*

The experience of William S. Godbe illustrates what, in former days, excommunication from the Mormon church meant to an apostate. The following extract is from a manuscript written by Mr. Godbe, and placed in my hands by one of his sons:

"After I was excommunicated, it was said by the people that in ninety days—to use their own terse, if not elegant phraseology—'there wouldn't be a grease-spot' left of me, and to carry out that prediction the Zion Drug Store was started, and I found the competition too severe for me, and was forced to close out my business. I lost my trade on account of the strong feeling against me. I had a large establishment full of goods, and I owed money for part of these goods, and I found I could not collect. There was about $100,000 due me at that time, and practically the whole amount is due now. In a year or so after being cut off from the church, instead of being worth at least $100,000, which I should have been worth, I found myself owing that much, and paying interest at a rate that would average at least $1,000 a month. Well, to meet all that, I put myself to work with all my might and main, and commenced mining, as being about the only thing open to me, and finally succeeded in discharging my indebtedness and recovering my former footing. At the time I was excommunicated it was very unpleasant for me—it was terrific. The Mormons took advantage of the feelings against me on account of being excommunicated and did not pay me the money owing me, thinking it would have a tendency to crush me, as prophesied. Owing to this and the competition started against me, I was unable to continue."

Mr. Godbe and E. L. T. Harrison in 1869 established the Utah Magazine, in which appeared articles advocating the opening up and development of the mines, which was against the counsel of Brigham Young. Upon refusing to change the policy of the magazine in that respect, Mr. Godbe was excommunicated at the dictation of Brigham Young, as was Mr. Harrison. The charge against them, preferred by George Q. Cannon, was "apostasy on the grounds of the articles in the magazine mentioned, containing views on financial questions differing with those of President Young" as well as on account of an expressed belief "that members of the church had not only the right to think, but to express their ideas on such subjects."

At the trial, Apostle Woodruff, who appeared on behalf of the church, asked Mr. Godbe this question: "Do you believe that President Young has the right to dictate to you in all things temporal and spiritual?" In answer Mr. Godbe said that he did not believe in the extraordinary right claimed for Brigham Young but deemed it wise in commerce to be guided by commercial experience and the circumstances of the case. After Mr. Cannon had read the charges preferred against the accused, he was asked by Mr. Godbe if it was apostasy to differ honestly with the measures of the priesthood. The reply was "It is apostasy. A man may be honest even in hell." Daniel H. Wells, who was present, remarked that "the question might as well be asked whether a man had the right to differ honestly with the Almighty."

Henry W. Lawrence, who was intimate with Mr. Godbe, defended his friend and voted against his excommunication on the ground that what he was charged with was not wrong but praiseworthy. For doing so he was also, at the dictation of Brigham Young, afterward excommunicated. At that time he was very highly respected by all, and generally popular. He was engaged in the mercantile business and built up a large and lucrative trade which, if he had sacrificed his manhood, instead of defending his friend against an absurd charge, and had observed silence and remained in the church, would have in time made him very wealthy. His excommunication, however, as in the case of Mr. Godbe, took from him the mass of his Mormon customers, ruined his trade, and forced him to go out of the mercantile business. In my experience of more than threescore years and ten I have never known so great a financial sacrifice for principle as that made by W. S. Godbe and Henry W. Lawrence.

Notwithstanding Brigham Young's efforts to prevent it, mines were discovered and developed, and almost exclusively by the despised Gentile element, who, by their investments and consummate skill, have made the mining industry, next to agriculture, the most important and greatest asset of the State.

William S. Godbe and Henry W. Lawrence were infinitely better and wiser than their fanatical and relentless oppressor, Brigham Young, and at the time he was oppressing them I have no doubt, although heartless and tyrannical as his treatment of them showed him to be, he secretly respected them for their manly independence.

JOHN D. LEE.

# CHAPTER X.

**The Mountain Meadows Massacre and its Resulting Investigation; Shadowy Glimpses of the Endowment House Rites and Atonement by Blood, Proven by Church Authority.**

For a considerable time after arriving in the Territory I had disbelieved the frequent assertions I heard that the Mountain Meadows massacre was ordered by Mormon officials and was carried out by a militia force of Mormons led by John D. Lee.

The massacre of one hundred and thirty or more persons, among whom were gray-haired grandmothers, mothers, young daughters and sons, by members of a civilized and Christian race, was so revolting and showed such depravity and utter disregard of all religious restraint that I was loth to believe the assertions referred to.

Upon becoming acquainted with Stephen DeWolfe who, in 1860, was the editor of "Valley Tan," the first Gentile paper published in Utah, I expressed to him my disbelief of what I had heard asserted respecting the massacre. He replied that what I had heard was true; that he had carefully investigated the matter, and had published in the Valley Tan a true version of the crime. He subsequently gave me a copy of that paper, and the occurrences respecting the massacre therein stated were substantially the same as was afterward shown by the evidence in the first trial of John D. Lee. In an editorial he also asserted that the Mormons had perpetrated other horrible crimes, and that none of the participants had been prosecuted by the Mormon authorities. After the appearance of that editorial a committee of Mormons, of which Jeter Clinton, the police magistrate of Salt Lake City was spokesman, waited upon Mr. DeWolfe and demanded a retraction of what he had written. Mr. Clinton stated that unless the retraction was made he would not be responsible for the safety of Mr. DeWolfe, as the editorial had created great excitement among the people, and many threats of violence had been made against its author. The next editorial written by Mr. DeWolfe after the demand to retract had been made upon him, and which met with his refusal, contained the following:

"The threats made against me for making statements which I, in common with almost every man in this valley not connected with the Mormon church, believe to be true, afford proof, if no other was found, of the correctness of all that I said about the insecurity of life here to such as fall under the ban of the Church authorities, and I have not a word of retraction to make of any line or paragraph which I have written on this subject; on the contrary, reiterate again my firm belief of the truth of all I have said, and take the risk of whatever consequences may result from a repetition of my former statement. In addition to that statement I will add that murder has been sanctioned from the pulpit of the Mormon tabernacle in this city, and there is incontestible proof that men have been murdered in this Territory whose death was deliberated about and decided upon in meetings over which a person holding a high position in the Mormon church presided. Neither do I fear the hierachial authorities' priestly curses when engaged in a cause that I believe just and righteous. Nor will threats or intimidation lead me to shrink from the performance of any known duty."

The next day after the committee had waited on Mr. De-Wolfe, Arthur Stainer, a hunchback, bookkeeper for Brigham Young, entered the office of Mr. DeWolfe, who arose to greet him. Stainer approached with uplifted hands and pronounced upon him in the most solemn manner, and in the name of Jesus Christ, a curse. In relating the incident to me Mr. DeWolfe laughingly said, "he cursed me from head to foot, and wound up by cursing my powers and parts of procreation, at which I took him by the collar and ejected him from my office." Mr. DeWolfe became my law partner, and was afterwards appointed by President Cleveland to the office of district judge of the Territory of Montana.

\*  \*  \*  \*  \*  \*  \*  \*  \*  \*  \*  \*

In 1859 a gentleman by the name of Wm. H. Rogers accompanied Judge Cradlebaugh to Cedar City. The purpose for which the judge went is disclosed by a letter written by Mr. Rogers and published by Mr. DeWolfe in Valley Tan on February 29, 1860, from which the following extracts are made:

"Owing to the disadvantages in the location of Cedar City, some of the inhabitants had moved away. There were in consequence a good many vacant houses in that place, and the judge obtained the use of one of them to stay in while there, and for the purpose of a courtroom.

"As soon as it became known that the judge intended holding court, was to investigate the circumstances of the Mountain Meadows massacre, and that he would have troops to insure protection and enforce his writs, if necessary, several persons visited him at his room at a late hour of the night, and informed him of different facts concerning the massacre.

"All those that called stated that it would be at the risk of their lives if it became known that they had communicated anything to him, and requested the judge if he met them in public in the daytime not to recognize them as persons that he had before seen.

"One of the men confessed that he participated in the massacre, and gave the following account of it:

"Previous to the massacre there was a council held at Cedar City in which President Haight and Bishops Higbee[1] and Lee participated. At this council a large number of men residing in Cedar City and in other settlements were appointed to perform the work of despatching the emigrants. The men selected for this purpose were instructed to resort, well armed, at a given time, to a spring or small stream lying a short distance to the left of the road leading into the Meadows, and not very far from Hamblin's ranch, but concealed by intervening hills.

"This was the place of rendezvous; and here the men, when they arrived, painted and otherwise disguised themselves to resemble Indians.

"Thence they proceeded, early in the morning, by a path or trail which led from the place of rendezvous directly into the Meadows. By taking this route they could not be seen by anyone at Hamblin's. On arriving at the corral of the emigrants, they came upon several standing outside by a campfire. These were fired upon, and at the first discharge several of them fell dead or wounded; the remainder immediately ran to the inside of the corral, began fortifying themselves, and preparing for defense as well as they could. The attack continued in a desultory manner for four or five days. The corral was closely watched, and if any of the emigrants showed

---

[1] Bishop John M. Higbee was first counselor to Isaac C. Haight, president of Parowan Stake of Zion, which took in Cedar City and all that part of the country in which was included Mountain Meadows. Higbee was a major, and Haight a colonel in the territorial militia of which Brigham Young was commander-in-chief and Daniel H. Wells lieutenant-general. Both Higbee and Haight made many trips across the plains as captains of wagon trains, escorting the proselytes of the church into Zion, and were first among Brigham's "useful" men.

themselves they were instantly fired at from without. If they attempted to go to the spring, which was only a few yards distant, they were sure to fall by the fire of their assailants. In consequence of the almost certain death that resulted from any attempt to procure water, the emigrants, before the siege discontinued, suffered severely from thirst. The assailants finding that the emigrants could not be subdued by the means adopted, resorted to treachery and stratagem to accomplish what they had been unable to do by force. They returned to their place of rendezvous, there removed their disguise, and again appeared in their ordinary dress. After this Bishop Lee with a party of men returned to the camp of the emigrants bearing a white flag as a signal of truce. From the position of the corral the emigrants were able to see them some time before they reached it. As soon as they discovered the white flag they dressed a little girl in white and placed her at the entrance of the corral to indicate their friendly feelings to the persons bearing the flag. Lee and his party arriving, were invited into the corral where they stayed about an hour, talking with the emigrants about the attack which had been made upon them. Lee told them that the Indians had gone over the hills, and if they would lay down their arms and give up their property he and his party would conduct them back to Cedar City; but if they went out with their arms the Indians would look upon it as an unfriendly act and would again attack them. The emigrants, trusting to Lee's honor and the sincerity of his statements, consented to the terms proposed, left their property and all of their arms at the corral, and under the escort of Lee and his party started in the direction of Cedar City. After they had proceeded about a mile on their way, on a signal given by Bishop Higbee (which was 'brethren, do your duty'), the slaughter began."

"When we arrived at the Mountain Meadows in April, 1859, more than a year and a half after the massacre, the ground for a distance of more than a hundred yards around the central point was covered with skeletons and bones of human beings, interspersed in places with bunches of tangled and matted hair, which from its length evidently belonged to females. In places the bones of small children were laying side by side with those of grown persons, as if parent and child had met death at the same time.

"Small bonnets and scraps of female apparel were also to be seen in places on the ground, and like the bones of those who had worn them, were bleached from long exposure, but the shapes in many instances were entire. In a gulch or hole in the ravine by the side of the road a large number of leg and arm-bones, and also skulls, could be seen sticking above the surface as if they had been buried there, but the action of the weather and the digging of the wolves had again exposed them to light. The entire scene was one too horrible and sickening to adequately describe."

The facts respecting the massacre stated by Mr. Rogers were verified by the evidence in the first trial of Lee. I refer to Mr. Roger's statements because they show that the facts of the massacre were known and publicly announced as early as 1860. In addition, at an early day it had become a matter of general notoriety that John D. Lee and other high officials and members of the Mormon church had perpetrated the massacre. When I became convinced of the complicity of the Mormons in that crime, I made a memorandum of the facts and the names of the participants, as from time to time I learned them, with the intention of presenting them to the United States district attorney whenever, as I had no doubt would eventually be done, Congress passed laws under which the guilty parties could be indicted and convicted. Upon the passage of the Poland bill in 1874, its provisions made the United States marshal the executive officer of the district courts and the United States district attorney the prosecuting officer of those courts in all cases arising under the laws of the Territory, and thereby the territorial jury system was changed. After George Caesar Bates had been removed as United States attorney, and William Cary, in whom I had confidence, had been appointed, I presented to the latter my memorandum of facts, and urged him to take the steps necessary to present them before the grand jury. He did so, and John D. Lee and other Mormons were indicted. When the case against Lee was set for trial Mr. Cary requested me to assist him, which I did. The evidence at the trial showed conclusively that at a meeting in Cedar City composed of leading officials of the Mormon church and a number of its prominent members, it was decided to destroy the emigrants, and the steps to be taken in the accomplishment of that end were there and then inaugurated; also, that after the emigrants had been induced by treachery, in the manner stated in the letter of Mr. Rogers, to place themselves under the protection of Lee and his party, then the preconcerted plans of the massacre were carried out. It was developed that a number of Indians were placed in concealment in a clump of cedars and oaks near the road, several hundred yards from the emigrant corral. The wounded men and seventeen little children, too young to expose the awful crime, were placed in wagons. The women and the other children were formed into a separate procession, the men were arranged in rank, and by the side of each was placed a Mormon assassin armed with a gun, ostensibly to protect the emigrants. The wagons containing the wounded men and young children, under order, moved ahead, the women and other children followed at some distance behind the wagons, and the men with their ostensible guards followed at a distance of about one hundred yards in the rear. When the women and other children reached the ambuscade of the Indians, the signal agreed upon was given by Bishop Higbee, and each fiendish Mormon guard shot or cut the throat of the defenseless victim he was pretendedly guarding. The Indians, not more merciless than the white-skinned Mormons present, rushed from ambush and slaughtered the helpless women the innocent children and the wounded men in the wagons were slain.

At Lee's camp on the evening before the massacre there had been a meeting at which Isaac C. Haight, John M. Higbee, and other officials high in Mormon councils, as well as officers in the territorial militia, were present. At this meeting was concocted the treachery by which the emigrants were induced to give up their arms and property, and to trust Lee and his party to their doom.

The Mountain Meadows massacre was more atrocious than either the massacre of Glencoe or the night of St. Bartholomew. Fifty-two of the participating conspirators belonged to an organization called the Church of Jesus Christ of Latter-day Saints. That fact appeared from the evidence in the first trial of Lee, and suggests the query, What influence engendered such a fiendish spirit as that horrible crime showed its participants possessed? Certainly not the teachings of Jesus Christ, for in no church under the sun in which the ethics of Christ are taught and enjoined, could any thought of perpetrating such a crime arise in the mind of any of its adherents. That spirit beyond all reasonable doubt was actuated by the pernicious influence exerted upon

88

the Mormon perpetrators of the crime by the oath-bound covenants, sermons and teachings of the church to which they belonged. This assertion is supported by the court proceedings and extensive quotations which immediately follow.

In 1889 a number of Mormon aliens made application to be admitted to citizenship in the district court. Objection to the admission of John Moore and Walter Edgar, two of the applicants, was made on the ground which will appear from the following extracts of the report of the proceedings reported by Frank E. McGurrin, official reporter:

The Court: "In the matter of the application of John Moore and Walter Edgar to be admitted to citizenship, objection was made to their admittance as citizens, because it was shown that they were members of the Church of Jesus Christ of Latter-day Saints, and had been through the endowment house. It was stated that it could be shown that those who had been through the endowment house—if not all members of that church—had been required to take oath, or had taken an oath, or entered into an obligation of some kind that would be incompatible with their duties as citizens of the United States; that the oath they were required to take there was incompatible with the oath they were required to take when becoming citizens. In the case of the applicants Moore and Edgar and several others of a similar character, the further hearing of the testimony has been continued until this morning for the purpose of giving the objectors a chance to offer the testimony, which they claimed they could furnish. The court is now ready to hear any testimony they may offer on that subject."

Mr. Baskin: "May it please the court, on account of the importance of this question, and the general interest the public has in excluding all persons from being naturalized who are not strictly competent, Mr. Dickson and myself have been requested to appear and participate in this examination, with the permission of the court."

The Court: "Counsel will be permitted to appear and conduct the examination of witnesses, and counsel for the applicants or any person offering to act as counsel for them, or on behalf of the church, may appear also, and cross-examine witnesses, and offer evidence on their side. If they have evidence to show that such oaths or obligations were not entered into, or any evidence that may tend to explain, they may be at liberty to present it."

LeGrand Young and James H. Moyle appeared as attorneys for the applicants. Twenty-five witnesses were examined, and after the arguments of the attorneys the matter was taken under advisement. Judge Anderson afterward delivered an opinion, in which he said:

"In the application the usual evidence on behalf of the applicants as to residence, moral character, etc., was introduced at a former hearing, and was deemed sufficient. Objection was made, however, to the admission of John Moore and William Edgar upon the ground that they were members of the Mormon church, and also because they had gone through the endowment house of that church, and there had taken an oath or obligation incompatible with the oath of citizenship, which they would be required to take if admitted.

"The claim is made by those who objected to the admission to citizenship of these persons that the Mormon church is and always has been a treasonable organization, and in its teaching and its practices hostile to the government of the United States, disobedient to its laws and seeking its overthrow; and that the oath administered to the members in the endowment house, binds them, under a penalty of death, to implicit obedience in all things, temporal as well as spiritual, to the priesthood, and to avenge the death of the prophets, Joseph and Hyrum Smith, upon the government and people of the United States. The taking of further testimony at this time is for the purpose of determining whether or not these allegations are true. Those objecting to the rights of the applicants to be admitted to citizenship, introduced eleven witnesses who have been members of the Church of Jesus Christ of Latter-day Saints. Several of these witnesses had held the position of bishop in the church, and all had gone through the endowment house and participated in its ceremony. The testimony of these witnesses was to the effect that every member of the church was expected to go through the endowment house, and that they nearly all do so; that marriages are usually solemnized there, and that those who are married elsewhere go through the endowment house ceremony at as early a date thereafter as practicable, in order that the martial relations shall continue through eternity. That these ceremonies occupy the greater part of a day, and include the taking of an oath, obligation, or covenant, by all who receive their endowments, that they will avenge the blood of the prophets, Joseph and Hyrum Smith, upon the government of the United States and will enjoin this obligation upon their children unto the third and fourth generations; that they will obey the priesthood in all things, and will never reveal the secrets of the endowment house, under the penalty of having their throats cut from ear to ear, their bowels torn out, and their hearts cut out of their bodies. The right arm is anointed that it may be strong to avenge the blood of the prophets. An undergarment, a sort of combination of shirt and drawers called an endowment robe, is then put on, and is to be worn ever after. On this robe near the throat, and over the heart, and in the region of the abdomen, are certain marks or designs intended to remind the wearer of the penalties that will be inflicted in case of a violation of the oath, obligation or covenant, he or she has taken or made.

"On behalf of the applicants, fourteen witnesses testified concerning the endowment ceremony, but all of them declined to state what oaths are taken, or what obligations or covenants are entered into, or what penalties are attached to their violation; and these witnesses, when asked for their reasons of declining to answer, stated that they did so on a point of honor, while several stated that they had forgotten what was said about avenging the blood of the prophets. John Henry Smith, one of the twelve apostles of the church, testified that all that was said in the endowment ceremony about avenging the blood of the prophets, is said in a lecture, in which the ninth and tenth verses of the sixth chapter of Revelations are recited. Other witnesses for the applicants testified that this is the only place in the ceremony where the avenging of the blood of the prophets is mentioned. John Clark, a witness for the applicants, testified that he took some obligations, made some promises, entered into some covenants in the endowment house, and wore his endowment robes, but did not know the significance of the slit over the heart. E. L. T. Harrison, another of applicants' witnesses, testified that he had a clear recollection; that his right arm was washed and something said about his being made stronger to avenge the death of the prophets, and that the names of Joseph and Hyrum Smith were not mentioned, but were understood to be among the number whose blood was to be avenged; and E. G. Wooley, a witness for the applicants, testified that they were to pray for the Lord to avenge the blood of the prophets. Every other witness for the applicants who was asked the question, stated that Joseph and Hyrum Smith were understood to be included among the prophets whose blood was to be avenged. The witnesses for the applicants, while refusing to disclose the oaths, promises and covenants of the endowment ceremony, and the penalties attached thereto, testified generally that there was nothing in the ceremony inconsistent with loyalty to the government of the United States, and that the government was not mentioned. One of the objects of this investigation is to ascertain whether the oaths and obligations of the endowment house are incompatible with good citizenship. The refusal of applicants' witnesses to state specifically what oaths, obligations or covenants are taken, or entered into in the ceremonies, renders their testimony of but little value and tends to confirm rather than contradict, the evidence on this point offered by the objectors. The evidence established beyond a reasonable doubt that the endowment ceremonies are inconsistent with the oath an applicant for citizenship is required to take, and that the oaths, obligations, and covenants there made or entered into are incompatible with the obligations and duties of citizens of the United States. The applications of John Moore and Walter Edgar, both of whom were shown on the former examination to be members of the Mormon church, and who have gone through the endowment house, are therefore denied."

As showing the character of the testimony of the witnesses on behalf of the applicants, that of James H. Moyle and John Henry Smith, nephew of the prophet, Joseph Smith, are here set out. Mr. Moyle took the stand as a witness for applicants. Being duly sworn, he testified that he was a member of the Mormon church, and had been through the endowment house twice, once when married, and once ten or twelve years ago.

Mr. Dickson: Did you take your endowments at that time? A. I took my endowments both times.

Q. Did you take any oaths at that time? A. No, sir.

Q. Or covenant? A. No, sir.

Q. What? A. Well, covenant—excuse me; certainly, I took a number of covenants.

Q. Did you take any obligations upon yourself? A. Yes, sir.

Q. With reference to the priesthood? A. In what respect?

Q. Obedience to the priesthood? A. No, sir.

Q. Nothing of the kind? A. No, sir.

Q. Not even by implication? A. No, sir; not even by implication.

Q. Are you testifying without any mental reservation about it? A. I am, positively, without any mental reservation whatever.

Q. Was there any penalty explained to you, or spoken of as a consequence of the violation of your covenants? A. That I decline to answer.

Q. Why? A. Simply because it is a matter which I regard as sacred; I say, that there was no covenant or nothing that was done there in which I, in any way—

Q. Just answer my question, sir? A. I decline to answer.

[Note—The Questions and Answers, where found herein, are true abstracts of the court records, and this being obvious to the reader, the usual "quotation marks" signifying converse have been omitted for reasons of appearance, and expedience and facility for the casual reader.—Ed.]

Q. Then stop when you decline to answer. A. Yes, sir; I decline to answer.

Mr. Dickson: That is all.

Witness: And in behalf of my declaration to the court, I want to say this, that my reason for it is this, that there was nothing, no promise made, but for chastity and for honor, and for good conduct; there was nothing said by which I bound myself in any way against the government, or made or vowed that I would in any way act in antagonism to the government, or that has any bearing or relevancy to this issue.

Mr. Dickson: Now are you through? A. As to those matters that I regard as secret and sacred I decline to answer.

Q. Are you through now? A. Because it has nothing to do with the case.

Q. Have you finished? A. I do not know whether I have or not. If you have anything to ask, I am ready to hear.

Q. I don't want to interrupt you. Are you through with your explanation? A. I am prepared to hear you.

Q. Was there anything said by any person in your hearing about 'avenging the death of the prophets?' A. Yes, sir.

Q. What was that? A. It would be a matter of impossibility for me to relate what it is.

Q. I mean the prophets, Joseph and Hyrum? A. Nothing whatever.

Q. The martyred prophets? A. The martyred prophets, yes.

Q. What was it? A. It was nothing more nor less than this: The passage of scripture—I can't recall it. If I had the bible here I could find it. It is in the book of Revelations; it runs something like this—"Oh, Lord, holy and true, how long shall our blood remain unavenged." It was something of that kind, and I am not certain but what—my recollection is, that there was nothing said in connection with that as a matter of instruction. I will state this much in order that the matter may be fully explained—that in the process of receiving endowments there are addresses delivered by the elders who are officiating; and in one address instruction is given that we should pray that God would avenge the blood of the martyred prophets. That is all.

Q. That is all? A. That is all.

Q. Wasn't there a penalty of death pronounced there? Wasn't it explained to you that the penalty of a violation of any of your covenants would be death? A. I decline to answer.

Q. That—you decline to answer; all right.

Mr. Baskin: Wasn't one of these penalties that you should have your throat cut across? A. With reference to what covenant?

Q. Well, with reference to the covenant you took there?
A. I decline to answer.

Q. Wasn't the penalty that your bowels should be torn out? A. I decline to answer that unless you tell me what you want me to answer.

Q. And that your heart should be torn out? A. (No response.)

Mr. Baskin: That's all. (Thereupon the witness left the stand.)

The direct examination of John Henry Smith, one of the twelve apostles, by LeGrand Young, in-chief, is as follows:

Q. I will ask you, Mr. Smith, if, in the course of the administration of the ceremonies there in the endowment house, there is any covenant or oath or affirmation made by, or required of, those passing through there—that they will avenge the blood of the prophet on this nation, or its people, or against the government of the United States? Has there ever been, since you first went through the endowment house? A. I absolutely declare that there was no such oath, or such covenant, nor such bond entered into by me; nor did I ever administer such an oath, covenant, or bond to any man, that could be construed by any reasonable construction of language, anyway upon the earth, to mean a thing of that kind; and will say here for myself, that had any man presented to me an oath that would have bound me to become a deliberate enemy of my country that I love and respect, I would have repudiated it upon the spot.

Q. Is there any thing in the endowment ceremony that teaches, promises, or in any way countenances the right of one man to shed the blood of another. A. No, sir.

Q. Is there any thing in the teachings of the church from the first revelation to the last? A. No, sir.

Cross-examination by Mr. Dickson: Q. I understand you to say that you have a very deep affection for your country. A. I have, sir.

Q. You mean, by "country," the United States? A. I have, sir.

Q. And, that if you had been required to enter into any covenants or obligations of any character which was antagonistic to your duty as a citizen of your country, you would have promptly repudiated it? A. I say so, even at that early age.

Q. And that has always been your attitude? A. That is today, and was then.

Q. Are you a polygamist? A. Yes, sir.

Q. When did you enter into polygamy? A. I entered into it twelve years ago.

94

Q. Didn't you know that that was against a law of your country? A. I knew that there was a contest as to the constitutionality of a law that had been passed by Congress.

Q. Didn't you know that that was against the law of your country, and that the law had been declared prior to that, to be a constitutional and valid law? A. No, sir.

Q. Did you continue after the passage of the law of 1882 to live in violation of it? A. I decline to answer that question.

Q. If you did continue to live in violation of that law after you knew that its constitutionality had been upheld by the supreme court of the United States, would you still maintain that you have a deep affection for the laws of your country? A. Yes, sir. The law of Congress was directed against the principle of my faith, and that principle of my faith was introduced, acknowledged, and had been taught and established for nearly forty years.

Q. Didn't you know that the Congress of the United States, as early as 1862, prohibited the practice of polygamy in the Territory of Utah? A. No, sir. It prohibited the practice of bigamy in the Territory of Utah.

Q. Well, what distinction do you make between bigamy and polygamy? A. I make this distinction—that a bigamist is a man that marries a wife, and then marries another, deceiving the first by not permitting her to know that he has married a second, or the second to know that he had married the first.

Q. According to your understanding, if the first and second wife, at the time of the second marriage had knowledge of situation of the man, that there is no bigamy. Is that it? A. Yes, sir.

Q. Do you believe in the revelation of "celestial" marriage? A. Yes, sir.

Q. Do you understand that revelation to be to this effect— that if the first wife refuses to consent to her husband taking a second wife, she shall be damned? A. I understand that principle; and a good many women have taken that chance. Under the Mormon theory they shall be damned.

Q. What part of that revelation do you reject? A. I accept the whole revelation.

Q. If, believing in that revelation, you felt it your duty to take the second living wife for time as well as eternity, and your first wife withheld her consent, would you not yield obedience to the will of God, and take a second wife. A. Yes, sir. If I felt to do it.

(After some discussion between the counsel, the court ruled: "The question of whether the constitutionality of the law had been passed upon or not is immaterial, because until the supreme court of the United States had held the law unconstitutional, it is the duty of the citizens to obey it.")

Q. Knowing that there was a law upon the statute books of the United States making it a crime for you or any other man in this Territory who had a wife living to take another wife, didn't you violate that law? A. Yes, sir. I did violate that law upon the statute books. I did this upon the basis that it was unconstitutional.

Q. After you knew the constitutionality of this class of legislation had been upheld, you still continued to violate that law, didn't you? A. I decline to answer.

Q. If you did continue to violate it after you knew its constitutionality was upheld, don't you say that where the law of the land comes in conflict with what you believe, as revealed to your church, that you will follow the latter and reject the former? A. When the law of the land takes my religion that is established and fixed, and that I have practiced and observed, while the constitution of the United States shall remain I shall think I am protected in the practice and observance of my religion so long as I wrong no other being. As I remarked, I had taken upon myself an agreement and covenant that was a perpetual one. Were I outside of that condition in regard to that matter, I would be reasonably a free man.

Q. Isn't it true that your church, through its recognized officers and teachers and leaders, has taught for years, publicly and privately, that the Kingdom of God was now established on the earth in the form of the Church of Jesus Christ of Latter-day Saints? A. I have heard them use that name.

Q. And you have heard every apostle of the church teach that doctrine, have you not? A. Not as a doctrine, but announce it, in the course of talk, "this is the Kingdom of God."

Q. And say it was the duty of the people—meaning the members of the church—to follow the counsels of the men at the head of the church in respect to building up the Kingdom of God on earth, haven't you? A. Yes, sir.

Q. Weren't the people instructed to pray the Lord to avenge the blood of the prophets, and teach that to their children and their children's children? A. I have no remembrance of any such instructions—of that positive kind.

Q. Well, that they were instructed to pray to the Lord to avenge the blood of the prophet, wasn't that it? A. I decline to answer any further questions with regard to that.

Q. What penalties were attached with regard to the violation of the covenants that you took in the endowment house? A. I decline to make any statement.

Q. Wasn't one of the penalties, "that you would have your throat cut?" A. I decline to answer. (And the witness declined to answer all questions asked him on that subject.)

Witness: Your Honor, I would like to make one statement right here, and that is this: That Oliver Cowdrey, the immediate friend and associate of Joseph Smith, apostatized from the Mormon church. He was never killed. He knew all that Joseph Smith knew. David Whitmore and Martin Harris, who were his immediate associates, apostatized from the church. They were never hurt, in any degree. Every one of them died outside of the church. And the fact that Mr. Baskin, who is a pronounced enemy, and has been from the first—and I have always respected him for his honesty—has never let up for a minute; he has fought the Mormons from the first until this day, and as viciously as any man ever did.

Mr. Dickson: What is the penalty for going against the Lord's anointed and heads of the church? A. I decline to answer to penalties.

Q. How long had you married your first wife until you took a second? (No answer.)

Dr. Heber John Richards, another witness for the applicants, upon cross-examination, testified as follows:

Q. You say there was no covenant to avenge the blood of the prophets upon this nation. A. None that I heard of.

Q. What was said about avenging the blood of the prophets? A. In the fore part of the ceremony, in the anointing, they anointed my arm, that it might be strong to avenge the blood of the prophets, and that was all that was said.

Q. What was said about avenging the blood of Joseph and Hyrum? A. Nothing whatever about Joseph and Hyrum; but I recollect it was just "prophets."

Q. What obligation did you take with reference to obedience to the priesthood in all things? A. If any, it has slipped my mind, I don't remember.

Q. What teachings was there in reference to polygamy? A. I don't remember anything being said about polygamy.

Q. Did you take any obligation under penalty? I wish you would state it in substance. A. I couldn't do it—I couldn't do it if I was willing, and I don't feel willing to.

Q. Well, doctor, it has been stated upon the witness stand that if a man apostatized from the church, the duty of those who have been through the endowment house, was to go and murder or kill him. Did you hear anything of that sort? A. No, sir. I can explain to you, what I understood by that was simply this: That after I had become a member of the church, if I then fell away, I could get remission if I went voluntarily and asked for the atonement of my blood, but not without it; it must come by my desire, the same as baptism does. If I was taken out and baptized against my will, it would do me no good; and if I was killed against my will it would do me no good.

Q. And it would be appropriate when they made the request for some brother to shed his blood? A. Yes, some person who was authorized to do so.

Q. And it wouldn't be murder? A. It wouldn't be murder—it would be murder probably in the eyes of the law, but not in the eyes of the church.

Q. And that was taught? A. That was taught.

\*    \*    \*    \*    \*    \*    \*    \*    \*    \*    \*

Miss Owens was converted in England by a man named Miles. Having plighted her troth to him, she was induced to accompany him to Utah before they married as he was desirous of having the marriage ceremony performed in the endowment house. Shortly after arriving in Salt Lake City she ascertained that Miles was also engaged to be married to a Miss Spencer, and that Miles intended to marry them both at the same time in the endowment house. To this Miss Owens most strenuously objected; but being so far away from her native home, among strangers, she was finally prevailed upon to consent on condition that she should be made the first and legal wife of Miles, and Miss Spencer the second. After the parties had gone through the ceremonies of the endowment house, at a social entertainment given in honor of the newly married parties at the residence of Angus Cannon, the fact was revealed to Miss Owens that she had been deceived, and in place of becoming the first wife by the ceremony, she was only a plural one. She rebelled, and at her instance Miles was criminally prosecuted and convicted. Shortly after the ceremony was performed, she made a statement of what transpired in the endowment house, from which the following is an extract:

"\* \* \* Joseph F. Smith then came to where we were all waiting, and told us that if we wanted to back out, now was our time, because we should not be able afterward, and that we were bound to go right through. All those who wanted to go through were told to hold up their hands, which, of course, everyone did, believing that all the good and holy things that were to be seen and heard in the House of the Lord were yet to come. He then told us that if ever any of us attempted to reveal what we saw and heard in the House, our memories would be blighted, and we should be everlastingly damned, for they were things too holy to be spoken of between each other after we had left the endowment house. We were then told to be very quiet, and listen. Joseph F. Smith then went away.

"They then proceeded to give us the first grip of the Aaronic, or lesser priesthood, which consists in putting the thumb on the index finger and clasping the hands round. We were then made to swear to obey the laws of the Mormon church and all they enjoin, in preference to those of the United States. The penalty for revealing this grip and oath is that you will have your throat cut from ear to ear, and your tongue torn out from your mouth. The sign of the penalty is drawing the hand, with the thumb pointing towards the throat, sharply across, and bringing the arm to the level of the square, and with the hand upraised to heaven, swearing to abide the same.

"Then came a man in and said that the Gospel had been again restored to the earth, and that an Angel had revealed it to a young boy named Joseph Smith, and that all the gifts, blessings and prophecies of old had been restored with it, and this last revelation was to be called the Latter-day Dispensation. The priests pretended joyfully to accept this, and said it was the very thing they were in search of, nothing else having had the power to satisfy them. They then proceeded to give us the first grip of the Melchisedek, or higher priesthood, which is said to be the same that Christ held. The thumb is placed on the knuckle of the index finger, which is placed straight along the hand, while the lower part of the hand is clasped with the remaining fingers. The robe for this grip was changed from the right to the left shoulder. We were then made to swear to avenge the death of Joseph Smith, the martyr, together with that of his brother Hyrum, on this American nation, that we would teach our children, and children's children, to do so. The penalty for this grip and oath was disembowelment."

Scores of apostate Mormons of credibility who have gone through the endowment ceremonies have, in confidence, stated to me that such oaths were administered. Numerous authors of books have also stated that they were so administered. Among them are Mrs. Stenhouse, authoress of "Tell It All," and Ann Eliza Young, the nineteenth wife of Brigham, who went through the endowment ceremony when she was married to that alleged holy prophet, and whose writings expose many secret practices of the church.

From the foregoing when viewed in connection with the extracts of Mormon sermons, here following, I do not think that any unbiased person will doubt the fact that such oaths were administered in the endowment house, and that those sermons inspired the infernal spirit displayed at the Mountain Meadows massacre.

The following extracts are from sermons published officially in the Journal of Discourses from time to time, that were delivered before the perpetration of the Mountain Meadows Massacre, and are referred to as follows:

(Brigham Young in Vol. III, page 247). "A few of the men and women who go into the House of the Lord and receive their endowments, and in the most sacred manner make covenants before the Almighty, go and violate those covenants, You say, 'that man ought to die for transgressing the law of God'. Suppose you found your brother in bed with your wife and put a javelin into both of them? You would be justified, and they would atone for their sins and be received into the Kingdom of God. I would at once do so in such a case and under such circumstances. I have no wife whom I love so well that I would not put a javelin through her heart, and I would do it with clean hands; but you who trifle with your covenants, be careful, lest in judging you will be judged. There is not a man or woman who violates the covenants made with their God who will not be required to pay the debt. The blood of Christ will never wipe that out. Your own blood must atone for it."

(Idem, Vol. II, page 255). "At the present, the enemies of all righteousness have the lead, and say, 'Now, you poor Mormons, are you not afraid that we can muster our thousands and destroy every one of you?' Go to hell, say I, and be damned, for you will go there, and you are damned already."

(Ibid., page 311). "It was asked this morning how we could obtain redress for wrongs. I will tell you how it could be done. We could take the same law that they have taken—mobocracy—and if any miserable scoundrels come here, cut their throats." (All the people said, "amen.")

(Ibid., page 317). "I have never yet talked as rough in these mountains as I did in the States when they killed Joseph. I then said boldly and aloud, 'If ever a man should lay his hands on me and say, on account of my religion, "thou art my prisoner" the Lord Almighty helping me, I would send that man to hell across lots.' I feel so now. Let mobocrats keep their hands off me or I will send them where they belong. I am always prepared for such an emergency."

(Brigham in Vol. I, page 83). "Now you Gladdenites, keep your tongues still, lest sudden destruction come upon you! I will tell you of a dream that I had last night. I dreamed that I was in the midst of a people who were dressed in rags and tatters. They had turbans upon their heads, and these were also hanging in tatters. The rags were of many coloro, and when the people moved they were all in motion. Their object in this appeared to be to attract attention. Said they to me, 'we are Mormons, Brother Brigham.' 'No, you are not,' I replied. 'We have been,' said they. And they began to jump and caper about and dance, and their rags of many colors were all in motion to attract the attention of the people. I said, 'You are not Saints—you are a disgrace to them.' Said they, 'We have been Mormons.' By and by came along some mobocrats, and they greeted them with, 'how do you do, sir; I am very happy to see you.' They kept on that way for an hour. I felt ashamed of them, for they were in my eyes a disgrace to Mormonism. Then I saw two ruffians whom I knew to be mobbers and murderers, and they crept into a bed where one of my wives and children were. I said, 'you, that call yourselves brethren, tell me: Is this the fashion among you?' They said, Oh! they are good men, they are gentlemen. With that, I took my large bowie knife that I used to wear as a bosom pin, and cut one of their throats from ear to ear, saying, 'Go to hell across lots.' The other one said, 'You dare not serve me so.' I instantly sprang at him, seized him by the hair of the head, and, bringing him down, cut his throat and sent him after his comrade, and told them both if they would behave themselves they should yet live, but if they did not, I would unjoint their necks. At this I awoke. I say, rather than an apostate should flourish here, I will unsheath my bowie knife and conquer or die! [Great commotion in the congregation, and a simultaneous burst of feeling assenting to the declaration.] Now, you nasty apostates, clear out, or judgment will be put to the line, and righteousness to the plummet  *  *  *  "

(Idem, Vol. III, page 247). "There is no man or woman who violates the covenants made with their God that will not be required to pay the debt. The blood of Christ will never wipe that out. Your blood must atone for it, and the judgment of the Almighty will come sooner or later, and every man and woman will have to atone for breaking their covenants."

(Idem, Vol. V, page 78). "But woe, woe, to that man who comes here to unlawfully interfere with my affairs. Woe, woe, to those men who come here to unlawfully interfere and meddle with me and this people. I swore in Nauvoo, when my enemies were looking me in the face, that I would send them to hell across lots if they meddled with me, and I asked no odds of all hell today."

(Idem, Vol. III, page 226). "The time is coming when justice will be laid to the line and righteousness to the plummet—when we shall take the old broadsword and ask, 'Are you for God?' and if you are not heartily on the Lord's side, you shall be hewn down."

(Idem, Vol. V, page 6). "If men come here and do not behave themselves, they will not only find the Saints whom they talked so much about biting their horses' heels, but the scoundrels will find something biting their heels. I wish such characters would let the boys have a chance to lay their hands on them. In my plain remarks I merely call things by their right names."

(Idem, Vol. III, page 50). "We are yet obliged to have devils in our community. We could not build up the Kingdom without them. Many of you know that you can not get your endowments without the devil being present. Indeed, we cannot make rapid progress without the devils I know that it frightens the righteous sectarian to think that we have so many devils with us—so many miserable, poor curses. Bless your souls, we could not prosper in the Kingdom of God without them. We must have those among us who will steal our fence-poles, who go and steal hay from their neighbor's haystack, or go into his cornfield and steal corn and leave the fence down. Nearly every ax that is dropped in the canyon must be picked up by them, and the scores of lost watches, gold rings, breast pins, etc., must get into their hands, though they will not wear them in your sight. It is essentially necessary to have such characters here. Live here, then, you poor, miserable curses, until the time of retribution, when your heads will have to be severed from your bodies. Just let the Almighty say, 'lay judgment to the line and righteousness to the plummet,' and the time of thieves is short in the community. What do you suppose they would say in old Massachusetts should they hear that the Latter-day Saints had received a revelation or commandment to lay judgment to the line and righteousness to the plummet? What would they say in old Connecticut? They would raise a universal howl of 'How wicked those Mormons are. They are killing the evil-doers who are among them.' What do I care for the wrath of man, more than I do for the chickens that run in my dooryard? I am here to teach the ways of the Lord, and lead men to life everlasting, but if they have not a mind to go there, I wish them to keep out of my path. I want the Elders of Israel to understand that if they are exposed in their stealing, lying, deceiving wickedness and covetousness which is idolatry, they must not fly in a passion about it, for we calculate to expose you from time to time as we please, when we can get time to notice you."

(Heber Kimball in Vol. IV, page 357). "I have no doubt there will be hundreds who will leave us, and go away to our enemies. I wish they would this fall; it might save us much trouble; and if men turn traitors to God and His servants, their blood will surely be spilled, or else they will be damned, and that, too, according to their covenants."

(Orson Hyde in Vol. I, pages 71-72.) "I will suppose a case: That there is a large flock of sheep on the prairie, and here are shepherds, also, who watch over them with care. It is generally the case that the shepherds are provided with most excellent dogs that understand their business. * * * Suppose the shepherd should discover a wolf approaching the flock, what would he likely do? Why, we should suppose that if the wolf was in proper distance, that he would kill him at once. In short, he would shoot him down—kill him on the spot. If the wolf was not within shot, we would naturally suppose he would set the dogs[2] on him—and you are aware, I have no doubt, that these shepherd dogs have very pointed teeth and are very active. It is some times the case the shepherd, perhaps, has not with him the necessary arms to destroy the wolf, but in such a case, he would set the faithful dogs on it, and by that means accomplish its destruction. * * * Now, was Jesus Christ the good shepherd? Yes; what the faithful shepherd is to the sheep, so is the Savior to his followers. He has gone, and left on the earth other shepherds who stand in the place of Jesus Christ to take care of the flock. If you say the priesthood or authorities of the Church are the shepherds, and the church is the flock, you can make your own application of this figure. It is not at all necessary for me to do it."

(Heber Kimball in Vol. I, page 160). "I have to do the work he [Brigham] tells me to do, and you have to do the same, and he has to do the work told him by the Great Master."

(Heber Kimball was in charge of the Tithing House when this sermon was delivered—Vol. V, page 135). "If you want a pound of coffee or tea, or a pair of shoes, it is 'Come, Brother Heber, go quick and get me what I want. If you don't, I will go and tell Brother Brigham.' Brother Brigham! go and be damned. I wish such characters were in hell, where they belong. [Voice, 'they are there']. I know it, and it is that which makes them wiggle so, the poor, miserable devils. They would make Our Father and God a drudge—make Him do their dirty work—kill those poor devils and every poor rotten hearted curse in our midst. With them it is, 'Lord, kill them—kill them, damn them —kill them, Lord.' We intend to kill the poor cusses ourselves."

From a sermon delivered by Brigham Young in 1855 and published in the Deseret News:

---

[2]Mr. Hyde's allegory in fable form can be well read between the lines. "Set the dogs," it is evident, meant the Danites, or "church police," as they termed themselves.

103

"Have not this people of God a right to baptize a sinner, to save him when he commits those crimes that can only be atoned for by shedding his blood? We would not kill a man, of course, unless we killed him to save him. Do you think it would be any sin to kill me if I were to break my covenants? Would you kill me if I break the covenants of God, and you had the spirit of God? Yes; and the more spirit of God I had, the more I should strive to save your souls by spilling your blood when you had committed sin that could not be remitted by baptism."

\* \* \* \* \* \* \* \* \* \* \* \*

I quote further from the opinion of Judge Anderson in the naturalization matter before referred to, as follows:

"The evidence also shows that blood atonement is one of the doctrines of the church under which, for certain offenses, the offender shall suffer death as the only means of atoning for this transgression, and that any member of the church has a right to shed his blood. In a discourse delivered September 21, 1856 Brigham Young said:

" 'There are sins which men commit for which they cannot receive forgiveness in this world or in the world to come; and if they had their eyes open to their true condition they would be perfectly willing to have their blood spilled upon the ground, that the smoke thereof might ascend to heaven as an offering for their sins; whereas, if such is not the case they will stick to them and remain upon them in the spirit world. I know when you hear my brethren telling about cutting people off from the earth you consider it strong doctrine; but it is to save them. It is true that the blood of the Son of God was shed for sin through the fall, and those committed by men, yet men commit sins which it [the blood] never can remit. As it was in ancient days, so it is in our day, and though the principles are taught publicly from this stand, still the people do not understand them, that the law is precisely the same. There are sins that can be atoned for by an offering upon an altar as in ancient days, and there are sins that the blood of a lamb, or of a calf, or of turtle doves, cannot remit; but they must be atoned for by the blood of the man. That is the reason why men talk to you as they do from this stand. They understand the doctrine, and throw out a few words about it. You have been taught that doctrine, but you did not understand it.'

"And again on the eighth day of February, 1857, in a discourse in the tabernacle, President Young used the following language (Deseret News, Vol. VI, page 397):

" 'But now I say, in the name of the Lord, that if this people will sin no more, but faithfully live their religion, their sins will be forgiven them without taking life. You are aware

104

that when Brother [Governor] Cummings came to the point of loving our neighbors, he could Yes or No as the case might be. That is true, but I want to connect it with the doctrine you have heard in the bible. When will we love our neighbors as ourselves? In the first place, Jesus said that no man hateth his own flesh. It is admitted by all, every person loves himself. Now if we do rightly love ourselves, we want to be saved and continue to exist; we want to go into the Kingdom where we can enjoy eternity, and see no more sorrow and death. This is the desire of every person believing in God. Now, take a person in this congregation who has knowledge of being saved in the Kingdom of God and Our Father; and being an exalted one, who knows and understands the principle of eternal life, and sees the beauty and excellency of the eternity when compared with the vain and foolish things of the world, and suppose he is overtaken in a gross fault and has committed a sin which he knows will deprive him of that exaltation which he desires and that he cannot attain to it without the shedding of his blood, and knows that by having his blood shed he will atone for that sin and be saved and exalted with the Gods—Is there a man or a woman in this house that would not say "shed my blood that I may be saved and exalted with the Gods?" All mankind love themselves, and let this principle be known by an individual and he would be glad to have his blood shed. That would be loving themselves until eternal exaltation. Will you love your brothers and sisters likewise when they have committed a sin that cannot be atoned for without the shedding of their blood? Will you love that man or woman well enough to shed their blood? That is what Jesus meant. He never told a man or a woman to love their enemies in their wickedness. He never intended such a thing. I could refer you to plenty of instances where men have been righteously slain in order to atone for their sins. I have seen scores and hundreds of people for whom there would have been a chance in the last resurrection if their lives had been taken, and their blood spilt upon the ground as a smoking incense to the Almighty, but who are now angels to the devil until our elder Brother, Jesus Christ raises them up to conquer death, hell, and the grave. I have known a great many men who have left the church for whom there is no chance whatever of exaltation, but if their blood had been spilled it would have been better for them. The wickedness and ignorance of the nation forbid this principle being in full force. But the time will come when the law of God will be in full force. This is loving our neighbor as ourselves. If he needs help, help him; and if he needs salvation, and it is necessary to spill his blood upon the ground in order that he may be saved, spill it. And if any of you, who understand the principles of eternity, if you have committed sins requiring the shedding of blood, except the sin unto death, you should not be satisfied nor rest until your blood should be

105

spilt, that you might gain the salvation you desire. That is the way to love mankind. **Now brethren and sisters, will you live your religion? How many hundreds of times have I asked that question—Will the Latter-day Saints live their religion?' "**

"President Jedediah M. Grant, in a discourse March 12, 1854, on the subject that he calls Covenant Breakers—that is, those who leave the Mormon church—used the following language:

" 'Then what ought this meek people, who keep the commandments of God, do unto them. "Nay," says one, "they ought to pray to the Lord to kill them." I want to know if you wish the Lord to come down and do all your dirty work? Many of the Latter-day Saints will pray, and petition, and supplicate the Lord to do a thousand things that they themselves would be ashamed to do. When a man prays for a thing, he ought to be willing to perform it himself; but if the Latter-day Saints should put to death the covenant-breakers, it would try the faith of the very meek, just and pious ones among them; it would cause a great deal of whining in Israel. Then there was another old commandment. The Lord commanded them not to pity the persons whom they kill, but to execute the law of God upon persons worthy of death. This should be done by the entire congregation, showing no pity. I have thought there would have to be quite a revolution among the Mormons before such a commandment could be obeyed completely by them. The Mormons have a great deal of sympathy. For instance, if they get a man before a tribunal administering the law of the land, and succeed in getting a rope around his neck, and having him done up like a dead dog, it is all right; but if the church and Kingdom of God should step forth and execute the law of God, oh, what a burst of Mormon sympathy it would cause! I wish we were in a situation favorable to our doing that which is justifiable before God without any contaminating influence of Gentile amalgamation, laws and traditions, that the prophet of the people of God might lay the axe at the root of the tree and every tree that bringeth not forth good fruit might be hewn down. What! do you think the people would do right and keep the law of God by actually putting to death the transgressor? Putting to death the covenant-breakers would exhibit the law of God, no matter by whom it was done—that is my opinion. You talk of the doings of the different governments, the United States, if you please, what do they do with traitors—what mode do they adopt to punish them? Do traitors to the government forfeit their lives? Examine also the doings of other earthly governments on this point, and you will find the same practice universal. I am not aware that there are any exceptions, but people will look into the books of theology and argue that the people of God have a right to try people for fellowship, but they have no right to try them on property or life. That makes the devil laugh, saying,

"I have got them on the hook now. They can cut them off and I will put eight or ten spirits worse than they are into their tabernacles and send them back to mob them." '

"In September, 1857, Brigham Young, in an address delivered in this city and found in Vol. V, Journal of Discourses, used the following language:

" '* * * There is high treason in Washington, and if the law was carried out, it would hang up many of them, and the very act of James K. Polk, in having five hundred of our men[3] while we were making our way out of the country, under an agreement forced upon us, would have hung him between the heavens and the earth if the laws had been faithfully carried out. And now, if they can send a force[4] against this people, we have every constitutional and legal right to send them to hell, and we calculate to send them there * * * Our enemies had better count the cost, for if they continue the job they will want to let it out to subcontractors before they get half through with it. If they persist in sending **troops here, I want the people of the West and the East to understand** that it will not be safe for them to cross the plains.'

"An effort was made to show that blood atonement, as preached by Brigham Young and Jedediah Grant, is not now the doctrine of the church, and a pamphlet containing an address on this subject by Elder Charles W. Penrose* in October, 1884, was offered in evidence; but in this pamphlet Mr. Penrose sustains the doctrine of blood atonement as preached by Brigham Young and President Grant: * * *

(Page 18). " 'Now, according to the doctrine of President Brigham Young, the blood of Jesus Christ, as I have shown you, atoned for the original sin, and for sins that men commit, and yet there are sins which men commit for which they cannot receive any benefit through the shedding of Christ's blood. Is that a true doctrine? It is true, if the bible is true. That is bible doctrine.'

(Page 36). " 'Now, Brother Jedediah M. Grant and Brigham Young, because of the transgression of the people, spoke as I have quoted. This was the time of the reformation, and the fears of evil-doers was worked upon to induce reform, and hence the strong language used at that time. Do we need the same language now? I hope not; but if there was any need of it, it would be just as applicable now as then.'

(Page 43). " 'These are some of the ideas entertained by the Latter-day Saints on the subject of blood atonement. After baptized persons have made sacred covenants with God and then

---

[3]See Chapter XVII, referring to Mormon Battalion.
[4]The advance of General Albert Sidney Johnston's army.
*At present Penrose is one of the First Presidency of the Mormon Church.

committed deadly sins, the only atonement they can make is the shedding of their blood. At the same time, because of the laws of the land and the prejudice of the nation and the ignorance of the world, this law cannot be carried out; but when the time comes that the law of God should be in full force upon the earth, then this penalty will be inflicted for those crimes committed by persons under covenant not to commit them.' "

"Whether such language as the above instigated the Mountain Meadows massacre, or whether that horrible butchery was done by direct command of Brigham Young, will probably never be known, but it is a part of the history of the Territory, that about that time a party of peaceful emigrants who were passing through Utah on their way to California, consisting of about one hundred and thirty men, women and children, were mercilessly butchered by men under the command of John D. Lee and Capt. Wm. H. Dame, both Mormons in high standing."

*     *     *     *     *     *     *     *     *     *     *     *

Soon after the assassination of Dr. Robinson, an inquest was held at which ex-Governor John B. Weller made in substance the following apt remarks to the jury:

"*   *   *   The founder of the Christian religion preached good will amongst men, instead of calling into action the worst passions of the human breast. 'Blessed,' said He, 'are the peacemakers.' Did He not teach obedience to the law and respect to the powers that be? Did He not say 'thou shalt love thy neighbor as thyself.' Did He not say 'love your enemies and pray for those who despitefully treat and persecute you?' Why—when surrounded by His enemies and nailed to the cross—He extended His eyes towards Heaven, and with His dying breath exclaimed 'Father forgive them; they know not what they do!' How inconsistent are these sentiments, promulgated by our illustrious Savior, with the doctrines taught by the modern prophet in the tabernacle."

It was shown by the evidence at the first trial of Lee that the emigrants after leaving Salt Lake City on their journey south encountered unfriendly neighborhoods, and the inhabitants who were Mormons refused to sell them anything. Robert Kershaw, a very intelligent witness, at the first trial of Lee, testified that he was living in Beaver City and saw the emigrants pass through; that previously George A. Smith had arrived and preached in the public square. He said the emigrants were coming, and forbade the people selling them anything under the penalty of being disfellowshiped; that John Morgan traded a small cheese for a bedquilt and was cut off from the church. In his own words, he said:

GEORGE A. SMITH.

"The emigrants camped in front of my house. I had a good garden, and they wanted to buy vegetables. I refused to trade with them. Samuel Dodge, a policeman, stood by the train, and intimidated people from trading with the emigrants."

Having learned that Mrs. Julia F. Thompson, who came to Utah soon after the first settlement was made, had heard Smith preach at Beaver City against the approaching emigrants, and knowing that she was a lady of ability, high standing, and of undoubted veracity, I called at her home in Salt Lake City on December 14, 1912, where she made to me the statement following:

"At the time of the massacre of the Arkansas emigrants I resided in Beaver City. A short time before they reached there, George A. Smith, on a Sunday, preached a sermon at which I was present. He informed the people that the emigrants were coming, and forbade selling anything to them. Afterwards it was common talk among the neighbors that they had been forbidden by the church authorities to deal with the emigrants. After they arrived in Beaver and camped near there, Mrs. Morgan, who did the washing for our family, knowing that I had been making cheese, came and asked me for one. I said, 'You want to sell it to the emigrants?' She said, 'Yes; I can sell it to them for a coverlet, and will do it because when my husband goes into the canyon he takes one of mine, and I sleep cold.' I told her that there were spies around, and if she did it she would be disfellowshiped, as orders had been given that anyone who sold the emigrants anything would be disfellowshiped. I gave her one cheese and told her she might have two if she wanted them. She sold the one I gave her to the emigrants. Shortly afterward I went to church one Sunday, and both Mrs. Morgan and her husband were disfellowshiped because she sold that cheese to the emigrants. The motion for their disfellowship was submitted to the vote of the congregation, and all hands went up in favor of the motion except mine. I did not vote. Afterward, at another church meeting I attended, Mrs. Morgan and her husband expressed their sorrow for disobeying the counsel not to trade with the emigrants, and were restored to fellowship."

Mrs. Thompson further stated that one or two years before the massacre she heard Col. W. H. Dame preach a sermon in Parowan, in which he said: "If you wives and sisters in passing by, see the head of a husband or brother upon the street, you must not ask any reasons. It is none of your business."

Lee in his confession stated that: "Inasmuch as this lot (the emigrants) had men among them that helped kill the prophet in the Carthage jail, the killing of them would be keeping our oaths and avenging the blood of the prophets." He further stated that in a conversation he had with President Haight respecting Brother Dan McFarland, after the massacre, he (Haight) said, "Dan will make a great warrior." "Why do you think so?" Lee asked. "Well, Dan came to me and said, 'You must get me another knife, because the one I have has no good stuff in it, for the edge turned when I cut a fellow's throat at the Meadows. I caught one of the devils that was trying to get away, and when I cut his throat, it took all of the edge off of my knife.' I tell you, that boy will make a warrior."

A number of the victims of the massacre had their throats cut, just in the same way as Isaac Potter, one of the victims of the Coalville murderers, (page 10) who had his throat cut from ear to ear, after he had been instantly killed and was lying prostrate upon the ground from the discharge of a shotgun in his back at close range. Other similar cases have been stated to me, and were given in the testimony at the trials of John D. Lee.

There is no doubt in my mind that all such cases were inspired by the throat-cutting sermons and oath-bound covenants of the Mormon church. The blood-thirsty spirit revealed by these sermons conclusively shows that their authors had vengeful and malignant hearts. To call an organization in which such sermons were tolerated, and afterwards reproduced and perpetuated in its official publications, the "Church of Jesus Christ of Latter-day Saints," is a disgraceful profanation of the sacred name of Jesus Christ. These disgusting sermons of Brigham Young not only emphasize the absurdity of his assumption of divine agency, but resemble the ravings of a vicious lunatic, and are such as no Christian would deliver.

Klingensmith testified that Bishop-Major John M. Higbee cut one man's throat; that women were lying around with their throats cut, and some with their heads smashed in; that he branded some of the cattle—about fifty head—with a cross, which was the church brand; that he attended a Conference held in Salt Lake City on October 5, 1857, where he met Lee, who told him that he had told Brigham Young everything that had transpired at the Mountain Meadows massacre; that the next day Lee, Charley Hopkins and himself met in President Young's office; that the president received them well, took them to his barn and showed them his horses, carriages and other fine things. He told the witness, who had control of the property, to turn it over to Lee, as he was Indian agent anyway, and the disposal of the property belonged to him; that Brigham Young then turned to the witness and said: "What you know about this affair, do not tell to anyone; do not talk about it among yourselves."

On cross-examination, this witness further testified that his first knowledge of the emigrants was that they had been ordered away from Salt Lake City and were coming down through the settlements; that he heard from President Haight that the people were forbidden to trade with them; that in council meeting in Cedar City he said the emigrants were coming down, and that they must be destroyed; that before the emigrants arrived, President Haight preached against trading with them; that when the order was given at the time the emigrants marched out of their corral he shot at the man by whose side he was marching; that witness was cut off from the church four or five years ago, and resigned his bishopric in 1868 or 1869; was not in full fellowship thereafter; that President Haight told him that he sold fifty head of the cattle to Hooper; that witness was afraid of personal violence if he should offer any active opposition; did not consider his life would be safe, and others were in the same position; that his fear grew out of his long experience; had seen one man put away, and had heard of other such cases; took part in the matter through personal fear; had heard of Mr. Anderson being put away, and also three others who had disobeyed counsel.

E. W. Thompson testified that he saw the emigrant train pass through Beaver City; saw men and women in the company; that they seemed to be a respectable class of people. He had previously heard that the emigrants were coming. At a meeting held in the city, the bishop read a letter counseling the people not to trade with the emigrants.

Wm. Roberts testified that he saw the emigrants in Red Creek Bottoms; that there was quite a number of families in the train; that Colonel Dame preached about them at Parowan, and that he said, "You must not sell them any provisions."

James McGuffie, one of the witnesses in behalf of the objectors in the naturalization investigation before mentioned, testified as follows:

Q. Do you know whether or not after the massacre, John D. Lee continued to be on terms of friendship with Brigham Young? A. Oh, yes; and he got more wives. Had two sealed to him the very year he committed that atrocious murder. I was as well acquainted with John D. Lee as I could be with any man.

Mr. Baskin: Was he afterwards a member of the legislature? A. Yes, sir; and Wm. H. Dame, too.

Mr. Dickson: What I want to get at is, whether you know, of your own knowledge, that after the massacre John D. Lee continued to be on terms of friendship with the president of the church? A. Oh, yes, and got two more women after that. Got two at a lick; an English girl—she died.

Mr. Baskin: Now, I understood you to say that you took an obligation to obey the priesthood in all matters? A. Yes, in all things.

Q. Was there any penalty attached to your disobedience to the priesthood in the ordeal through which you passed? A. There was nothing farther than that the throat was to be cut and the belly ripped out. I think that is plenty enough.

Q. Do you know William Laney? A. Yes, I knew him well. He lived about five rods below my house at the time of the Mountain Meadows massacre.

Q. Do you know of his having furnished that band of emigrants with supplies? A. Yes; Laney recognized in the company a young man named Harris as being the son of a man that had been a great friend to him, and treated him kindly when he was on a Mormon mission in Tennessee. Laney invited the young man to supper at his house, and invited him to come and get his breakfast; and the young man, after he got his breakfast, saw the onions growing in the dooryard, and said that he would like to have a few of them; and Laney said, "Well, take all you want, and welcome," and he took them; and then Dame sent Barney Carter, one of the Destroying Angels, who tore a picket out of the fence and hit Laney side of the head. The man has never been sound in his mind since, just because he let the onions go to that man. It was Laney's only offense.

Q. What position did Dame hold in the church at that time? A. He was the colonel in the armed battalion, and was a high priest of the Mormon church of the Parowan Branch in 1857.

In John D. Lee's confession, which was made only after it was certain he would be executed, is contained in substance the same statement respecting the assault upon Laney as that made by McGuffie.

William Bradshaw testified that after the emigrants passed, Haight preached in Cedar City at a Sunday meeting, and said "Some old fool had been tampering with the Indians; if he had kept aloof, the emigrants would have been dead and in their graves by this time. Never mind," he added, "they have only gone farther into the net." He had also forbade the people from trading with the emigrants at a previous meeting; after the massacre, he had preached in a meeting that nothing was to be said about it.

It appears from the testimony, which was very voluminous, that a large portion of the emigrants' property was sold to the Mormons in Cedar City at public auction, and that as the people in that vicinity had not much money, most of the property so sold was paid for in grain. In answer to the question, "What was done with the grain?" asked by me of a number of the witnesses who testified to that fact, they invariably replied: "It was put in the tithing house granary."

\* \* \* \* \* \* \* \* \* \* \* \*

In 1877 Geo. Caesar Bates came to my office and stated that while he and his partner had appeared and participated in the defense of John D. Lee, at the first trial, they were employed to do so by Brigham Young, "trustee in trust" of the Mormon church; that he contemplated bringing a suit against the church to recover for the services so performed, as payment of a large portion thereof had been refused by Brigham, and that he desired me and my partner, Mr. DeWolf, to act as his attorneys in the case; that he had prepared the complaint, which he handed me. Upon reading it, I consented to act as his attorney, and instituted a suit. The following is an extract from the complaint:

"In the Third District Court of Utah Territory: Geo. C. Bates, Plaintiff, vs. The Church of Jesus Christ of Latter-day Saints, Defendant.

"Plaintiff alleges that on the 17th day of August, 1875, the defendant was indebted to the firm of Sutherland & Bates, attorneys at law, in the sum of $5,000.00 for work, labor, care and diligence of the firm, performed and bestowed

113

by them as attorneys, of and for the defendants at its instance and request, in and about and concerning the indictment, defense and trial of John D. Lee; and for fees due, and of right payable to said firm in respect thereof, and for necessary money spent by said firm in and about said work, labor and employment for defendant at its instance and request; that the said Sutherland had transferred and assigned his interest in said claim to the plaintiff."

The church had been incorporated by an act of the territorial legislature. Williams & Young, attorneys of the church, interposed a demurrer to the complaint on the ground that the employment of Sutherland & Bates to defend Lee was not within the scope of the corporate powers granted by said act. Upon expressing my opinion to Mr. Bates that the demurrer would be sustained by the court, he requested me to prepare, if that should occur, a complaint based upon the ground that Brigham Young, by assuming to act in the matter for the church, without authority, rendered himself liable. The demurrer having been sustained, I drew a complaint, as requested, and sought Mr. Bates for the purpose of having him verify it, but instead of finding him, I ascertained that he had entered into a written marriage contract with a "doctoress," and that they had left the Territory.

In the chapter of Bancroft's History of Utah, on the subject of the Mountain Meadows massacre trial, page 565, N. 46, it is stated that "Sutherland & Bates were the attorneys of the first presidency." They were not employed by Lee. After the evidence of the prosecution at the first trial was introduced, as it implicated both Brigham and Geo. A. Smith, those attorneys protracted the trial until the ex parte affidavits of Brigham and Smith, hereinafter mentioned, arrived. They then offered them in evidence, but upon the objection of the prosecution they were rejected. As the evidence tended strongly to show that both Brigham and Geo. A. Smith were accomplices of the crime, they sought to break its force by said ex parte affidavits. No doubt these affidavits had that effect upon members of the Mormon church, but not upon outsiders, for when these affidavits were critically examined, in the light of well established facts, the inference that both Brigham and Smith were accessories became more apparent. The context of the affidavit of Brigham was as follows:

"First: State your age and the present condition of your health, and whether in your present condition you could travel to attend in person at Beaver the court now sitting there. If not state why.

"Answer: To the first interrogatory he says: I am in my seventy-fifth year. It would be a great risk, both to my health and life for me to travel to Beaver at the present time. I am, and have been for some time, an invalid.

"Second: What offices, either ecclesiastical, civil or military, did you hold in the year 1857?

"Answer: I was Governor of this Territory, ex officio Superintendent of Indian Affairs, and the President of the Church of Jesus Christ of Latter-day Saints, during the year 1857.

"Third: State the condition of affairs between the Territory of Utah and the Federal Government in the summer and fall of 1857.

"Answer: In May, or June, 1857, United States mails for Utah were stopped by the Government, and all communication by mail was shut off. An army of the United States was en route for Utah, with the ostensible design of destroying the Latter-day Saints, according to the reports that reached us from the East.

"Fourth: Were there any United States judges here during the summer and fall of 1857?

"Answer: To the best of my recollection there was no United States judge here in the latter part of 1857.

"Fifth: State what you know about trains of emigrants passing through the Territory to the West, and particularly about a company from Arkansas, en route for California, passing through this city in the summer or fall of 1857.

"Answer: As usual, emigrant trains were passing through our Territory for the West. I heard it rumored that a company from Arkansas en route to California had passed through the city.

"Sixth: Was this Arkansas company of emigrants ordered away from Salt Lake City by yourself, or anyone in authority under you?

"Answer: No, not that I know of. I never heard of any such thing, and certainly no such order was given by the Acting Governor.

"Seventh: Was any counsel or instruction given by any person to the citizens of Utah, not to sell grain, or trade with the emigrant trains passing through Utah at that time? If so, what were those instructions and that counsel?

"Answer: Yes; counsel and advice was given to the citizens not to sell grain to the emigrants to feed their stock, but let them have sufficient for themselves, if they were out. The simple reason for this was that for several years our

115

crops have been short, and the prospect was at that time that we might have trouble with the United States army then en route for this place, and we wanted to reserve the grain for food. The citizens of the Territory were counseled not to feed grain even to their own stock. No person was ever punished or called in question for furnishing supplies to the emigrants within my knowledge.

"Eighth: When did you first hear of the attack and destruction of the Arkansas company at Mountain Meadows in September, 1857?

"Answer: I did not learn anything of the attack or destruction of the Arkansas company until some time after it had occurred—then only by a floating rumor.

"Ninth: Did John D. Lee report to you at any time after this massacre, what had been done at that massacre, and if so, what did you reply to him in reference thereto?

"Answer: Within some two or three months after the massacre, he called at my office and had much to say with regard to the Indians; their being stirred up to anger and threatening the settlements of the whites, and then commenced giving an account of the massacre. I told him to stop, as from what I had already learned by rumor, I did not wish my feelings harrowed with a recital of the details.

"Tenth: Did Philip Klingensmith call at your office with John D. Lee at the time of Lee making his report, and did you at this time order Smith to turn over the stock to Lee, and order them not to talk about the massacre?

"Answer: No; he did not call with John D. Lee, and I have no recollection of his ever speaking to me, or I to him, concerning the massacre, or anything pertaining to the property.

"Eleventh: Did you ever give any directions concerning the property taken from the emigrants at the Mountain Meadows massacre, or know anything as to its disposition?

"Answer: No; I never gave any directions concerning the property taken from the company of emigrants at the Mountain Meadows massacre, nor did I know anything of that property or its disposal, and I do not to this day, except from public rumor.

"Twelfth: Why did you not, as Governor of Utah Territory, institute proceedings forthwith to investigate that massacre and bring the guilty authors to justice?

"Answer: Because another governor had been appointed by the President of the United States, and was then on the way here to take my place, and I did not know how soon he might arrive and because the United States judges were not in the Territory.

"Thirteenth: Did you, about the tenth of September, 1857, receive a communication from Isaac C. Haight, or any

116

other person of Cedar City, concerning a company of emigrants called the Arkansas company?

"Answer: I did receive a communication from Isaac C. Haight, or John D. Lee, who was then a farmer for the Indians.

"Fourteenth: Have you that communication?

"Answer: I have not. I have made diligent search for it, but cannot find it.

"Fifteenth: Did you answer that communication?

"Answer: I did, to Isaac C. Haight, who was then Acting President at Cedar City.

"Sixteenth: Will you state the substance of your letter to him?

"Answer: Yes; it was to let this company of emigrants, and all companies of emigrants, pass through the country unmolested, and to allay the angry feelings of the Indians as much as possible.

"(Signed) BRIGHAM YOUNG.

"Subscribed and sworn to before me this 30th day of July, A. D. 1875.

"WILLIAM CLAYTON, Notary Public."

Brigham admits that he was governor and ex officio superintendent of Indian affairs. Note the flimsy excuse which he makes in his twelfth answer for neglecting to investigate the massacre and bring the guilty parties to justice. Governor Cummings, Brigham's successor, did not arrive until March 12, 1858, six months after the massacre. His second excuse in that answer is as ridiculous, and even more damaging than the first flimsy one. It did not require the presence of a United States judge to investigate the massacre. If the presence of a judge had been necessary, the probate judge of the county in which the crime was committed, under the provisions of the statutes of the Territory, exercised general criminal jurisdiction. An investigation could have been made by a justice of the peace, acting as a committing magistrate, and both the territorial marshal and the sheriff had authority to act as executive officers in the matter, and that both the attorney general of the Territory and the district attorney of the county had authority to institute proceedings. All of the territorial officers named were members of Brigham's church and owed their appointment or election to him, for he exercised at that time absolute control of the political affairs of the Territory. The probate courts continued for many years after the massacre, and until the decision of the case of Ferris

v. Higley, in 1874, to exercise general criminal jurisdiction, and the executive and prosecuting officers mentioned continued to perform the duties of executive and prosecuting officers conferred by the Utah statutes until the passage of the Poland bill in 1874, and, under the decision of the United States supreme court in the case of Englebrecht v. Clinton, during all of that time were the proper executive and prosecuting officers of the district courts in all cases arising under territorial laws.

The perpetrators of the massacre were subject to prosecution only under the territorial statute defining and punishing the crime of homicide. At any time during which said officers exercised the authority conferred upon them by the territorial legislature, Brigham Young, by exercising his power could beyond any doubt have legitimately caused the guilty parties to be indicted and punished. And as fifty-two high officers and members of the church of which he was the president participated in the crime, it was his manifest duty, both as an officer and as a citizen and church leader, to exercise his power and influence to accomplish that righteous end. It would undoubtedly have been effected long before the lapse of seventeen years, if he had, in earnest, publicly ordered the prosecution of the perpetrators of the massacre. For, such an order made in good faith would have been regarded as a divine command by most of the inhabitants of the Territory and the Mormon civil authorities.

Judge Cradlebaugh, of the second judicial district, held a term of court at Provo in March, 1859, ten months after Brigham had made the offer to Governor Cummings referred to hereafter, and impaneled a grand jury of Mormons, especially instructing them to investigate the massacre. In his charge he said:

"* * * I said to you in the outset that a great number of cases had come to my knowledge of crimes having been committed through the country, and I shall take the liberty of naming a few of them. The persons committing those offenses have not been prosecuted, the reasons why I cannot tell, but it strikes me that outside influences have prevented it. If you do your duty you will not neglect to inquire into those matters, or allow the offenders to go unpunished. I may mention the Mountain Meadows murders, where a whole train was cut off, except a few children who were too young to give evidence in court. It has been claimed that this offense was committed by Indians, but there is evidence that there were others who were engaging in it besides. When the Indians commit crimes they are not so discriminate as to save children; they would not be so particular as to save the children and kill the rest. I say, that you may look at all the crimes that have been committed in the western country by the Indians and there is no case where they have been so careful as to save the innocent children. But if this be not enough, we have evidence to prove that there were others engaged in it.

"A large body of persons leaving Cedar City, armed, and after getting away were organized, and went and returned with the spoil. Now, there are persons who know that there were others engaged in the crime; I brought a young man with me who saw persons go out in wagons with arms, others on horseback; they were away a day or two and came back with the spoil. The Indians complain that in the distribution of the property they did not get their share; they seem to think that the parties engaged with them kept the best and gave them the worst. The chief, there (Kanosh), is equally amenable to law, and liable to be punished, and I suppose it is well known that he was engaged in assisting to exterminate the hundred persons that were in that train. I might name to you persons who were there; a great number of them I have had named to me. And yet, notwithstanding this crime has been committed, there has been no effort made to punish those individuals. I say, then, gentlemen, it is your duty to look after that, and if it is a fact that they have been guilty of that offense, indict them, send for them, and then have them brought before this court. * * * It is not pleasant to talk about these things, but the crimes have been committed, and, if you desire, you can investigate them. My desire is that the responsibility shall be with the grand jury, and not with the court; all the responsibility shall be with you, and the question is with you, whether you will bring those persons to trial."

Judge Cradlebaugh kept the grand jury in session for two weeks, but they failed to pay any attention to his instructions, and after being severely reprimanded by him were discharged. An opportunity was thus afforded Brigham, if he had been in earnest in the offer to Governor Cummings to lend his aid in bringing the guilty to justice; but instead of doing so he opposed the efforts of the judge and disparaged him, as shown in his scurrilous letter to Secretary Belknap, written March 12, 1872, in which he said:

"I pledged myself to Alford Cummings, Governor of Utah Territory, to lend him and the court every assistance in my power in men and means to thoroughly investigate the Mountain Meadows massacre, and bring the guilty parties to justice. That offer I have made again and again, and although it has not been accepted, I have neither doubt nor fear that the perpetrators of that tragedy will meet their just reward. But sending an armed force is not the means of furthering the ends of justice, although it may serve an excellent purpose in exciting popular clamor against the Mormons. In 1859 Judge Cradlebaugh employed a military force to attempt the arrest of those alleged criminals. He engaged in all about four hundred men, some of whom were civilians, reputed gamblers, thieves, and other camp-followers, who were doubtless intended for jurors, as his associate, Judge Eccles, had just done in another district; but these accomplished absolutely nothing further than plundering hen roosts and rendering themselves obnoxious to the citizens on their line of march."

He could have brought the guilty parties to justice any time during a period of sixteen years, if he chose to exercise the power, which the following extract from a sermon delivered by him in March, 1863, shows that he knew he possessed:

"When a company of emigrants were traveling on the southern route to California, nearly all of the company were destroyed by Indians. The unfortunate affair has been laid to the charge of the whites. A certain judge that was in the Territory wanted the whole army to accompany him into Iron county to try the whites for the murder of that company of emigrants. I told Governor Cummings that if he would take an unprejudiced judge into that district where that horrid affair occurred, I would pledge myself that every man in that region around about should be forthcoming when called for, to be condemned or acquitted, as an impartial and unprejudiced judge and jury should decide, and I pledged him that the courts should be protected from any violation or hindrance in the prosecution of the law; and if any were guilty of the blood of those who suffered in the Mountain Meadows massacre, let them suffer the penalty of the law: but to this day they have not touched the matter for fear the Mormons will be acquitted from the charge of having a hand in it, and our enemies would thus be deprived of a favorite topic to talk about when urging hostilities against us—'The Mountain Meadows massacre! only to think of the Mountain Meadows massacre!'"

If Brigham made the foregoing "pledge" to Gov. Cummings, he well knew that under the statutes, hereinbefore referred to, the district court could only use Mormon instrumentalities in the prosecution, and that without a special order from him to the grand jury and the Mormon officials of the court, no indictment could be found. The offer was one of Brigham's crafty tricks, for he knew if it were accepted that any efforts made in pursuance thereof would be abortive.

As Governor and ex officio superintendent of Indian affairs, it was Brigham's imperative duty to investigate the massacre himself, after it was reported to him by Lee, even if the Indians alone had committed it; but he failed to do so. An investigation by him would have soon shown the complicity of at least fifty-two members of the church of which he was president, seer and revelator, and that among those members were several of his subordinate church officers.

Lee alleged in his confession that when attending the October Conference of the church, a month or six weeks after the massacre, he made a full statement of the facts to Brigham and gave him the names of the Mormons engaged. If this was true, an investigation for the purpose of ascertaining the facts was wholly unnecessary. Being in possession of that knowledge, Brigham's simple official duty only required him to have the guilty parties arrested, and collect and sell the property of the emigrants for the use of the unfortunate children who were spared. His failure to take charge of and sell the property of the massacred emigrants, and procure the arrest and conviction of the guilty can only be rationally accounted for on the ground that he was an accessory either before or after the commission of the crime.

In answer to the eleventh question in his affidavit: "Did you ever give any directions concerning the property taken from the emigrants at the Mountain Meadows massacre, or know anything as to its disposition?" Brigham replied: "No; I never gave any directions concerning the property taken from the company of emigrants at the Mountain Meadows massacre, nor did I know anything of that property or its disposal, and do not to this day, except from public rumor."

He must have known that seventeen little children had been saved, for two of them were given shortly after the massacre to Mrs. Cook, who at the time was a teacher of music in his family at Salt Lake City, and who afterwards became a client of mine and stated to me these facts. The other children were scattered around among the Mormons. The number of small children showed that the emigrant train was a very large one, and that the emigrants must have had in their possession a large amount of property.

That Brigham fully knew is shown by an extract from the report of Mr. Forney, a special agent sent out to investigate the affair, and to collect the children and send them to Arkansas to friends and relatives. Concerning the wrongful and unconscionable claims presented to him by a number of the inhabitants of the Territory relating to the orphans surviving the massacre, he says:

"In pursuance to directions from the Indian department, I forward the accounts of expenses incurred in recovering, maintaining, and finally sending to Fort Leavenworth, the seventeen children surviving the Mountain Meadows massacre, in September, 1857. I respectfully invite your attention to Abstract No. 1, which contains the accounts of expenses for said children. I rejected a number of claims against the government for these children, for different alleged expenses. There were a number of claims for purchasing the children from the Indians, by persons with whom Mr. Hamblin [Brigham's interpreter] found them; when it is a well-known fact that they did not live among the Indians one hour. I charged to the account of the children part of Mr. Hamblin's wages. The amount of claims presented to me on account of the children by persons in the southern portion of Territory, amount to over seven thousand dollars, of which amount I only paid twenty-nine hundred and sixty-one dollars and seventy-seven cents. Those I have paid I considered strictly and entirely proper." (Senate Executive Document No. 42, page 71, q. v. further on.)

If Brigham Young had possessed official integrity or common humanity, and really was not an accessory, he would not have been guilty of the criminal nonfeasance in office which is shown by answer eleven, but would have promptly taken vigorous steps to prevent the unfortunate children spared from being robbed by the wretches who murdered their parents and elder brothers and sisters. His criminal nonfeasance in this respect, and in failing to take any steps to bring the criminals to justice, in view of the facts disclosed, was such as only an accessory either before or after the fact would have been guilty of.

Not only does his criminal nonfeasance in office show his complicity as accessory, but there are positive statements and other matters which strongly tend to prove that fact. John D. Lee in his confession states:

"When I arrived in the city, I went to President Young's house, and gave him a full detailed statement of the whole affair from first to last. I gave him the names of every man that was present at the massacre. He said to me, 'When you get home I want you to sit down and write a long letter, and give me an account of the affair, charging it to the Indians. You sign the letter as "Farmer to the Indians," and direct it to me as Indian agent. I can make use of such a letter to keep off dangerous and troublesome inquiries.'"

Lee in substance further stated that in pursuance of that request he sent the following letter to Brigham Young, and thought he had managed the affair nicely:

"Harmony, Washington Co. Ut.

"November 20th, 1857.

"To his Excellency, B. Young, exofficio Superintendent of Indian Affairs.

"Dear Sir: My report under the date of May 11th, 1857, relative to the Indians over whom I have charge as Farmer, showed a friendly relation between them and the whites, which doubtless would have continued to increase, had not the white man been the first aggressor, as was the case with Capt. Fancher's company of emigrants passing through to California about the middle of September last, on Corn creek, fifteen miles south of Fillmore City, Millard county. The company there poisoned the meat of an ox which they gave to the Pahvant Indians to eat, causing four of them to die immediately, besides poisoning a number more. The company also poisoned the water where they encamped, killing the cattle of the settlers. This unguarded policy, planned in wickedness by this company, raised the ire of the Indians, which soon spread to the southern tribe, firing them up with revenge till blood was in their path, and as the breach according to their traditions was a national one, consequently any portion of the nation was liable to atone for that offense. About the 22nd of September, Captain Fancher and company fell victims to their wrath near Mountain Meadows; their cattle and horses were shot down in every direction, and their wagons and property mostly committed to the flames." * * * * * *

123

5

In the ninth answer of his affidavit, Brigham admits that Lee had called at his office, and when the latter commenced giving an account of the massacre, he told Lee to stop, as from what he had already learned by rumor, he did not wish his "feelings harrowed up with the recital of the details." That he possessed such sensitive and humane feelings, as this answer was evidently intended to convey, is disproved by the numerous cut-throat, blood-atoning sermons delivered by him to members of his church previous to the massacre. It is "passing strange" if Brigham with his known sagacity did not discover the untruthfulness of Lee's letter. He certainly must have known, and before Lee's letter—written more than three months after the massacre—that seventeen children were spared. The existence of this fact was what first caused federal officials of the Territory to suspect that the massacre was not the work of the Indians, and led to the investigation by them which disclosed that the crime was committed by Mormons, as it was generally known that in massacres by Indians they kill, indiscriminately, both children and adults. Again, if the massacre had been the work of Indians, some of them would have been killed by the emigrants in defense of their wives and children, as many of the Mormons would have been if their strategy had not been successful. It is strange, "passing strange," if the failure of Lee to state in that letter that Indians were killed did not attract the attention of Brigham and arouse his suspicion that Lee's letter was untrue. It is evident, however, that that letter was among many of Brigham's foxy devices to divert attention from unpleasant facts. Again, Klingensmith testified that at the October conference following the massacre he met Lee, who said to him that he had told Brigham Young everything that had transpired; that the next day Lee, Charley Hopkins and he met in Brigham's office, and that Brigham told Klingensmith, who had control of the property of the emigrants, to turn it over to Lee, as he was Indian agent anyway, and the disposition of the property properly belonged to him; and also said: "What you know about this affair, do not tell to any one, do not talk about it among yourselves."

\*   \*   \*   \*   \*   \*   \*   \*   \*   \*   \*   \*

At the second trial of John D. Lee the following was elicted in the examination of Jacob Hamblin by William Howard, United States attorney:

Q. Tell what else Lee told you. A. Well, he spoke of many little incidents.

Q. Mention any of those incidents. A. There were two young ladies brought out.

Q. By whom? A. By an Indian chief at Cedar City, and he asked him (Lee) what he should do with them, and the Indian killed one and he killed the other.

Q. Tell the story he told you. A. That is about it.

Q. Where were these young girls brought from; did he say? A. From a thicket of oak brush where they were concealed.

Q. Tell just what he said about that. A. The Indian killed one and he cut the other one's throat, is what he said.

Q. Who cut the other's throat? A. Mr. Lee.

Q. Tell us all the details of the conversation and killing. A. Well, he said they were all killed, as he supposed; that the chief of Cedar City then brought out the young ladies.

Q. What did he say the chief said to him? A. Asked what should be done with them.

Q. What else did the chief say? A. He said they didn't ought to be killed.

Q. Did the chief say to Lee why they should not be killed? A. Well, he said they were pretty and he wanted to save them.

Q. What did he tell you that he said to the chief? A. That according to the orders [the orders he had] they were too old and big to let live.

Q. What did he say he told the chief to do? A. The chief shot one of them.

Q. Who killed the other? A. He did, he said.

Q. How? A. He threw her down and cut her throat.

Q. Did you ascertain in that conversation, or subsequently, where it was they were killed? A. When I got home I asked my Indian boy and we went out to where this took place, and we saw two young ladies lying there with their throats cut.

Q. What was the condition of their bodies? A. They were rather in a putrefied state; their throats were cut; I didn't look further than that.

Q. What were their ages? A. Looked about fourteen or fifteen.

This witness also testified that Lee told him the other circumstances of the massacre, and how the emigrants were betrayed and induced to surrender. On cross-examination by Mr. Bishop, he answered as follows:

Q. Have you ever given this conversation that you had with Lee to anyone—to the public generally? A. I have no recollection of it.

Q. Have you ever given a report of it to any of your superiors in the church, or officers over you? A. Well, I did speak of it to President Young and George A. Smith.

Q. Did you give them the whole facts? A. I gave them some more than I have here, because I recollected more of it.

Q. When did you do that? A. Pretty soon after it happened.

Q. You are certain you told it fuller than you have told it here on the stand? A. I told them everything I could.

Q. Who else did you tell it to? A. I have no recollection of telling it to any one else.

Q. Why have you not told it before this time? A. Because I did not feel like it.

Q. Why did you not feel like it? You felt and knew that a great crime had been committed, did you not? A. I felt that a great crime had been committed, but Brigham Young told me that "as soon as we can get a court of justice we will ferret this thing out—but till then, don't say anything about it."

Jacob Hamblin was Brigham Young's Indian interpreter, and his testimony not only furnishes additional proof that Brigham Young was informed of the facts of the massacre shortly after its perpetration, but also corroborates the statements of Lee and Klingensmith that Brigham advised them not to talk about the occurrence.

Again, if Brigham was not an accomplice, why did he employ Sutherland & Bates to defend Lee? The letter of Lee was one of Brigham's devices to conceal from the public and the officers of the federal government the real participants of the crime, and the dishonest use he made of it is shown by the following letter written by him over a year after the massacre, and after being fully informed as to its horrible details by Lee and Jacob Hamblin:

"Office of Superintendent of Indian Affairs.
"Salt Lake City, Utah, Jan. 6, 1858.
"Hon. James W. Denver, Commissioner of Indian Affairs, Washington, D. C.
"Sir: On or about the middle of September, a company of emigrants traveling by the southern route to California poisoned the meat of an ox that died and gave it to the Indians to

126

eat. This caused the immediate death of four of their tribe and poisoning several others. This company also poisoned the water where they were encamped. This occurred at Corn creek, fifteen miles south of Fillmore City. I quote from a letter written to me by John D. Lee, Farmer of the Indians in Iron and Washington county. 'About the 22nd of September Capt. Fancher and a company fell victims to the Indians' wrath near Mountain Meadows; their cattle and horses were cut down in every direction and their wagons and property mostly committed to the flames. Lamentable as this case truly is, it is the only natural consequence of that fatal policy which treats the Indians like the wolves or other ferocious beasts.
\* \* \*"

No one knew better than Brigham that this letter was untrue, and that the charges there made against the emigrants were concocted by the assassins who murdered them. The letter, in connection with Lee's viewed in the light of the facts disclosed respecting the massacre, and Brigham Young's relations thereto, is most damaging, and is additional evidence that he was an accessory after, if not before, the fact.

The following extracts from newspapers show how Brigham's affidavit was regarded by the hundreds who commented thereon:

"As a literary curiosity, Brigham Young's affidavit deserves respectable consideration. It is indeed calculated to put the prophet in quite a new light before the world. Evidently there has been a terrible mistake somewhere. He has never been the autocrat supposed. He has never had authority over the Mormons. He did not know anything of the Mountain Meadows massacre until, by floating rumor, two months after it. But when at length, in a casual way it came to his knowledge that the people of his church had butchered one hundred and thirty defenseless men, women and children, he was so overcome that he could not bear to hear the details. And then according to his statement, he absolutely dropped the matter. Seeing, however, that his neglect to take any action might appear strange to the world, he offered as an explanation of this that 'I did not examine into the matter because another governor was appointed, and enroute to the Territory; and because no United States judges were here.' Really, this is too bad. It is adding insult to injury for a man in Young's position to affront the intelligence of the nation with so bald and so puerile a tissue of flummery as this. So clumsily is it constructed, moreover, that it affords cumulative proof that he possessed the necessary authority in the premises."—Sacramento Record.

"Brigham Young's affidavit in the Mountain Meadows massacre case at Beaver, Utah, is a very thin document. He pretends that he never really got an account of the affair. Vague rumors he admits had reached his ears of a deed over which every family in the United States was shuddering, but neither enough nor sufficient definite information to suggest to him the desirability of investigating the matter. Nay, it is even added in the affidavit that when Lee, a long time after the affair, proposed to tell him something about it, he refused to have his feelings harrowed up by a recital of the details. The transparent hypocrisy of the entire affidavit is the strongest evidence of Brigham's complicity in the whole business."— St. Albion (Vt.) Advertiser.

"The Mormons are making a desperate effort to clear Brigham Young of the Mountain Meadows massacre, but they will never succeed in convincing the world that the old sinner was not guilty of participation in the preliminary to that inhuman outrage, nor that the work of butchery was not perpetrated with his sanction, if not by his positive command." —Leavenworth Commercial.

"Brigham Young was the High Priest and Governor, and is still the head of the church. No one who knows the extent of his power over his dupes, and the spirit in which he wielded this power so long as he thought himself at a safe distance from the eyes of the world, can doubt for a moment that this massacre lies at his door, either as a result of his direct order or at least the natural and necessary result of his teachings."—Helena (Mont.) Herald.

On pages 708-709, Vol. I, of Whitney's history, is the following:

"Of the militia ordered or lured to the scene of the massacre by Lee and Klingensmith, nearly all were young men who acted in innocence of evil under military orders; in most instances they took no part in the actual killing. It was not until 1870 that Lee's complicity was established; and when upon investigation and recommendation of Apostle Erastus Snow made to President Young, it was reported and unanimously carried in council of the Apostles held in Salt Lake City, that John D. Lee be expelled from the church."

At the time of the massacre Brigham Young was not only governor and Indian superintendent, but also, under the organic act of the Territory, commander-in-chief of the militia, and yet according to Whitney, Lee's complicity in the massacre was not established until thirteen years thereafter. Up to that time neither Lee nor any of the other numerous participants, except Klingensmith, who had revealed the crime, had been disciplined by the church, but continued in full fellowship; nor were any of the numerous church members, except Lee, Haight and Klingensmith, who were active participants in the massacre, ever disfellowshiped by the church on account of their active participation in that brutal crime; nor has any of them except Lee ever been punished.

It appears from the testimony that Geo. A. Smith—who, according to Whitney's history, left Salt Lake City on his journey south at the end of July—delivered a sermon in the public square of Beaver City in which he stated that the emigrants were coming, and forbade the people to sell them anything, under penalty of being disfellowshiped, and that other sermons to the same effect were delivered by him. In his ex parte affidavit introduced in evidence by Mr. Howard, district attorney, at the second trial of Lee, Smith admits that he preached several times on his way south, and also on his return; that he advised the people to furnish all emigrant companies passing through the Territory with what they might actually want for breadstuff for the support of themselves and families; but advised the pepole not to feed their grain to their own stock, nor to sell it to the emigrants for that purpose."

Brigham, to strengthen Smith's assertion, in his answer to the seventh question asked in his affidavit, stated that he had given the same advice. Both Brigham's and Smith's affidavits were sworn to on the same day, before the same notary public, and were evidently intended to be used for the same purpose, i. e., to break the force of the testimony in the first Lee trial, which showed that Geo. A. Smith on his trip south had forbidden the people to deal with the emigrants. The affidavit of Smith raises the question of veracity between himself and the witnesses who testified that he forbade the people to trade with the emigrants. Which of these contradictory statements is true must be determined by the extrinsic testimony and circumstances throwing light upon the question. The reason why, as stated by Smith, he was moved to advise his people to furnish the emigrants with necessary food is not apparent, nor can it be imagined why he should do so. Did he fear that it would not be done unless he advised it? It is not presumable that he had any such fears, for his people were members of a civilized and Christian race of men, and to refuse to sell necessary food to an emigrant company among which were so many women and little children, or to any company, would have been characteristic only of barbarians; nor is it presumable that if he had given such advice that the emigrants would have experienced any difficulty whatever in obtaining necessary food. But if Smith's sermons were such as stated by Robert Kershaw and Mrs. Thompson it is presumable—as Smith was one of the counselors of Brigham Young and therefore a member of the high priesthood—that in view of the consequences of violating the oaths of obedience to the priesthood the emigrants would be unable to procure necessary food.

The reason assigned by both Smith and Brigham for advising the people not to sell their grain to emigrants is very flimsy. A great majority of the trains passing through the Territory took the northern route, by way of Soda Springs. A very limited number ever took the southern route on account of the hardship of crossing the unavoidable sandy desert. Nearly all the trains were hauled by oxen, and very few by mules. All the animals engaged in moving the trains subsisted on the natural pasturage of the plains. No grain was carried to feed the work-animals, and but a very limited quantity was carried to feed to saddle-horses used for scouting purposes, and usually there were not more than two or three of such. If an emigrant was in need of grain for feed he would certainly purchase oats or barley and not breadstuff, and he would never think of feeding grain to oxen. I will venture to say that the grain purchased annually by emigrants passing over the southern route in comparison to the local supply was not more than as a drop in a bucket of water.

Smith's journey through the south of Utah apparently was a natural proceeding, often indulged in by the directing heads of the church as a sort of a verbal roundup and inspection of the faithful. And almost simultaneously with the appearance of Smith, according to all accruing testimony, the local mouthpieces of the church began sermons in which they informed their adherents of the approaching emigrants, and not only forbade the sale or barter of anything with the invaders, but denounced them as mobocrats and enemies of the Mormons, and various other covert slanders. This statement in Lee's confession fully indicates Smith's design respecting the emigrants:

"In August, about ten days before the emigrants arrived, Gen. Geo. A. Smith called upon me. He said, 'I have sent down here by the old boss, Brigham Young, to instruct the brethren of different settlements not to sell any grain to our enemies. Suppose an emigrant train should come along through the southern country, making threats against our people and bragging of the part they took in helping to kill the prophets—what do you think the brethren would do with them? Would they be permitted to go their way, or would the brethren pitch into them and give them a good drubbing?' To which I replied: 'I am sure they would be wiped out if they had been making threats against our people. Unless emigrants have a pass from Brigham Young or some one in authority, they will certainly never get safely through this country.' My reply pleased him very much; he laughed heartily, and said: 'Do you really believe the brethren would make it lively for such a train?' I said 'Yes, sir. I know they will, unless they are protected by a pass or positive order of Governor Young, as the people are all bitter against the Gentiles, and full of religious zeal, and anxious to avenge the blood of the prophets.' The only reply which he made, was to the effect that on his way down from Salt Lake City, he had had a long talk with Major Haight on the same subject, and that Haight had assured him that the emigrants who came along without a pass from Governor Young could not escape from the Territory. We then rode along for some distance, when he again turned to me and said 'Brother Lee, I am satisfied that the brethren are under the influence of the reformation, and they will do just as you say they will with the wicked emigrants that come through the country, making threats and abusing our people.' I have been told by Joseph Wood, Thomas T. Willis and many others, that they heard Geo. A. Smith preach in Cedar City during that trip, and that he told the people that the emigrants were coming, and that they must not sell the company any grain or provisions, for they were a mob of villains and outlaws, and enemies of God and the Mormon people."

Mr. Bishop, who was Lee's real attorney, in his preface to Lee's confession, stated that:

"After all chance of escape had vanished and death was certain, the better nature of Lee overcame his superstition and fanaticism, and he gave me his confession of the facts connected with the massacre and requested me to publish the same. Why he refused to confess at an earlier day and save his own life by placing the guilt where it belonged, is a question which is answered by the statement that he was still a slave to his endowment and Danite oaths, and trusted until too late to the promises of protection by Brigham Young."

A false statement respecting Smith could not benefit Lee in any possible way, nor could he gain anything by falsely implicating any innocent person, and, in view of the well known facts and circumstances, it is clear that he has not done so in his confession.

The following synopsis of my closing speech to the jury at the first trial of Lee was made by Mr. Lockley, then the editor of the Salt Lake Tribune, who was present at the trial:

"Mr. Baskin made the closing argument for the prosecution. He commented upon the charge of the opposing counsel, that the case was being tried by popular clamor, and that the prosecution addressed itself to the prejudice of the audience and jury, and said by the severe arraignment of the people of the United States, and the peoples' attorneys, a stranger would be in doubt who was really on trial. It had been admitted that murder was committed, heinous in nature and revolting in its details. The fact is well known that at the time of the massacre not over one hundred Gentiles were living in the Territory. The speaker dwelt briefly upon the organization of the Nauvoo Legion, and said that 'it was a militia body obnoxious to public sentiment, a brutal instrument of an ecclesiastical despotism, and part and parcel of the Mormon church. Its highest officers were leaders of that church.' He severely criticized the length of time the crime had been allowed to slumber, and quoted from the Utah statutes to show that the execution of the law was in the hands of the Mormon authorities; that the territorial marshal appointed by the legislature summoned the grand and petit jurors; that the attorney general appointed by the same body was the prosecuting officer of the district courts until last year, when an act of Congress changed the judicial system of Utah, vesting the power to prosecute criminals in the United States district attorney, and that the probate courts exercised general criminal jurisdiction. He said 'the blame for delay in instituting a judicial investigation into the violation of crime rests solely with the Mormon authorities, who, having the power entirely in their own hands, have thrown every impediment in the way of executing the law.' To make this disgraceful fact more apparent, the speaker pointed to one of the prisoner's counsel who long held the office of prosecuting attorney for the judicial district, and whose duty during his tenure of office it was to bring his client to justice, and said that 'Congress at last having

132

acted, unpunished crimes are being investigated and offenders who have long enjoyed security brought to the bar of justice.'

" 'The counsel for the defense says that we ask you to "convict Lee, because he is a Mormon." Such an assertion is an insult to your intelligence. The first witness described the scene at the Mountain Meadows a few days after the occurrence, and the second witness a few weeks later. Their testimony established the corpus delicti. Klingensmith, a former bishop of the Mormon church, because of his position, was made a conspicuous actor in the crime. Because he was an active participant, and testified to that fact, he has been made the subject of vituperation and invective, and persistent effort is made to break down his testimony. If it were all stricken out, the charge is still conclusively proved. The prisoner's counsel have asked to what possible use a man like Klingensmith can be put. He is fit to obey counsel, a cardinal duty enjoined upon every good Saint. He is fit to be a polygamist bishop, and help build up "the Kingdom." He is fit to carry out the orders of his ecclesiastical superiors, and murder and spoliate at the command of alleged God-chosen servants. So long as he confined himself to these functions he was fit for preferment in the hierarchial ranks and not a word against his character was spoken, but now that he has come out from the charnel house, and has shaken his soul clear of the delusions that held it in bondage, and shown a willingness to atone for his past offenses by ridding his conscience of this appalling crime, he instantly loses all of his past sanctity and becomes "a monster of such hideous mien, that is to be hated needs but to be seen".'

" 'From the accumulation of testimony upon the point there can be no doubt that the emigrants surrendered their arms and committed to Lee the care of their young children, and then followed in the death procession. Defendant's counsel asked the jury to believe that this was done in good faith with the intention of rescuing the emigrants from the Indians who were menacing them. Is not such a request an insult to common intelligence? If deliverance was meant, why compel them to surrender their arms? Why take from the mother's breast the nursing baby? Why lead them into an ambuscade of Indians? The whole execution of the plot shows murderous design, and to believe otherwise is to do violence to common sense. When the victims were slain, the whites dispersed unmolested to their homes. If the Indians had committed the massacre, their passions being whetted with blood, they would have further gratified their savage rage by an assault upon the white men present. But the testimony shows that, instead, Indians tricked out in the clothing of the slain, went to Cedar City and washed bloody garments in the ditches, and that there was no excitement among them, and none of the citizens feared any attack; that Brigham Young was governor of the Territory and exofficio Indian superintendent. Had he been an honest and faithful official—had be been a Christian gentleman—he would have diligently collected the vast property of the emigrants and sold it—at the high prices that such property brought at that time in the Territory—for the benefit of the innocent little children, made fatherless and motherless by the Mormon fiends who ruthlessly murdered their fathers, mothers, and their older brothers and sisters. But instead of performing that official and humane duty, he suffered much of the property to be sold at public auction to the assassins of the emigrants, and many of the cattle to be branded with the church brand.

"'If there is a man on this jury who has been through that sink of iniquity, the endowment house, and wears endowment garments on his limbs, he will not find a verdict according to the law and testimony. He parted with his manhood when he swore blashphemous oaths which bind him a lifelong slave to the Mormon priesthood. He divested himself of his individuality, and is under obligation to think and act as he is directed.

"'Judge Sutherland asks the question, Why did not the witness Klingensmith and Joel White object to the massacre, instead of engaging in it? I answer, simply because they were members of an organization in which upon their oaths, they had bound themselves to obey the priesthood, and in which they had been made cowards—craven cowards and obedient serfs. All of the defendants attorneys who have addressed you, have denounced Bill Hickman and have severely criticized the prosecution for summoning him as a witness. They failed, however, to state what has made him odious and notorious. Gentlemen, it was his connection with Brigham Young, and the crimes which he, as one of the chief Danites of the Mormon church, committed. Both Hickman, and [also] the fifty Mormons who participated in the massacre, have made themselves infamous by obeying their church leaders. I have no doubt that both Lee and the church officials of Cedar City under whose orders that crime was committed, at the October Conference following the massacre, which they attended, as usual, partoook of the sacrament commemorative of the suffering and death of Jesus Christ, whose mission on the earth was one of mercy, and who said "Blessed are the Merciful."

"'With what joy must the beleaguered emigrants have hailed the approach of that white flag, the emblem of peace and mercy, in the hands of a man whose white skin denoted that he was a Christian and coming to their rescue? My God! what a sad mistake they made when they trusted that man who, with a lying tongue, induced them to give up their arms which was their only means of defense; and Oh! what must have been their horror when the onslaught upon them in their defenseless condition was began by the white men whose protection had been promised, and by the secreted Indians upon their helpless women and children. The horror of the scene is indescribable. About one hundred and twenty-five of the survivors of the emigrants were foully betrayed under a flag of truce, and in the space of a few minutes after the assault upon them began they were ruthlessly murdered by fifty-two white men called "Latter-day Saints," aided by an ambuscade of Indians. The evidence shows that the Mormons in the vincinity of the massacre, under the influence of the infamous organization to which they had subjected themselves, had lost their manhood and had become so servile that they made no effort to prevent that awful crime, and when those who participated in it were ordered out by their church leaders, they went to the scene of the slaughter like dumb cattle; and when they were at the Meadows, as testified to by young Pierce, Pollock and other witnesses, the talk among them was that the emigrants were to be destroyed; and yet not one among that assemblage of at least fifty-two members of the so-called Church of Jesus Christ of Latter-day Saints possessed manhood enough to make the least objection to the commission of that atrocious crime.

" 'What was done with the property of the emigrants? The evidence shows that it was sold at auction and bought by the inhabitants of Cedar City; that the bulk of it was appropriated by the men who murdered the parents of those little orphan children. I arraign Brigham Young as an accessory of the massacre, because considering the power he had over his people, no man, bishop, or any other subordinate officer, would have dared to take such an important step, or engage in such heinous scheme, if he hadn't the direct or implied sanction of the head of the church. The evidence shows that the leaders in that massacre were leaders in the Mormon church at Cedar City. I not only arraign Brigham Young as accessory before the fact of the massacre, but also as having violated his oath of office in failing to do what both his official duty and the common dictates of humanity required of him, which was to prevent the little children who were saved from being robbed; to have the property of the emigrants collected and sold and the proceeds appropriated to the nurture and education of those children. In place of doing that, this man with almost omnipotent power over his people, when the news was carried to him that the fathers, mothers and friends of those children had been butchered like dogs by Latter-day Saints and savage Indians combined, ordered the property to be delivered to John D. Lee, one of the chief perpetrators of the massacre.

" 'Gentlemen of the jury, in concluding, I again say, as I said before, I do not know whether any members of the Mormon church are on this jury, or even one man who has been bound by the shackles and subjected to the influence which led Klingensmith, Joel White, William Young, and each and all of the others engaged in that massacre, to march out to the Mountain Meadows and ruthlessly bathe their hands in the blood of offenseless men, women and children. If any one of this jury is a member of the Mormon church, I don't expect any verdict. In short, if any member of this jury has upon him the endowment garments received in that iniquitous grease-vat, the endowment house, where he took an oath of obedience and laid down his individuality, no evidence can be introduced in a case like this one that would induce such a man, as long as he is under that pernicuous influence, to find a verdict of guilty, and I do not expect it'."

The evidence at the first trial of Lee as conclusively showed his guilt as the second one did. Mr. Bishop in his preface to Lee's confession, stated, respecting these trials:

"Mormonism prevented conviction at the first trial, and at the second, Mormonism caused conviction—Brigham and his worshipers deserted Lee and marked him as a victim that should suffer to save the church from censure on account of the crimes it had ordered."

I have not the least doubt that to appease the universal adverse sentiment shown by the general expressions of disgust and indignation by the newspapers of the country caused by the exposures made at the first trial, Brigham Young entered into an arrangement with District Attorney Howard, that a Mormon jury should be impaneled to convict Lee; that the affidavits of Brigham Young and Smith, and their letters should be offered in evidence by Howard, and that he should exonerate the authorities of the Mormon church of complicity in the massacre. Mr. Howard, when he offered these affidavits and letters, said, "These papers have been submitted to the attorneys for the defense, and they consent to their introduction. I now file them and place them in evidence." Mr. Bishop, one of the attorneys of Lee, replied as follows:

"May it please your honor: While denying that these documents are legal evidence, we wish to see what length the prosecution will go in this court against the defendant by law or without law. Our opinion as attorneys is opposed to the evidence, but our client insists that it be admitted. Let the evidence go in, and with it all besides that the authorities of the church at Salt Lake City have unearthed for the perusal of Brother Howard. We now know we are fighting the indictment, and also the secret forces and power of the Mormon church."

Mr. Howard knew that the prisoner was entitled, under the provisions of the constitution, to a trial by an impartial jury, and to be confronted by the witnesses against him; that he had a right to cross-examine the witnesses of the prosecution, and that said ex parte affidavits and letters were incompetent, and had no possible bearing in the case; that their only effect was to place on record a denial of any complicity of either Brigham or Smith in the commission of the massacre. No doubt they were given to Howard, and offered by him in evidence in pursuance of a previous arrangement with Young and Smith, or with some one representing them.

Daniel H. Wells, one of the witnesses whose memory was so bad in the Reynolds case, went to Beaver City, about two hundred and fifty miles from Salt Lake City, to testify in the case; and the only testimony given by him was that "In 1857 John D. Lee was Farmer to the Indians, was popular with them, and had previously held the office of major in the militia." These facts were of no importance to the prosecution whatever, and could have been easily proved by hundreds of persons living in the vicinity of Beaver City where the trial was held.

The jury which convicted Lee was composed exclusively of Mormons, all the Gentiles who qualified on their voir dire having been peremptorily challenged by Howard. This was not a natural thing for any district attorney to do, but his object for so doing was evidently to have Lee convicted by a Mormon jury. Howard, in his closing speech to the jury, said that he had unanswerable evidence that the authorities of the Mormon church did not know of the butchery till after it was committed, and that then Lee had knowingly misrepresented the facts to President Young, seeking to keep him in ignorance of the truth.

When I learned from the newspapers that all the Gentiles had been challenged off the jury, and that Daniel H. Wells was present at the trial, I stated then that John D. Lee was doomed; and while there was no shadow of doubt of his guilt he was entitled to a trial by a jury which was not subject to any outside influence, and had not been packed for the purpose of securing his conviction by a Mormon jury. I do not believe that any Mormon jury at that time, or any jury before Congress changed the judicial system of the Territory, would have convicted Lee, or any one of the perpetrators of the numerous homicides which for many years had been committed with impunity in the Territory, unless its members had been either directly or indirectly advised that it was the wish of the high priesthood that it should be done. Would the high priesthood interfere with the jury? This question is answered by the following sermons of Jedediah M. Grant, one of Brigham's counselors, reported in Vol. III, page 233, of the Journal of Discourses:

"Last Sunday the president chastised some of the apostles and bishops who were on the grand jury. Did he fully succeed in clearing away the fog which surrounded them and in removing the blindness from their eyes? No, for they could go to their rooms and again disagree, though to their credit it must be admitted that a brief explanation made them unanimous in their action. Not long ago I heard that in a certain case, the Traverse jury, were eleven to one, and what is more singular, the one was alone right in his views of the case. Seven got into the fog to suck and eat the filth of a Gentile court."

While the guilt of Lee was as conclusively proved by the evidence at his first trial as at the second trial, yet at the first the jury, composed of three Gentiles, eight Mormons and one jack-Mormon, disagreed, the Gentiles having voted for conviction, and the Mormons and jack-Mormon for acquittal.[5]

Elder Chas. W. Penrose, in defending the church and Brigham Young in an address delivered in a Mormon assembly hall in Salt Lake City on October 26, 1884, said:

"At the second trial (of Lee) the evidence was plain and direct as to his complicity in the massacre; he was convicted by Mormon testimony, and a verdict of guilty was brought in against him by a Mormon jury. I have a list of their names, all members of the Mormon church. Strange thing, was it not, to have a Mormon jury? It would be singular in these times. But John D. Lee was convicted by a Mormon jury, a thing said by some of the newspapers, extracts which I have read to you, to be impossible."

The impaneling of that Mormon jury and the conviction of Lee by it was, indeed, strange—amazingly strange. One day in 1867, when I was walking up Main street in Salt Lake city with John Chislet, one of the persons who crossed the

---

[5]During the long contest which was waged between the Gentiles and Mormons, there were a few (comparatively) mercenary and fawning Gentile residents of the Territory. These were called jack-Mormons, because they tried to obtain from the Mormon masses business favors and patronage by fulsome laudation of the Priesthood, and by espousing the cause of the Church party, and denouncing the measures of the Liberal party.

plains with one of the celebrated hand-cart trains, but who afterwards apostatized from the church, he pointed to a carriage which was approaching at a few yards distance, and said: "That man in the carriage with Brigham Young is John D. Lee, the leader of the Mountain Meadows massacre, and the carriage in which they are riding is one which the emigrants had owned." That was the first time I had seen Lee. The carriage was accompanied by Brigham's mounted, sacred, guard. The next time I saw Lee was at his first trial, and I recognized him as the man whom I had before seen in the carriage with Brigham Young.

Whitney's version of the massacre is most disgusting to any one conversant with the facts. He not only libels the emigrants himself, but also gives currency to slanders invented and circulated by the wretches who murdered them. In Vol. I, pages 693, 694, 695, is the following:

"Whatever had been the conduct of these companies when they encountered the Utah outposts of the East there seems to be no question that not long after their arrival in Salt Lake valley they gave abundant evidence of their hostility and vindictiveness.

"During their entire journey through the Territory they appear to have conducted themselves in the most offensive manner. They swaggered through the town declaring their intention, as soon as they should have conveyed their women and children to a place of safety, to return with military force sufficient to complete such destruction of the Mormons as the United States soldiery might leave unfinished.

"They averred that the murdered leaders of the church had received their tardy deserts, and gave the impression, if they did not positively boast, that in their company were hands which had been reddened with the Prophet's blood. Nor were their offenses confined to harrowing and insulting words. They acted like a band of marauders, preying upon the possessions of those through whose country they traveled, and committed all manner of petty indignities upon person and property. Still greater crimes were charged to them by the Indians. They were said to have not only wantonly shot some of the braves, but were known to have poisoned beef where the savages would likely get it. Several deaths attributed to this cause occurred among the Indians near Fillmore, and numbers of their animals perished through drinking water from springs poisoned by the emigrants when about breaking camp. * * * Against this company, as stated, was laid the fearful charge of injecting poison into the carcass of one of

139

their oxen, first having learned that the Indians would be likely to eat the meat, and of throwing packages of poison into the springs. In other ways they contrived to render themselves obnoxious to the settlers and hateful to the natives."

The charges there made are absolutely false; but if they were even true, making them either as a justification or in mitigation of the murder of innocent women and children, or even of the murder of those guilty of the silly charges, was disgraceful in the extreme. If any such crimes had in fact been committed, the proper course to pursue would have been to punish the guilty ones by due process of law. Most of the victims of that class of homicides, which in former days in the Territory were committed with impunity, were also foully slandered.

Bancroft, in his History of Utah, on page 550, states:

"It was Saturday evening when the Arkansas families encamped at the Mountain Meadows. On the Sabbath-day they rested, and at the usual hour, one of them conducted divine services in a large tent, as had been their custom throughout their journey. At break of day on the seventh of September while the men were lighting their campfires, they were fired upon by Indians, or white men disguised as Indians, and more than twenty were killed or wounded."

Mr. Forney, as superintendent of Indian affairs, made a close investigation into the details of the massacre, and in his official report dated at Salt Lake City, 1859, Senate Document, No. 42, 36th Congress, First Session, pages 87-88, said:

"A massacre of such unparalleled magnitude on American soil must sooner or later demand thorough investigation. I have availed myself during the last twelve months of every opportunity to obtain reliable information about the said emigrant company, and the alleged causes of and circumstances which led to their treacherous sacrifice.

"Mormons have been accused of aiding the Indians in the commission of this crime. I commenced my inquiries without prejudice or selfish motive, and with a hope that, in the progress of my inquiries, facts would enable me to exculpate all white men from any participation in this tragedy, and saddle the guilt exclusive upon the Indians, but, unfortunately, every step in my inquiries satisfied me that the Indians acted only a secondary part. Conflicting statements were made to me of the behavior of this emigrant company while traveling through the Territory. I have accordingly deemed it a matter of material importance to make a strict inquiry to obtain reliable information on this subject, not that bad conduct on their part could in any degree palliate the enormity of the crime, or be regarded as any extenuation. My object was common justice to the surviving orphans. The result of my inquiries enables me to say that the company conducted themselves with propriety. They were camped several days at Corn creek, Fillmore valley, adjacent to one of our Indian farms.

"Persons have informed me that, whilst there encamped, they poisoned a large spring with arsenic and the meat of a dead ox with strychnine. This ox died, unquestionably, from eating a poisonous weed which grows in most of the valleys here. Persons in the southern part of the Territory told me last spring, when on a southern trip, that from fifteen to twenty Pahvant Indians (of those on Corn creek farm) died from drinking the water of the poisoned spring and eating of the poisoned meat. Other equally unreasonable stories were told me about these unfortunate people.

"That an emigrant company, as respectable as I believe this was, would carry along several pounds of arsenic and strychnine, apparently for no other purpose than to poison cattle and Indians, is too improbable to be true. I cannot learn that the Pahvants had any difficulty with these people. The massacre took place only about one hundred miles south of Corn creek, and yet not any of those Indians were present. Bad white men have magnified a natural cause to aid them in exciting the southern Indians, hoping that, by so doing, they could be relied upon to exterminate the said company and escape detection themselves."

In the early seventies, when I was in Washington trying to procure legislation on the Utah problem, I became acquainted with a member of Congress whose name I have forgotten, from the district in Arkansas from which the emigrants came. I drew a bill granting to each of the survivors of the massacre a quarter section of the public land of the United States on account of the injustice done them when small children by the governor and superintendent of Indian affairs of the Territory in permitting them to be robbed by the assassins of their parents. That member introduced the bill, but it was not passed.

I stated to him the charges which had been made against the emigrants, and it made him very indignant. He said that the charges were infamous slander, because the families and persons composing the company were honest, moral and most highly respected in the community in which they had resided.

He also stated to me in substance the following respecting the emigrants: "Two young men went from Arkansas to California in the early days of the gold excitement; that they were very successful and acquired considerable wealth; and that they either purchased or procured an option on one of the large Mexican grants in Southern California; that they returned to their native State and induced a number of their relatives and neighbors, who were in comfortable circumstances, to sell their homes and property and form a company to colonize the land mentioned; that the train made up by them was not loaded with the kind of merchandise usually transported over the plains, but with the various articles necessary for household purposes, and agricultural implements, and that a considerable number of blooded horses and cattle for breeding purposes were selected and bought. The amount invested by the emigrants in the enterprise, he stated, must have been considerably more than one hundred thousand dollars.

James H. Berry, a United States Senator from Arkansas, in a speech made by him in the Smoot case, reported in the Congressional Record of February 12, 1907, said:

"In 1857 I lived in the County of Carroll, State of Arkansas. In the spring of that year there left that county, and two adjoining counties, between a hundred and forty and a hundred and fifty—including men, women and children—emigrants for California. They consisted of the **best citizens** of that county. It was a large train. It excited much interest throughout the section of country from which they went. They had about 600 head of cattle, several mule teams, a number of wagons, and each head of a family had more or less money; how much I do not know. Late in the fall or the early winter the news came back that the train had been assaulted by the Indians far out west, and that every soul had perished. Later on there came the news that some, the children—how many we did not at that time know—were saved, and that they were in the hands of the Mormons in Utah. Our senators and representatives here called upon the Interior Department. An agent, a Mr. Forney, was sent there by the Commissioner of Indian Affairs. He gathered those children together, sixteen of them, who had been preserved from the massacre on that fatal 13th [11th] day of September. He brought those children back to Leavenworth, and there Colonel Mitchell of our county went and met them and took them in charge. I was a boy seventeen years old on that day when they were brought to the village court house. I saw them as they were lined up on the benches, and Col. Mitchell told the people whose children they were, at least, whose he thought they were. There were sixteen of them. One little girl, I distinctly remember had an arm broken by a gunshot wound. It had not united and the arm hung dangling by her side. I have seen much of life since that day; I have seen war along the lines of the Border States in all of its horrors; but no scene in my life was ever so impressed upon my mind as that which I saw there that day presented by those little children, their fathers, mothers, brothers and sisters dead on the far-off plains of Utah, and they absolutely without means, with no human being to look to. When he (Mr. Forney) first got the children, he reported to the Secretary of the Interior, and you will find it in the report of the Commissioner of Indian Affairs, that they had been so frightened and scared by the Mormons that he could get nothing from them; that they would not talk; and that it was long before he could gain their confidence. The eldest of them was five or six years of age, and perhaps there was one seven years of age. But when they got back to Leavenworth, and from there to Arkansas they had lost the fears that had been instilled in them by the Mormon families in which they had lived. They could not tell much, but they could tell that white men and not all Indians assisted in the massacre. They could tell it was a white man who came into their corral and induced the emigrants to give up their guns; that it was white men that drove the wagons in which they rode; that it was white men who shot the wounded men who had been placed in one of the wagons."

The children were sent back to Arkansas by Mr. Forney in 1859, so that at the time of the dreadful occurrence the eldest of them were only four or five years old.

The speech of Senator Berry, even if there was no other evidence of the fact, shows beyond question the high character of the emigrants, and that Whitney's statements respecting them are false.

The high character of the emigrants is also stated in the following quotation from the "Rocky Mountain Saints," by Stenhouse:

"In addition to the ordinary transportation wagons of emigrants, they had several riding carriages, which betokened the social class of life in which some of the emigrants had moved before setting out on the adventure of western colonization.  *  *  *  In that company there were men, women, and children of every age, from the venerable patriarch to the baby in arms. It was a bevy of families related to each other by the ties of consanguinity and marriage, with here and there in the train a neighbor who desired to share with them the chances of fortune in the proposed new homes on the golden shores of the Pacific. One of their number had been a Methodist preacher, and probably most of the adults were members of that denomination. They were moral in language and conduct, and united regularly in morning and evening prayers. On Sundays they did not travel, but observed it as a day of sacred rest for man and beast. At the appointed hour of service, this brother-preacher assembled his fellow travelers in a large tent which served as a meeting house within their wagon circled camp, for the usual religious exercises, and there, on the low, boundless prairies, or in higher altitudes at the base of snow-capped mountains, he addressed them as fervently, and with as much soul-inspiring faith, as if his auditory had been seated comfortably within the old church walls at home; and they, too, sang their hymns of praise with grateful, feeling souls, and with hearts impressed with the realization that man was but a speck in the presence of that grand and limitless nature that surrounded them, and of which they were but a microscopic part. Those who passed the company en route, or traveled with them a part of the way, were favorably impressed with their society, and spoke of them in the kindest terms as an exceedingly fine company of emigrants, such as was seldom seen on the plains. * * * A gentleman, a friend of the author, traveled with the Arkansas company from Fort Bridger to Salt Lake City, and speaks of them in the highest terms; he never traveled with more pleasant companions."

Mrs. Stenhouse, in her work, "Tell It All," said:

"My old friend, Eli B. Kelsey, traveled with them (the emigrants) from Fort Bridger to Salt Lake City, and he spoke of them in the highest terms * * * that they traveled along in the most orderly fashion, without hurry or confusion. On Sunday they rested, and one of their number, who had been a Methodist preacher, conducted divine service."

None of the witnesses in the Lee trials testified that the emigrants had poisoned the springs or dead animals, except in the first trial, when Elisha Hoops, who was placed upon the stand by the defendant, testified that in September, 1857, he accompanied Geo. A. Smith, Jesse N. Smith and ex-Bishop Farnsworth as far north as Fillmore; that they camped at Corn creek, and found the Arkansas emigrants encamped there about one hundred and fifty yards distant; that an ox lay dead between the two camps, and just as witnesses' party was about to start he saw a little German doctor who belonged to the emigrant company, draw a two-edged dagger with silver guard, such as gentlemen carry, and make three thrusts into the ox; that he produced a small, half-ounce vial, filled with a light colored liquid,

144

which he poured into the knife holes. On cross-examination by me, he stated that the Smiths and Bishop Farnsworth were in the wagon when the ox was tampered with, but didn't know if they saw it; did not call their attention to it, and no mention was made of the occurrence; that ten or fifteen minutes after the German had "pizened" the ox, some Indians came up and dickered with him for it. They finally gave him buckskins, and then began skinning the ox. He supposed the Indians wanted the hide to cut up into soles for moccasins, but didn't know how long they were flaying the animal as his party was driving away at the time.

The story told by Hoops was a very improbable one. He had seen the little German doctor at work upon the ox just as his party was about to start. Ten or fifteen minutes subsequently a dicker was made with some Indians for the "infected" carcass, which the Indians must have known that the emigrants would soon leave. On his further cross-examination, his efforts to explain his statement were so ridiculous that he became a laughing-stock in the courtroom. He further stated that the emigrants also put small bags of "pizen" in the spring at Corn creek. The volume of water issuing from that spring was so great that it would have required more than an ordinary amount of poison to produce any deadly effect. Hoops showed himself on the witness stand, not only to be a false witness, but a fool as well.

In Vol. I, page 782, of Whitney's history, is the following:

"Though there was a plenitude of rumors as to the persons who knew the internal history of the massacre, a degree of difficulty was encountered in determining who were actually in possession of that knowledge. This may have been partly owing to the obligation of secrecy placed upon all who were at the Meadows on the fatal day; but the greatest impediment in the way of obtaining the requisite information was the action of the officers themselves in shaping their course, as Judge Cradlebaugh had formerly done for a crusade against the Mormon church and its leaders. They thereby forced members of that organization to stand aloof and refrain from extending the aid which otherwise would have been willingly given. It was vain to say to them that only guilty persons would be pursued. They knew better. The memory of the conspiracy of the McKean clique against the church leaders which had been overthrown by the United States Supreme Court was yet fresh in their minds. McKean was still in office; a prosecution of the case by Baskin was prospective, while Boreman, judge in the second judicial district, with U. S. Attorney Cary and U. S. Marshal Maxwell were ardent followers of the chief justice in his anti-Mormon mission."

The quiescence of the Mormon masses regarding the massacre is a most remarkably anomaly; and to have occurred on such an occasion in an American community is shocking and unmistakably discloses the viciousness of the organization of which the Mormon masses, at the time of the massacre, were members. Their quiescence, however, is not as reprehensible as the inaction of the high church officials and Mormon territorial officers, whose duty it was to move promptly in the matter, and as they could have easily done if they so desired, procure the arrest and conviction of the fiendish communicants of their church, who, under a flag of truce, treacherously disarmed and foully murdered the innocent and confiding emigrants. Whitney further states:

"The first reports were that the Indians, several hundred in number, had attacked and slain some of the emigrants, and that men were needed to guard the remnant and bury the dead. It was upon this call to Colonel Haight that John M. Higbee, a major in one of the battalions of militia, on Thursday the 8th, set out with a body of men and wagons for the Meadows. His force was not numerous, and the men were not all supplied with arms. Some were teamsters and others took along picks and spades. They reached their destination early Wednesday morning, only to find that there had been no such bloodshed as had been reported, and that the emigrants were making good their defense. But they found an angry host of Indians bent on bloodshed, and outnumbering ten to one of their own forces. An attempt by the militia to assist the emigrants would have transferred to themselves the Indian attack. During that day and the next, awaiting further orders, they lay in camp, near to but out of sight of the entrenched emigrants, who were on the other side of a small hill. Thursday brought slight reinforcements, but by this time more Indians had arrived upon the scene. The whites who were from Santa Clara county believed as did Higbee's men, that they were summoned there on a mission of mercy to bury the dead and protect the survivors, but the fury of the Indians was uncontrollable."

In the light of Lee's confession, and the unrefuted evidence at both trials of Lee, which not only corroborated the material facts contained in that confession, but also conclusively showed that the massacre was ordered and planned by Mormon church officials who were also officers of the militia, and was treacherously and inhumanely executed by the militia and an Indian auxiliary force under the leadership of John D. Lee. Whitney's version of the massacre is "as dishonest as it is despicable," and again verifies the assertion of Brigham Young, heretofore referred to, that "we have the greatest and smoothest liars in the world."

It is not reasonable that the subordinate church authorities at Cedar City would have taken steps to murder the emigrants had they not been instructed to do so by an order of their superior officers. Of course such an order was not, and could not be shown, except by circumstantial or oral evidence. This could have been furnished only by the church officer at Cedar City to whom it was (in my opinion) communicated by George A. Smith on his southern trip, made for that purpose; but to have so testified he would have violated his oath-bound endowment covenants by disclosing the fact, and thereby subjected himself to the fearful penalty he would incur for violating that oath.

There was no direct evidence in the trials of Lee, nor is it stated in Lee's confession, that any order was given either by Brigham or Smith to massacre the emigrants. Isaac C. Haight, of Cedar City, was the president of the Parowan stake of Zion, and as such was the chief or presiding officer of the local church government in the Mormon settlements in the vicinity of the Mountain Meadows. It was shown by the evidence in said trials that he was the first and chief instigator of the massacre, and soon after the visit of George A. Smith began to move in the matter and was an active participant until the massacre was accomplished. He afterward permitted much of the property to be sold at auction in Cedar City, where he resided, and the grain which was received in payment for most of it to be put in the church tithing house granaries. The subordinate church officers who participated in the massacre were John M. Higbee, first counselor to Haight, and William H. Dame and Philip Klingensmith, who were bishops. Lee was not a church officer, but being government Indian farmer, he was the only person who could procure the assistance of the Indians, and was selected to perform that service. That both Lee and the other Mormon laymen acted under the orders of Haight, and which were sanctioned by his superior church officials clearly appears from the facts and circumstances disclosed. It is not a reasonable hypothesis that they voluntarily assembled to commit such a horrible crime without being commanded to do so by some person or persons whose commands they were obligated to obey. I have before shown the nature of the obligations by which members of the Mormon church bind themselves, on their oaths, to obey the priesthood in both temporal and spiritual affairs.

147

When Haight and his subordinate church officers determined to destroy the emigrants, to accomplish it the services of a sufficient number of their co-religionists was necessary. Therefore the order under which the latter assembled and acted was an obvious and essential one, and was stated by Lee, in his confession, as follows:

"Those who were connected with the massacre, and took part in the transaction, were moved by a religious duty. All were acting under the orders of and by command of their church leaders. The immediate order for killing the emigrants came from those in authority at Cedar City. I and those with me acted by virtue of positive orders from Brother Haight and his associates. Before starting on my mission to the Mountain Meadows, I was told by Brother Haight that his orders to me were the result of full consultation with Bishop Dame, and all in authority."

This statement was corroborated in the trials of Lee. It is not probable that Haight, who was the first one to move in the matters at Cedar City, and so soon after the visit of Geo. A. Smith, acted without the sanction of his superior church officers at Salt Lake City. After Smith made his journey to Cedar City, the church authorities in the various settlements through which he passed and preached, began to slander the emigrants and forbid the members of the church furnishing any of them with necessary supplies. While there is no direct evidence that Smith ordered the massacre, there is very strong circumstantial evidence that an order for the massacre of the emigrants was delivered by Smith at the time he visted Cedar City, to President Haight. Unless Haight revealed the fact, which it is improbable he would do except to his subordinate church officers on their pledge of secrecy, it could not be shown. It is not therefore a matter of surprise that no direct evidence that such an order was given, was elicted at the trials of Lee. The omissions and commissions of Brigham Young hereinbefore stated conclusively show that he was accessory to the massacre of the offenseless emigrants at the Mountain Meadows. There were many more than sixteen children in the emigrant train, and only those who were old enough to coherently state the facts of the massacre if they had been permitted to live, were killed. Many of those not slaughtered were too young to know even their own names. It appears from Senator Berry's speech, before quoted, the parentage of the unfortunate children who were saved was not known, but merely "supposed." By a most revolting massacre and heartless robbery, planned and executed under the leadership of high officials of an organization claimed to be the **"Church of Jesus Christ,"** those innocent children were left "absolutely without means, with no human being to look to." "If there isn't a Hell, there ought to be."

Whitney, in his history, Vol. I, page 707, states that "the orphans, seventeen in number, ranging in age from three months to seven years, were taken to Cedar City and distributed among the families in the vicinity."

149

# CHAPTER XI.

## The Danites, or "Destroying Angels."

The Danites were an organization in the Mormon church. Its existence was stated by Bill Hickman in his confession made to me. He gave me the names of more than a score of its active members, among whom were a number of reputed notorious Danite assassins. He stated that the members were bound by their covenants to execute the orders of the priesthood, and that when a direct order or intimation was given to "use up" anyone, it was always executed by one or more of the members, according to the circumstances of the case. That such an organization existed is conclusively shown by the numerous mysterious murders which were never investigated by the executive officers of the Territory, or any attempt made to prosecute the guilty parties. The Mormon sermons, the confessions of Hickman and Lee, and numerous other circumstances made plain its existence. Hickman confessed to me that he personally knew of thirteen persons having been murdered, some of them by him, and others by various Danites; that at one time he murdered a man by the name of Buck at the personal request of Brigham Young. Hickman's statement of this affair in his published confession is substantially the same as given to me, in fuller detail, and is as follows:

"A messenger came from the city and told me I was wanted at Brigham Young's office immediately. I mounted my horse and was in town in an hour, and went to Young's office. He asked me if I had 'seen the boys.' I asked him 'What boys?' and he answered 'George Grant and William Kimball.' I told him I had not. I then told him I had got word to come to his office, and wished to know what was wanted. He answered, 'The boys have made a bad job of trying to put a man out of the way. They all got drunk, bruised up a fellow, and he got away from them at the point of the mountain, came back to this city, and is telling all that happened, which is making a big stink.' He said I must 'get him out of the way, and use him up.' He told me to go and find the boys, meaning Generals Grant and Kimball, both being acting generals in the militia at that time, and arrange

BILL HICKMAN.

things with them so as to have him taken care of. I found them, and they told me O. P. Rockwell [a notorious Danite], with a party, had made a bad job and wanted help, and I had been sent for to wind it up. Said they, 'did Brigham tell you what was up?' I told them he did, and had sent me to them to arrange things. They told me they had things fixed: that when the party to which this man belonged first came into the Territory, all had stopped twelve miles north of the city, and remained several weeks in the neighborhood where George Dalton lived; that Dalton was in town, and they had got him to see this man (whose name I never heard, only he was called 'Buck') and take him home with him, for he had confidence in Dalton. They said Dalton understood it, and they were waiting for me to come and meet him on the road. They then hunted up Dalton, and told him they had things all right now. Dalton was to leave town a little before sundown and pass the Hot Springs, three miles north of the city, and take the lower road, on which there was not much travel, and I was to meet him. I was to know his team because both of his horses were white. All being arranged, and the sun about an hour high, I got my horse, and the question was then asked how many men I wanted to go with me. I told them I did not want anyone. They said I must have somebody, and I told them I would take a man that was standing by, by the name of Meacham. They got him a horse, and we went to the place appointed, and just at dark the wagon came. We called it to halt. The man, Buck, got a shot through the head, and was put across the fence in a ditch. A rag was hung on a bush below the place. We returned to the city to General Grant, as per agreement, and found him at home with General Kimball, O. P. Rockwell and somebody else, whose name I do not recollect now. They asked if all was right, and I told them it was. They got spades, and we all went back, deepened the ditch, put him in and buried him, returned to Grant's, took some whiskey, and separated for the night. The next day Kimball and I went to Brigham Young, told him that 'Buck' was taken care of, and there would be no more stink about his stories. He said he was glad of it."

I remember distinctly that Hickman in relating that occurrence to me, said that Buck, when he was shot, sprang out of the wagon, and while he was struggling on the ground, Meacham dismounted and drove his bowie knife twice into his body. He was up to this event the sole survivor of the Aiken party, who were murdered by Porter Rockwell and his ever-ready assistants at the "point of the mountain" on the road to Lehi.

The church influence which made the perpetrators of the Mountain Meadows massacre fiends, evidently made the Danites fiends also. Among the many heartless murders committed by the Danites was that of Jesse P. Hartley, published in Hickman's confession as follows:

"Hartley was a young lawyer who had come to Salt Lake City the fall before, and had married a Miss Bullock of Provo, a respectable lady of good family. But word had come to Salt Lake (so said, I never knew whether it did or not) that he had been engaged in some counterfeiting affair. He was a fine looking, intelligent young man. He told me he had never worked any in his life, and was going to Fort Bridger or Green River to see if he could not get a job of clerking or something that he could do. But previous to this, at the April Conference, Brigham Young, before the congregation, gave him a tremendous blowing up, called him all sorts of bad names, and saying he ought to have his throat cut, which made him feel very bad. He declared he was not guilty of the charges. I saw Orson Hyde looking sour at him, and after he had been in camp an hour or two, Hyde told me he had orders from Brigham Young, if he (Hartley) came to Fort Supply, to have him used up. 'Now,' said he, 'I want you and George Boyd to do it.' I saw him and Boyd talking together; then Boyd came to me and said, 'its all right Bill, I'll help you to kill that fellow.' One of our teams was two or three miles behind and Orson Hyde wished me to go back and see if anything had happened to it. Boyd saddled his horse to go with me, but Hartley stepped up and said he would go if Boyd would let him have his horse. Orson Hyde said 'let him have your horse,' which Boyd did. Orson Hyde then whispered to me, 'now is your time; don't let him come back.' We started, and in about half a mile we had to cross the canyon stream, which was mid-side to our horses. While crossing, Hartley got a shot and fell dead in the creek. That evening, after supper was over, Orson Hyde called all the camp together and said he wanted a strong guard on that night for that fellow that had come to us in the forenoon had left the company. He was a bad man, and it was his opinion that he intended stealing horses that night. This was about as good a take-off as he could get up, but it was all nonsense. It would do well enough to tell, as everyone that did not know what had happened believed it."

In the early days of my experience in Utah, I frequently had cases which required me to go to the city of Provo, and when attending court there I lodged at Mr. Bullock's hotel. Having heard of the murder of Hartley, and that his wife was a sister of Mr Bullock, I asked him on one occasion, while stopping at his hotel, whether what I had heard respecting the murder of Hartley was true. He stated that Hartley had incurred the displeasure of Brigham Young, who at a public meeting had used strong language against Hartley, and had ordered him to leave the speakers stand; that on account of the charges made by Brigham, which Bullock said were not true, Hartley was put under the ban of the church, and decided to change his residence. He joined the company of Judge Appleby, and while leaving the Territory was murdered by Hickman. I asked Mr. Bullock if the matter had ever been investigated by the executive authorities, and he said it had not been, although it was generally known that Hickman had committed the crime. I also asked him why he had not instituted proceedings against Hickman. He shook his head significantly and replied, "Don't press me for an answer to that question."

The following account of the murder of Hartley, given by his wife thirteen years before the confession of Hickman, is contained in Mrs. Mary Etta V. Smith's book entitled, "Fifteen Years Residence with the Mormons," pages 309-310, and is as follows:

"I married Jesse Hartley knowing he was a Gentile in fact, though he passed for a Mormon; but that made no difference with me, because he was a noble man and sought only the right. Being my husband, he was brought into close contact with the heads of the church, and thus was soon enabled to learn of many things he did not approve of, and of which I was ignorant though brought up among the Saints, and which if known to the Gentiles would have greatly damaged us. I do not understand all he discovered, or all he did; but they found he had written against the church, and he was cut off, and the prophet required as an atonement for his sins that he should lay down his life; that he should be sacrificed in the endowment rooms, where such atonement is made. This I never knew until my husband told me—but it is true. They kill those there who have committed sins too great to be atoned for in any other way. The prophet says if they submit to this he can save them, otherwise they are lost. Oh, that is horrible! But my husband refused to be sacrificed, and so set out alone for the United States, thinking that there might be at least a hope of success. I told him when he left me and left his child, that he would be killed; and so he was.

"William Hickman and another Danite shot him in the canyons, and I have often since been obliged to cook for this man when he passed this way, knowing all the while he had killed my husband. My child soon followed his father, and I hope to die also, for why should I live? They have brought me here, where I wish to remain rather than return to Salt Lake where the murderers of my husband curse the earth, and roll in affluence, unpunished."

John D. Lee, in his confession, stated:

"When the Danites—or Destroying Angels—were placed on a man's track, that man died—certain, unless some providential act saved him. The church authorities used the law of the land, the laws of the church, and Danites, to enforce their orders and rid the community of those who were distasteful to the leaders. And I say as a fact, that there was no escape for anyone that the leaders of the church in southern Utah selected as a victim. It frequently happened that men became dissatisfied with the church and tried to leave the Territory. The authorities would try to convince such persons that they ought to remain, but if they insisted on going, they were informed that they had permission to do so. When the person had started off with his stock and property, it was nearly always the rule to send a lot of Danites to steal all of their stock and run it off into the mountains, so that in the majority of cases the people would return wholly broken up, and settle down again as obedient members of the church."

Many apostates have made similar statements to me, and before the completion of the Union Pacific railroad it was very hazardous for an apostate to leave the Territory with his family and property. In his confession, Lee states with particularity eight or nine murders which he knew were committed by the Danites, and some of the victims had their throats cut.

In the excavations made within the limits of Salt Lake City during the time I have resided there, many human skeletons have been exhumed in various parts of the city. The present City cemetery was established by the first settlers. I have never heard that it was ever the custom to bury the dead promiscuously throughout the city; and as no coffins were ever found in connection with any of these skeletons, it is evident that the death of the persons to whom they once belonged did not result from natural causes, but from the use of criminal means, and therefore the victims were not given a Christian burial. That the Danites were bound by their

154

covenants to execute the criminal orders of the high priest-hood against apostates and alleged enemies of the church is beyond question.

That such an organization existed is shown by the sermon of Orson Hyde, before quoted in which he referred to the "shepherd and his sharp-toothed dogs"; also in the sermon of Brigham, before mentioned, in which he said:

"If men come here and do not behave themselves, they will not only find the Saints, whom they talk so much about, biting their horses heels, but the scoundrels will find something biting **their** heels. I wish such characters would let the boys have a chance at them." * * *

Evidently reference is here made to the Danites. How many murders were secretly committed by that band of assassins will never be known, but an estimate may be made from the number mentioned in the confessions of Hickman and Lee, and the number of human skeletons which have been exhumed in Salt Lake City, the possessors of which were evidently murdered and buried without a knell, coffin, or Christian ceremony.

# CHAPTER XII.

## The Alleged "Revelation" of Polygamy.

Chapter II, book of Jacob in the Book of Mormon, page 132, contains the following sections:

"Sec. 22. And now I make an end of speaking unto you concerning this pride. And were it not that I must speak unto you concerning a greater crime, my heart would rejoice in me because of you.

"Sec. 23. But the word of God burdens me because of your grosser crimes, for behold, thus sayeth the Lord, 'This people began to wax in iniquity, for they seek to excuse themselves in committing whoredom because of the things which were written concerning David and Solomon and his son.

"Sec. 24. 'Behold David and Solomon, who had many wives and concubines, which thing was abominable before me,' sayeth the Lord.

"Sec. 25. Wherefore, thus sayeth the Lord: 'I have led this people unto the land of Jerusalem by the power of mine arm, that I might raise up unto me a righteous branch from the fruit of the loins of Joseph.

"Sec. 26. 'Wherefore, I the Lord God will not suffer that this people shall do like unto them of old.'

"Sec. 27. Wherefore, my brethren, hear me, and hearken unto the word of the Lord, for there shall not any man among you have, save it be one wife, and concubines he shall have none."

Section 5, in Chapter III, page 134, is as follows:

"Behold the Lamanites, your brethren, whom ye hate because of their filthiness, and the cursings which have come upon their skins, are more righteous than you; for they have not forgotten the commandments of the Lord, which was given unto our fathers, that they should have, save it were one wife, and concubines they should have none."

It is a tenet of the Mormon church that the Book of Mormon is an inspired translation by Joseph Smith of certain hieroglyphics on golden plates which he, under the guidance of an angel, dug from a hill and was enabled to decipher by the aid of a peepstone called the Urim and Thummim, given him by an angel. That book first appeared in 1830. Thirteen years thereafter

Smith claimed to have received the alleged revelation of polygamy, and it began thus:

"Verily, thus saith the Lord, Unto you, my servant Joseph, that inasmuch as you have inquired of my hand to know and understand wherein I the Lord justified my servants Abraham, Isaac and Jacob, as also Moses, David and Solomon, my servants, as touching the principle and doctrine of their having many wives and concubines. Behold and lo, I am the Lord thy God, and will answer thee touching these matters."

In view of the quotations which I have made from the Book of Mormon, this would have been the natural answer to Joseph's request, so far as it relates to David and Solomon:

"My dearly beloved servant, have you so soon forgotten that in the Book of Mormon which I have inspired you to translate, I stated in most positive and unambiguous terms that the acts of David, and Solomon his son, in having many wives and concubines was abominable before me and rendered them less righteous than the filthy Lamanites, for they have not forgotten the commandments of the Lord which was given unto their fathers, that they should have, save it were one wife, and concubines they should have none."

But the answer to Joseph's inquiry given in the alleged revelation is as follows:

"David also received many wives and concubines, as also Solomon and Moses, my servants, as also many of my servants from the beginning of Creation until this time, and in nothing did they sin, save in those things which they received not from me. David's wives and concubines were given unto him by me by the hand of Nathan, my servant, and others of the prophets who had the keys of power, and in none of these things did he sin again against me, save in the case of Uriah and his wife."

This, in express terms, justifies both concubinage and polygamy as well, and explicitly contradicts the statements on the same subject made in the Book of Mormon, and is sufficient alone to discredit the alleged revelation and to brand its author as having been a superlative fraud. That he is such is equally apparent from the following portions of that revelation:

"Verily, I say unto you a commandment I gave unto my handmaid Emma Smith, your wife, whom I have given unto you, that she stay herself, and partake not of that which I commanded you to offer unto her; for I did it, saith the Lord, to prove you all, as I did Abraham, and that I might require an offering at your hands, by covenant and sacrifice, and let

157

mine handmaid Emma Smith receive all those that have been given unto my servant Joseph, and who are virtuous and pure before me; and those who are not pure, and have said they were, shall be destroyed, saith the Lord; for I am the Lord, thy God, and ye shall obey My voice, and I command my handmaid Emma Smith to abide and cleave unto my servant Joseph and none else. But if she will not abide this commandment, she shall be destroyed, saith the Lord, for I am the Lord, thy God, and I will destroy her if she abide not in my law; but if she will abide this commandment, then shall my servant Joseph do all things for her as he hath said, and I will bless him and give unto him an hundred-fold in this world of fathers and mothers, brothers and sisters, houses and lands, wives and children, and crown of eternal lives in the eternal world. * * * And again, verily I say, Let mine handmaid forgive my servant Joseph his trespasses, and then shall she be forgiven her trespasses wherein she hath trespassed against me, and I the Lord thy God will bless her, and multiply her and make her heart rejoice. * * * And again, verily, verily I say unto you, If any man, having a wife, who holds the keys of this power, and he teaches her the law of my priesthood as pertaining to these sayings, then shall she believe and administer unto him, or she shall be damned, sayeth the Lord, your God, for I will destroy her: for I will magnify my name upon all those who receive and abide in my law. Therefore, it shall be lawful if she receive not this law, for him to receive all things whatever I the Lord his God will give unto him because she did not believe and administer unto him according to my word: and she then becomes the transgressor; and he is exempt from the law of Sarah, who administered unto Abraham according to the law when I commanded Abraham to take Hagar to wife."

The following extract is from a sermon of Brigham Young delivered in 1874:

"Brother Geo. A. Smith has been reading a little of the revelation concerning celestial marriage, and I want to say to my sisters, that if they lift their heels against this revelation you will go to hell just as sure as you are living women. Emma, Joseph's wife, began teasing for the revelation. She said 'Joseph, you promised me that revelation, and if you are a man of your word, you will give it to me.' Joseph took it from his pocket and said, 'take it.' She went to the fireplace and put the candle under it and burned it, and she thought that was the end of it; and she will be damned just as sure as she is a living woman. Joseph used to say he would have her hereafter if he had to go to hell for her, and he will have to go to hell for her, as sure as he ever gets her."

John Henry Smith, who at the time of his death was one of the counselors of Joseph F. Smith, the president of the church, was in his examination hereinbefore mentioned, asked the question: "Do you understand that revelation to be to this effect, that if the first wife refuses to consent to her husband taking a second wife, 'she shall be damned'?" He answered: "I understand that principle. A good many women have taken that chance. Under the Mormon theory they shall be damned."

No true wife could, without stifling one of the strongest natural attributes with which woman has been endowed by her Creator, consent to or abide by the plural marriage of her husband, and to destroy or damn her, or send her to hell for refusing to submit to a thing so repugnant to her womanly nature as polygamy would be monstrously wicked and barbarous.

The claim of Joseph Smith that this tenet of the Mormon church was revealed to him by God, conclusively shows him to have been an impostor and pervert. To ascribe the authorship of such an infamous document as that alleged revelation to God is a monstrous profanation of His sacred name.

Whitney was evidently ashamed of that tenet of the Mormon church, for in his History of Utah he eliminated from the alleged revelation of polygamy, as published therein, the portions above quoted.

In the Deseret News of May 26, 1886, there appeared an affidavit of William Clayton, the person who wrote down the revelation of polygamy as dictated to him by Joseph Smith. In this affidavit Clayton says:

"In the month of February, 1843, Joseph informed me that he had other wives living besides his first wife, Emma, and in particular gave me to understand that Eliza R. Snow, Eliza Beman, Desdemona Fuller, and others, were his lawful wives in the sight of Heaven. On the 27th of April, 1843, the Prophet Joseph Smith married me to Margaret Moon, for time and eternity, at the residence of Heber C. Kimball, and on the 22d day of July, 1843, he married me according to the [celestial] order of the church to my first wife, Ruth. On the first day of May, 1843, I officiated in the office of Elder by marrying Lucy Walker to the Prophet Joseph Smith at his own residence. During this period the Prophet took several other wives, among the number I only remember Eliza Partridge, Emily Partridge, Sarah Ann Whitney, Helen Kimball and Flora Wadsworth. All these he acknowledged to me were his lawfully wedded wives, according to the celestial order."

The Deseret News, which is the official organ of the church, on May 20, 1886, contained the following:

"The revelation of celestial marriage, published in the Doctrine and Covenants, was given July 12th, 1843. The principles it contains, with further intelligence on the subject, was revealed to the Prophet many years before, but not formulated in writing for the church. Acting under instructions from the Lord, the Prophet had several wives sealed to him before the date of the revelation."

In February, 1844, the following appeared in the Times and Seasons, then the official publication of the Mormon church:

"Notice—As we have been credibly informed that an elder of the Church of Jesus Christ of Latter-day Saints by the name of Hyrum Brown has been preaching polygamy and other false and corrupt doctrines in the county of Lapeer, State of Michigan, this is to notify him and the church in general, that he has been cut off from the church for his iniquity, and he is further notified to appear at a Special Conference on the fifth of April next to answer to these charges.

(Signed) JOSEPH SMITH,
HYRUM SMITH,
Presidents of the Church."

John Taylor, at a public discussion with a divine in Boulogne, France, in July, 1850, in answer to the accusation made that the Mormon church tolerated the practice of polygamy, said: "We are accused here of polygamy, and actions the most indelicate, obscene and disgusting, such as none but a corrupt heart could have contrived; these things are too outrageous to admit of belief." Taylor at that time had at least eight plural wives living. In explanation of these denials, the Deseret News of May 20th, 1886, published the following:

"Polygamy, in the ordinary and Asiatic sense of the term, never was and is not now a tenet of the Latter-day Saints. Until the open enunciation of the doctrine of celestial marriage by the publication of the revelation on the subject in 1852, no elder was authorized to announce it to the world. The Almighty has revealed things on many occasions which was for his servants and not for the world. In the rise of the church, the Lord had occasion to admonish his servants in regard to revelations that were afterward permitted to be

160

published. 'I say unto you, hold your peace until I shall see fit to make all things public. I say unto you, hold your peace until I shall see fit to make all things known unto the world concerning the matter, and now I say unto you, keep these things from going abroad in the world until it is expedient to me.' Under these instructions the elders had no right to promulgate anything but that which they were authorized to teach, and when assailed by enemies and accused of practicing things which were really not countenanced in the church, they were justified in denying those imputations and at the same time avoiding the avowal of such doctrines as were not yet intended for the world. The course they have taken when necessary by commandment is all the ground which their accusers have for charging them with falsehood."

Whitney, in his history, Vol. I, page 216, states:

"Prior to the recording of this revelation, the Prophet had taught the doctrine privately, and he and other prominent elders had practiced it. But this was also in secret, owing to the great prejudice it was foreseen it would invoke. It was not avowed even to the masses of the Saints until after their removal from Illinois."

It is evident from the above that previous to the revelation, Joseph had been cohabiting with numerous women on the sly, and that a point had been reached when further concealment from the generality of his adherents was difficult, and knowing that his followers believed him to be a true prophet of God, he announced the revelation, intending by that ruse to justify his practices, reconcile his adherents and coerce his wife Emma to submit to his outrageous violations of her marital rights.

\* \* \* \* \* \* \* \* \* \* \* \*

The following extracts from revelations of Joseph Smith contained in the Doctrine and Covenants, which contains the most of his "revelations," shows the absurdity of the claim that he was an inspired prophet:

(Sec. 124, page 436.) "And now I say unto you, as pertaining to my boarding house, which I have commanded you to build for the boarding of strangers, that it be built unto my name, and let my name be named upon it, and let my servant Joseph and his house have place therein from generation to generation, for this anointing have I put upon his head that his blessings shall also be put upon the head of his posterity after him. And as I said unto Abraham concerning the kindreds of the earth, even so I say unto my servant Joseph,

161

In thee and in thy seed shall the kindred of the earth be blessed. Therefore let my servant, Joseph, and his seed after him, have place in that house from generation to generation for ever and ever, sayeth the Lord. And let the name of the house be called 'Nauvoo House,' and let it be a delightful habitation for man, and a resting place for the weary traveler, that he may contemplate the glory of Zion, and the glory of the cornerstone thereof. That he may receive also the counsel from those whom I have set to be as plants of renown, and as watchmen upon her walls. Behold, verily I say unto you, Let my servant George Miller, and my servant Lyman Wight, and my servant John Snyder, and my servant Peter Haws, organize themselves and appoint one of them to be president over their quorum for the purpose of building that house. And they shall form a constitution whereby they shall receive stock for the building of that house. And they shall not receive less than $50.00 for a share of stock in that house, and they shall be permitted to receive $15,000.00 from any one man for stock in that house, but they shall not be permitted to receive over $15,000.00 stock from any one man, and they shall not be permitted to receive any man as stockholder in this house, except the same shall pay his stock into their hands at the time he receives the stock."

As being extremely apropos to the foregoing covert plan of Joseph to have his poor dupes build for him a regal residence, the following extract of Colton, the metaphyscist, is interpolated:

"It is a curious paradox that precisely in proportion to our own intellectual weakness will be our credulity to those mysterious powers assumed by others; and in those regions of darkness and ignorance where man cannot effect even those things that are within the power of man, there we shall ever find that a blind belief in feats that are far beyond those powers has taken the deepest root in the minds of the deceived, and produced the richest harvest to the knavery of the deceiver."

(Page 241). "And now, verily I say, that it is expedient in me that my servant, Sydney Gilbert, after a few weeks, should return upon his business, and to his Agency in the Land of God; and that which he hath seen and heard may be made known unto my disciples, that they perish not. And for this cause I have spoken these things. And again I say unto you, that my servant, Isaac Morley, may not be tempted above that which he is able to bear, and counsel wrongfully to your heart, I give commandment that his farm should be sold."

(Page 242). "And it is not meet that my servants, Newell K. Whitney and Sydney Gilbert, should sell their store and their possessions, for this is not wisdom until the residue of the church which remaineth in this place shall go up unto the land of Zion."

One of the characteristic expressions of Brigham Young was "Tie up the calf, and the cow will not stray away from her home." To accomplish the end indicated by that expression, he forced (and was enabled to do so because he was generally regarded by his adherents as being the mouthpiece of God on earth) many of the wealthier and more influential members of his church into polygamy who would not, voluntarily, have married plural wives. A Mormon polygamist, if he should apostatize, would immediately, as Brigham well know, be ostracized by his former brethren, and could not hope by moving with his polygamous family away from a Mormon community, to escape proscription, or form respectable social relations elsewhere among Christian people. Therefore a member of the Mormon church, by marrying plural wives, figuratively tied up the calf, and if he afterwards apostatized from the church would have been placed in a most distressing position by his polygamous connections.

# CHAPTER XIII.

## The Policy of the Priesthood Was to Prevent Gentiles From Settling in the Territory, or to Acquire Property.

The hostility of the Priesthood to the settlement of Gentiles in the Territory is shown by its teachings, sermons, and also by the outrages perpetrated to prevent it. Brigham opposed the articles of the Utah Magazine which advocated the opening up of the mines on the ground that it would "open the floodgates to Gentile immigration," and procured the excommunication of Mr. Godbe, the proprietor of the magazine, as also Mr. Harrison, its editor, on the charge of having advocated the opening up of the mines in opposition to the counsel of Brigham Young. Brigham, in a sermon delivered in the tabernacle on the subject, said: "I would make a wall so thick and so high around the Territory that it would be impossible for the Gentiles to get over or through it."

The following is an extract from a sermon of Heber J. Kimball, copied from Bowles' book, entitled "Across the Continent":

"Ladies and gentlemen, good morning! I am going to talk to you by revelation. I never study my sermons, and when I get up to speak I never know what I am going to say, only as it is revealed to me from on high; then all I say is true. Could it help but be so when God communicates through me? * * * The Gentiles are our enemies. They are damned forever. They are thieves and murderers; and if they don't like what I say, they can got to hell—damn them."

In the case of the Church v. The United States, 136 U. S. Rep., page 49, Mr. Justice Bradley, in the opinion, said:

"It is unnecessary here to refer to the past history of the sect—to their defiance of the government's authority, to their attempt to establish an independent community, to their efforts **to drive from the Territory all who were not connected with them in communion and sympathy.** The tale is one of patience on the part of the American government and people, and of contempt of authority and resistance to law on the part of the Mormons."

The manner in which any considerable number of Gentiles were successfully prevented from settling in Utah until after the development of the mines and the completion of the Union Pacific railroad is shown by the following statement of facts:

The legislature of the State of Deseret, which was established by the Mormons previously to the meeting of the first territorial legislature in 1852, granted to Brigham Young, the governor of that State, and other officials of the Mormon church, the control of the most important canyons. The following is a sample of the acts granting such control:

"Be it ordained by the General Assembly of the State of Deseret: That Brigham Young have the sole control of City Creek and Canyon; and that he pay into the public treasury the sum of five hundred dollars therefor."

This act was approved by Governor Young, December 9, 1850, and in pursuance of that grant Brigham Young, by the erection of the Eagle Gate, closed the only entrance to City Creek canyon then existing; and from that time, and until long after my arrival in Salt Lake City in 1865, he exacted tribute from the inhabitants for the privilege of utilizing the natural, useful and extensive resources of that canyon. By that grant Brigham obtained a rich bonanza, and the eagle which still hovers over that gate is a fit emblem of the rapacity which exacted tribute from the masses for the privilege of enjoying that portion of the natural resources of the public domain within the limits of City Creek canyon. All of the acts of the Deseret legislature were re-enacted by the territorial legislature in 1852.

The most available agricultural land of the Territory was also monopolized likewise. Cities and small villages were at an early day started at the mouths of the various irrigating streams, and incorporated by acts of the State of Deseret and confirmed by the territorial legislature by similar acts. In each instance, the corporate boundaries included a large quantity of unoccupied agricultural land, notwithstanding that even the largest cities at that time had but a small number of inhabitants. The corporate limits of Cedar City is a fair sample of the other cities and villages, and is as follows: "Beginning at the mouth of Coal Creek canyon, thence north three miles, thence west six miles, thence south six miles, thence east six miles, thence north three miles to the place of beginning."

Cedar City was incorporated, as were many of the other cities and villages, at the first session of the territorial legislature in 1852. At that time Cedar City had only about one hundred inhabitants.

The homestead and preemption act of Congress expressly excludes from its operation land within the corporate limits of a city or town. By an act of the territorial legislature the surveyor-general was authorized and required to give to the person for whom he made a survey a certificate therefor, describing the tract, block or lot, and specifying its area, and provided that such certificate should be title of possession to the person holding it. Under that act as construed and enforced, no one had a right to take possession and hold any of the land so excluded from the homestead and preemption act without obtaining such certificate as the one mentioned. In view of the church policy of excluding Gentiles from settling in the Territory, it would have been useless for any Gentile to apply for such a certificate, and it would have been the height of folly, and dangerous for him, to have attempted to hold possession of any of the land so excluded without such a certificate. Among the incidents which show that the latter statement is correct, are the assassination of Dr. Robinson, and an occurrence told to me by Dr. Williamson, whose veracity was unquestionable, and which in substance is as follows:

During the same year that Dr. Robinson was assassinated, Dr. Williamson, intending to acquire the title to an unoccupied tract of land lying outside the inhabited portion of the city of Salt Lake, after surveying the same, and without applying to the surveyor-general for a certificate, erected a house thereon. On a night a few weeks afterwards, while the doctor and Captain Brown, a friend, were sitting in the house, they were arrested by a squad of masked men and forcibly taken to the Jordan river, which was near the doctor's house. On the brink of that stream their captors halted, and then began to bind the arms and legs of their prisoners. Captain Brown exclaimed, "If you intend to take our lives, as we are honorable men, for God's sake, shoot us instead of drowning us like dogs!" When Captain Brown made that exclamation, one of the masked men recognized him as a former acquaintance by whom he had been befriended in California, and having stated

166

that fact, he interceded to save the life of his former friend. The masked men after holding a short consultation offered to release the prisoners on condition that the doctor would promise to abandon his claim to said land, and not again take possession of it. The doctor promised, and both he and the captain were set free. Dr. Williamson recognized among his captors two members of the police force of Salt Lake City. Both Dr. Williamson and Captain Brown were Gentiles, and had previously been United States officers, the former as surgeon and the latter a captain on General Connor's staff at Camp Douglas.

The exclusion of the land at the mouth of the various irrigation streams of the Territory practically placed all of the available irrigation water under the control of the municipal corporations, and practically prevented homestead or preemption filings on land not within the corporate limits by outsiders. As the municipal boundaries in some instances are contiguous in different localities in Utah, a person can travel in places for many miles without being outside of the limits of a municipal corporation. The land monopoly thus secured was held in reserve by the priesthood for the future occupation of Latter-day Saints.

In connection with that monopoly, a company called the Perpetual Emigration Fund was incorporated by the territorial legislature. It was authorized to acquire by donation and otherwise, without limitation, both real and personal property. Section 10 of the act incorporating the company provided, "that the entire proceeds of the company should inure to a perpetual emigration fund for the poor, and the general business of the company would be devoted, under the direcion and supervision of the First Presidency of the church, to promote, facilitate and accomplish the emigration of the poor."

The numerous missionaries sent out by the church succeeded in proselyting many converts by representing to them that by joining the Mormon church and emigrating to Utah they would be assisted in acquiring ownership in land on which to establish homesteads of their own, and that the money necessary in accomplishing this, as also the expenses of their emigration, would be advanced to them by a company formed to assist the poor. Thousands of emigrants were brought to

Utah by that company and settled upon the land so monopolized by the church. They were required upon arrival in Utah to give their notes for money advanced bearing the high rates of interest prevalent there at that time. There existed in the Territory a general sentiment which made the indebtedness thus incurred a preferred one, and although ample time was given to the obligors in which to meet it, until discharged it was practically a mortgage on all the property subsequently acquired by them. Almost the entire population of the Territory was Mormon until several years after the completion of the Union Pacific railroad, and the mines had been developed by Gentiles. Previous to that time members of the church were prohibited by the priesthood from selling land to outsiders, or from patronizing Gentiles engaged in mercantile and other commercial pursuits, and to secure the observance of the latter prohibition, a sign, here reproduced, was always

placed over the entrance of each Mormon store and business house in obedience to an order of Brigham Young, and any Mormon who patronized a house over the entrance of which there was no such sign, if caught in doing so, incurred the displeasure of the priesthood and was liable to church "discipline" therefor. No doubt the priesthood thought that it had by the methods mentioned forestalled any extensive settlement in the Territory by Gentiles, but—

"The best laid schemes of mice and men
   Gang aft a-glee
And lea'e us nought but grief and pain
   For promised joy."

Brigham Young, by interdicting the discovery and development of the mines by his adherents, thwarted his well-laid schemes of exclusion. If, instead of prohibiting his followers from doing so, he had ordered them to prospect, they could have as readily—as was afterward done by outsiders—discovered the mines, formed mining districts, and made local mining laws under which locations of mining claims could have been made as would have enabled the Mormons to monopolize the mines in the Territory the same as was done respecting the available agricultural land.

The following testimony of Henry W. Lawrence, in the investigation of the naturalization cases before mentioned, shows the method resorted to by Brigham Young to prevent the opening up of the mines:

"The charge upon which I was excommunicated was a rather general charge of apostasy. Anything in disobedience to the priesthood was apostasy. * * * There are many theories connected with Mormonism that are pretty good— they are very winning to the outside world. The practical working of Mormonism is one thing, the theories are another. There were a great many things connected with it that were objectionable. When you would ask any one in authority they would say, 'Well, you don't understand. These things are all right, and if you only have faith—are faithful—you will understand them after a while.' We were taught to a certain extent to give up our individuality, not to think, not to reason.

"For some little time before we came out of the church Mr. Godbe and Mr. Harrison were printing what was called The Utah Magazine, the forerunner of the Tribune. The paper was started with the view of printing some advanced ideas or liberal thoughts to set the people to thinking. I realized that there were a great many things that were wrong, and we wanted to see them corrected. We were all in the church, and we wanted Mormonism to be true. We had grown up in the system, and we didn't want to follow something that was not what it represented itself to be. For about a year or two that magazine existed. The priesthood was supreme here in these mountains. To object to anything—to object to any of the counsels of Brigham Young or any of the leaders of the church—was considered, I won't say worthy of death, but of excommunication and ostracism which very few men could

169

afford to bear.  In temporal matters and in spiritual matters
it is the right of the priesthood to dictate in all things, the
people to give their unquestioned obedience.  We saw that the
course which we were pursuing, defying the government and
trying to ostracise and alienate the people from the government and the world would bring us into conflict with the
government and with civilization.  We wanted to prevent this
if we could.  It was considered quite a crime for any man
to advocate the opening of mines.  Brigham Young or the
priesthood used to say that whenever the Lord wanted the
mines open he would order them opened.  Of course, that
would be through the priesthood.

"They printed a piece on opening the mines.  At that
time they were building the Union Pacific railroad.  Brigham Young had contracts on that road, and he tried to control the wages of the workmen.  He taught that the wages of
workmen and all these temporal matters must be controled
by what was called the School of the Prophets.  Mr. Harrison
wrote a piece on Workmen's Wages in which he argued that
Supply and Demand should control the men's wages.  Brigham Young had never been opposed by anyone at that time.

"The charges were that they had printed things in the
Utah Magazine against the counsels and direction of the holy
priesthood.  George Q. Cannon was the 'prosecuting attorney.'
He stood right there (pointing), and he read that piece on the
Development of Mines as one of the evidences of the spirit of
apostasy.  That was the main charge against these men, that
they wanted to open up the mines here contrary to the directions and counsels of the holy priesthood.  The result was
that the vote was taken and they were cut off from the church.
Geo. A. Smith got right up there, and says: 'These two men
sitting there have blacker hearts than any men since the formation of the world.  They want to open up the mines and bring
all hell and the devil in here.'  When the contrary vote was
called for, Mr. Kelsey voted to sustain them.  He had been a
member of the church ever since the old Nauvoo days.  For
exercising the right to vote the contrary vote, Brigham Young
got up and says, 'I move that Eli B. Kelsey be cut off from
the church.'

"That vote was taken immediately, without a trial, when
the theory of the church is that every man shall have a fair
hearing before the members of the church.  [Kelsey was excommunicated.]  I remained in the church probably for a
month afterward.  I wanted to help bring about some re-
forms that I saw were necessary.  We wanted to see Mormonism made respectable so as to bear the light of the nineteenth
century.  I wasn't even then prepared to give up the church,
but they cited me to appear before the bishop in the eighth

ward, and some general charges were made against me, of a spirit of apostasy in sustaining Godbe and Harrison and their movement, and I was cut off from the church.

"They didn't give me a trial before the high council, nor allow any more public trials. The Mormon church claims to be the government and Kingdom of God—that is, a present, literal kingdom, with laws to govern and control its members and all its affairs—extended to the direction of the people in all things.

"When they first came here they had a provisional government called the State of Deseret; they included within their jurisdiction the whole country this side of Oregon on the north, east of the Sierra Nevadas; took in, I think, New Mexico. This was the extent of what they hoped and expected to get a State government for, and establish their kingdom, the kingdom that was set upon the earth no more to be thrown down. As the power developed they expected to control, not only this government of the United States, but the whole earth. They believed that because the government of the United States was established upon such a broad basis, so free and liberal in its provisions, this Kingdom of God could be established and increase until in time it would take possession of the government. That is the theory of the Mormon Kingdom of God. We used to sing a song here in early days, 'Brigham Young, he is our king.' It went to the tune of 'Du da.' It is a temporal and spiritual kingdom combined.

Nowhere in the teaching of the Mormon leaders—nowhere in their private ceremonies—are people taught to be loyal and true to the government of the United States. The general tenor of the teachings in early days was disloyalty to the government."

Several of General Connor's soldiers, stationed at Fort Douglas, being experienced miners were given leave by the general in 1862 to prospect for mines in the mountains, and upon discovering any, to locate the same. They discovered and located valuable mines both in Bingham Canyon and Stockton. In 1868, the phenomenally rich bonanza of the celebrated "Emma mine" was developed. That event directed the attention of the prospectors and miners of the Rocky mountains and West coast to the importance and extent of the mineral resources of Utah. As a consequence, the summer following brought from other mining regions into the mountains of Utah hundreds of practical prospectors and miners who were well equipped with the usual outfit of prospectors. They possessed extraordinary courage, energy and

171

ability. They were the kind of men that the church could not control and the Destroying Angels could not intimidate. Their discoveries and development of numerous productive and valuable mines, in connection with the completion of the Union Pacific railroad, induced a greatly increased immigration of Gentiles to the Territory, and large investments of outside capital. As mining and agriculture are the leading and most important sources of prosperity in Utah, if the mines had been monopolized by the Mormons as the agricultural land had been, the exclusion sought would have lasted for an indefinite period. From what has been accomplished in Colorado and other territories, where the natural laws of immigration were not interrupted, I confidently assert that if the Mormons had not settled in Utah, and there had not been any inhabitants there previous to the discovery and opening up of the mines, that State today would be richer and have a much greater population, and that there would at the present time be, if not on the site of Salt Lake City, somewhere in this State, a city corresponding to that of Denver. Utah's natural resources are greater than Colorado's, and there were many inhabitants in the valleys of Utah long before any settlements in Colorado were commenced. The policy of exclusion enforced by the priesthood, and the frequent diatribes uttered in Mormon pulpits against the Gentiles, made Ishmaelites of the Latter-day Saints, and the expression, "Those who are not for us are against us," became proverbial among them.

# CHAPTER XIV.

## The Edmunds-Tucker Bill and Its Effect.

I took no part in the Poland bill, the effective provisions of which were copied from the Cullom bill. Nor did I take any active part in the Edmunds bill of 1882, which also contained additional provisions of the Cullom bill, except to call Mr. Edmund's attention to the latter bill as containing the provisions required by the anomalous conditions in Utah. When the Edmunds-Tucker bill, which contained additional provisions of the Cullom bill and others more stringent, passed the Senate, the Gentiles of the Territory who were posted knew that a strenuous effort would be made by the priesthood to defeat it in the Judiciary Committee of the House, as through Mormon influence and money many other bills had been defeated in the committees to which they had been referred. Consequently, at a meeting of a large number of business Gentiles at the Walker House, I was selected to go to Washington, and on behalf of the Gentiles of the Territory to advocate the passage of that bill at its discussion before the Judiciary Committee of the House, to which it had been referred. Upon my arrival at Washington, I called upon Judge Randolph Tucker, chairman of the committee, with whom I was well acquainted, and stated to him the purpose for which I had been selected to visit Washington, requesting him to fix a day on which I could be heard by the committee in favor of the passage of the bill. He stated that on principle he was opposed to the arbitrary confiscation by the general government of property, and that as present advised he was not favorable to the clause of the bill confiscating the property of the church; and that while he had never, except in a casual way, given any attention to the Mormon question, his present inclination was against any radical and exceptional legislation on the subject. In reply, I said the evil of the polygamic anti-American system established and maintained by the priesthood of the Mormon church in Utah was radical and exceptional, and it required extraordinary measures to eradicate that evil,

173

and that the accomplishment of that desirable end could only be attained by adequate legislation by Congress; that as he had only given the matter casual attention, and as his position of chairman now imposed upon him the duty of making a thorough investigation of the subject, by his permission, I would furnish him with the offical documents and data necessary in making such an investigation, which without my assistance, would be difficult, if not impossible, for him to obtain. He replied that it was his intention to make a thorough investigation of the matter, and any documents bearing upon the subject which I might see proper to submit to the committee, through him, would receive due consideration. Shortly afterwards I placed in his hands the revised territorial statute of 1870 with a reference to the various provisions which I deemed had a material bearing upon the subject, among which were the act incorporating the Mormon church, and the clause of the organic act, in the sixth section of which it was provided that: "All laws passed by the legislature assembly and governor shall be submitted to Congress of the United States, and if disapproved shall be null and of no effect." The act incorporating the Mormon church authorized the church to hold and occupy (without limitation) real and personal estate; provided for the election at General Conference of the church, one trustee in trust, and not to exceed twelve assistant trustees; to receive, hold, buy, sell, and manage, use and control, real and personal property of the church, and authorized said trustees to receive real and personal property (without limitation), by gift, donation and bequest, and prohibited the transaction of any business in relation to buying, selling or otherwise disposing of church property, without the consent of the trustee in trust. From the passage of said act in 1851, Brigham Young until his death was trustee in trust of the church. The church was also authorized to solemnize marriages compatible with revelations, and pass laws for the government of the church, and for the punishment or forgiveness of all officers relative to fellowship, according to church covenants. The act also contained the following proviso, "Provided, however that each and every act or practice so established or adopted for law or custom shall relate to solemnities, sacraments, ceremonies, consecrations, endowments, tithing, marriage, fellowship, or the religious duties of man to his maker. Inasmuch as the doctrines, principles, practices or performances support virtue and increase morality, and are not inconsistent with or repugnant to the constitution of the United States, and are founded in the revelations of the Lord."

The power thus granted to acquire by purchase and gift, real and personal property without limitation was against public policy. The Mormon church had, in its corporate capacity, acquired extensive tracts of land, and was extensively engaged in secular pursuits, owned large herds of sheep, cattle and horses, and had invested large sums of church money in various money-making enterprises. A grant of such power to any corporation is indefensible and especially dangerous when, as in the case of the Mormon church it is given to an ecclesiastical corporation whose adherents concede its claims of the right by divine authority to govern in both spiritual and temporal affairs, and which derives an immense annual income from its law of tithing. The exercise by corporations of such dangerous power in the mother country was wisely restricted by the statutes of mortmain. The act incorporating the Mormon church clearly authorized the solemnization of plural marriage alleged to have been revealed to Joseph Smith. The character of the punishment which the church was authorized to inflict upon its members can be inferred from the character of the church endowments and covenants hereinbefore shown.

It was the manifest duty of Congress to disapprove that vicious act, and it is astonishing that it was permitted to remain in force for thirty-seven years. It was not disapproved by Congress until the enactment of the Edmunds-Tucker bill of 1887. By its disapproval the church corporation was dissolved and could no longer acquire or hold property. During its existence it had acquired large and valuable quantities of both real and personal property which was not, as is usual in the case of private corporations, represented by shares of stock. In the property so acquired no person had any specific interest or the right to any share of the proceeds resulting from the sale of said property provided for in the act dissolving the church corporation. Upon the disapproval of the act incorporating the church, as there was no person legally entitled to hold the property of the church or share in the proceeds of its sale by operation of law, it escheated to the United States. That result unavoidably followed the annulment of an extremely vicious charter of an ecclesiastical corporation. It is therefore apparent that the property of the church was not, as the mass of the Mormon people are taught to believe, arbitrarily confiscated by the Edmunds-Tucker act as a punishment of the Mormons, but necessarily followed the rightful and praiseworthy disapproval by that measure of a vicious and wrongful act of a Mormon legislature. Many persons throughout the country who are not members of the Mormon church believe that the Edmunds-Tucker act arbitrarily confiscated the church property, and regard the act as an oppressive one evidently because they have been misinformed respecting the facts, and do not know the circumstances which caused and justified the escheating of the church property. Upon the disapproval by Congress of the act incorporating the Mormon church and the dissolution of that corporation, and the escheating of the property which resulted therefrom, the sixteenth section of the Edmunds-Tucker act, in accordance with the settled practice of the courts in such instances, prescribed the method of winding up the affairs of the dissolved corporation, and is as follows:

"That it shall be the duty of the attorney general of the United States to cause such proceedings to be taken in the supreme court of the Territory of Utah as shall be proper to carry into effect the provisions of the preceding section, and to pay the debts and dispose of the property and assets of said corporation according to law. Said property and assets in excess of the debts, and the amount of any lawful claims established by the court against the same, shall escheat to the United States, and shall be taken, invested, and disposed of by the Secretary of the Interior under the direction of the President of the United States, for the benefit of common schools in said Territory."

The discussion was carried on at various meetings of the committee for several weeks, after which the committee unanimously adopted the report presented by Mr. Tucker, the chairman recommending the passage of the act; also a report recommending the passage of a resolution authorizing the amendment of the constitution of the United States defining polygamy and unlawful cohabitation, and vesting Congress with the power to legislate respecting the same. In Mr. Tucker's report of that resolution, he, among other things, said:

"The evils of the Mormon system are deeper than can be cured by ordinary legislation. To punish the offender may be accomplished by law, but to extirpate the system, to eradicate it from this Union of free and civilized commonwealths, will require a change in the constitution of the United States. If a polygamist can claim the privilege of having plural wives because of his religion, and the monogamist cannot because he has no such religion, or the former is granted immunity for his crime because of his conscience, which is refused to the latter, then a privilege to do the act and immunity from punishment for so doing will accord to one man that which is denied to another, and as a reward for the religion of the one and as a penalty for that of the other. In other words, if the fact that the Mormon belief in polygamy as commanded of God could prevent the government from punishing the Mormons for it, while it punished anti-Mormons, it would be preferring that religion to all others by shielding its adherents from a penalty inflicted without mercy on all who would not profess its creed; or if to prevent this preference the law was annulled entirely as to all, it would create the supremacy of this one system of religion over the civil authority of the government, and take from the government all power to mould its policy except in conformity to the Mormon creed. Polygamy could not be made a crime by the government because sanctioned by the Mormon religion! What better example of an established religion could be given than this would be? A union of Church and State in which the Church would be supreme, and the State subordinate."

After Wilford Woodruff, president of the Mormon church, issued the Manifesto advising the Latter-day Saints to refrain from contracting any marriages forbidden by the law of the land, Congress passed an act requiring that the escheated property be returned to the church, and the President of the United States granted an amnesty to all Mormon polygamists on condition that they would in the future obey the law against polygamy. (See Appendix).

At the discussion before the committee, the church was represented by the following named persons employed by it: Hon. Jefferson Chandler, distinguished attorney; Franklin S. Richards; A. M. Gibson; Hon. Geo. S. Boutwell; Epa Hunton,

177

ex-senator from Virgina, and Joseph A. West. John T. Caine, the delegate from Utah, also appeared and addressed the committee in opposition to the bill.

I represented the Gentiles.

In the territorial legislature of 1892 a majority of the upper house Committee on Memorials made a report recommending the passage of a memorial praying Congress to repeal the Poland act of 1874, the Edmunds law of 1882, and the Edmunds-Tucker act of 1887, and to admit the Territory into the Union.

James Glendinning and myself were the only members of that committee belonging to the Liberal party, and joined in a minority report which I drew up, and which is as follows:

"The majority of the Committee on Memorials, to whom was referred C. J. M. No. 2, having reported the same back and recommended its passage, and the minority being unable to concur in said report, or give assent to the statements contained in the memorial, respectfully submit the following minority report:

"'While Congress has the sole power to legislate for the government of the Territory, yet at an early day it adopted the method of governing the territories in all matters of local policy through the agency of the people inhabiting the territories. It was intended and expected that each Territory, in accordance with the true intent and spirit of the agency delegated to it, would pass and faithfully execute such laws as experience has pointed out as being essential to the proper regulation and government of American communities, and to the laying of the foundation of a new state on the American and democratic plan, with institutions in harmony with the other states of the Union. The Territory of Utah was given substantially the same Organic Act under which other territories have founded new and prosperous states, but in Utah the agency granted to the Territory by the Organic Act, under the domination of the Mormon church, has been used, not to lay the foundation of a new State on the American plan, but to establish a system which, as Mr. Tucker in his report on the Edmunds-Tucker Bill expressed it, "is directly antagonistic to all ideas of European and American civilization," and which as further expressed by Mr. Tucker, "presents the alternative of admitting a polygamous State into the Union, or one from which polygamy was excluded as a Territory, but may be restored by the new State after admission."

" 'Congress first expressed the sense of the nation against this abuse of territorial agency by the passage of the act against polygamy in 1862. This law for many years remained a dead letter on the statute, because under the laws passed by the legislature, the selection of the grand and petit juries was in the hands of territorial officers who yielded allegiance to the church and were subservient to its will. Congress was therefore forced to resort to additional legislation, and it passed the Poland bill of 1874. The provisions of this bill took from these faithless territorial officers all their power and established the present jury system of which the memorial complains.

" 'The law of 1862, after the passage of the Poland bill, still remained unexecuted, because under the law of 1862 the gist of the crime of polygamy was the solemnization of the marriage ceremony, and all polygamous marriages were performed in the secret precincts of the endowment house of the Mormon church, and those present were sworn under severe penalties to reveal nothing that therein transpired. Congress was therefore again forced to resort to legislation to prevent the execution of this law from being defeated. The Edmunds law of 1882 was accordingly passed. Its provisions were also complained of in the memorial.

" 'Notwithstanding the passage of these laws, still the opposition by the priesthood of the Mormon church to their execution was successfully continued, and Congress was again forced to resort to still more rigid measures. In 1887 the Edmunds-Tucker Law was passed.

" 'From these statements it will be seen that Congress was forced to pass the foregoing measures by the unjustifiable contumacy of a church, the membership of which embraces an overwhelming majority of the inhabitants of the Territory. The memorial aims at the repeal of these measures, and asks for the passage of a law by Congress which will place in the hands of this contumacious majority, powers far greater than any which have ever been extended to those territories which have at all times been true in the execution of their agency.

" 'The admission of the Territory into the Union is also asked for. The granting of this request would place the powers of the State in the hands of a church whose history and whose tenets make it both probable and possible that, protected by the safeguards which a State under our system would afford, the priesthood would revive the suspended revelation of polygamy. In determining the propriety of repealing the existing law of Congress referred to by the passage of either the Teller or Faulkner bills, what has been and is still being accomplished under those laws should be carefully considered.

" 'Immediately following the passage of the Edmunds-Tucker bill there came a boom unprecedented in the history of the Territory. Salt Lake City and Ogden, the now leading towns of the Territory, have doubled their population. The former has grown into a magnificent, metropolitan city. A school system which before was disgraceful, has given way to one which would be a credit to any community. The incommodious and poorly ventilated school houses (in Salt Lake City) have been replaced by others of modern architecture—roomy, convenient, well-lighted and properly ventilated.

" 'Large amounts of capital have been invested, and are still seeking investments. The industries and business of the Territory were never in such prosperous and healthy condition. The present advancement which is being made is as great as the most sanguine could expect, and nearly the entire Gentile population is satisfied with the present prosperity of the Territory and the promise of continued advancement. They do not feel that Utah has yet been freed from her humiliation and disgrace, but that she is being gradually lifted to the exalted position she would have occupied had she not been retarded by the opposition which forced Congress to enact and enforce the laws which have produced and still are producing such magic changes.

" 'In the opinion of the minority, the commercial and business interests of the whole Territory—the interests of both the Gentile and Mormon inhabitants alike—demand that the Territory be left alone, so far as congressional legislation is concerned, until the forces which are actively at work solve the Utah problem. If left alone, the desired end will be reached sooner; but the passage of either of the bills mentioned in the memorial (the Teller and Faulkner bills) will prove detrimental—will complicate the affairs of the Territory and prolong the time of final settlement of the Utah problem. In the opinion of the minority of your committee it would be dangerous and disastrous to admit the Territory into the Union before the constitution of the United States is amended so as to prohibit polygamy, and give to Congress jurisdiction to pass laws for its enforcement, and until after the lapse of sufficient time in which to test the sincerity of the new departure (the Manifesto), and until the Gentile population shall have become strong enough to protect themselves and American institutions in the new State.

" 'The charges made in the memorial against the Utah Commission are false. However, such charges are not a matter of surprise, because from the early infancy of the Territory up to the present time, few, if any, federal officers of the Territory who have been faithful and vigilant in the execution of the federal laws, have escaped vituperation and slander.' "

A bill containing the same provisions as the first and third sections of the Edmunds law of 1882 was passed by the territorial legislature in 1892. The first section of that law prohibited polygamy and prescribed the penalty for its violation; but it was as ineffective, for the reason which I have heretofore stated, as the anti-polygamy law of 1862 had been. The third section made the cohabitation of any male person with more than one woman in the Territory a misdemeanor, punishable by fine of not more than $300, or by imprisonment for not more than six months, or by both of said punishments. This section proved to be very effective, and its provisions are the only ones under which Mormon polygamists have ever been or can be successfully prosecuted in Utah.

During the term of that able and impartial judge, Chief Justice Charles S. Zane, numerous polygamist Mormons were convicted for violating the provisions of that section in the court over which he presided. The important decisions sustaining the laws of Congress relating to the Mormon problem delivered by him and for which he was decried by the leading members of the Mormon church, were all reviewed and affirmed by the supreme court of the United States.

As the first and third sections of the Edmunds laws remained in force from their passage in 1882 until the admission of Utah as a State in 1896, their re-enactment in 1892 by the Mormon territorial legislature was farcical and nugatory; because during the time the Edmunds law was in force it was paramount, and no prosecutions for the crimes therein prohibited were permissible under any act of the territorial legislature.

The evident purpose of said re-enactment was to induce the people of the United States to believe that polygamy and the temporal power of the priesthood no longer existed in the Territory, and thereby strengthen the memorial before mentioned and aid the movement for the admission of the Territory into the Union.

Section 4611 of the Revised Statutes of Utah of 1898 provides that "every person who has reason to believe that a crime or public offense has been committed, must make complaint against such person before some magistrate having authority to make inquiry of the same." If that section had been observed many members of the Mormon church who have been guilty of polygamy since the Woodruff manifesto, but who have escaped punishment, would at least have been exposed, if not convicted.

In order to exclude polygamous practices from the operation of that section, the Mormon members of the State legislature in 1901 passed a bill which amended it by adding the following provisions at the end of the same: "Provided, that no prosecution for adultery shall be commenced except on the complaint of the husband or legal wife of the accused, and no prosecution for unlawful cohabitation shall be commenced except on the complaint of the legal wife of the accused."

The evident purpose of that bill was to secure immunity to polygamy. Governor Heber M. Wells, though a Mormon and scion of a father deep in the depths of plural marriage, evinced his good sense and courage by vetoing the bill; but notwithstanding that the section sought to be amended has remained in force ever since its enactment, polygamy has been continually practiced with impunity by members of the Mormon church, and numerous new plural marriages have been entered into by them. In view of the fact that such marriages are secretly formed and have, except in a very few instances, always been successfully concealed, no doubt many unknown to those not members of the church have been solemnized since the manifesto. No doubt, too, there are many instances of the violation of the law against unlawful cohabitation by members of the church who had married plural wives previous to the manifesto, which are likewise unknown.

Since the manifesto, and the admission of the Territory as a State, many known plural marriages have been performed, and the Salt Lake Tribune has published two hundred and thirty such marriages which have occurred since the Woodruff mandate, and in the publication of each plural marriage the names and residence of the parties thereto were stated. Up to the present time not one of the guilty parties have ever been arrested by the civil authorities of the State.

# CHAPTER XV.

## The Cullom-Struble Bill the "Last Straw."

It is true, as alleged in Vol. III, page 720, of Whitney's history, that I carried to Washington a bill introduced by Senator Cullom in the Senate which was referred to the Senate Committee on Territories of which Mr. Cullom was a member, and was also introduced in the House by Mr. Struble and referred to the Committee on Territories, of which he was chairman. The bill was drawn by me, and provided in substance that no person living in plural or celestial marriage, or who taught, advised or counseled any person to enter into polygamy; or who was a member of or contributed to the support, aid or encouragement of any organization that taught or sanctioned that practice; or who participated or aided in the solemnization of any polygamous marriage, should vote, serve as juror or hold any office in the Territory. The bill also required each person, upon applying for registration as an elector, to show that he was qualified as such by taking the test-oath, the form of which was therein prescribed.

Mr. Whitney severely criticized that measure and my connection therewith. That its provisions were valid is clear, for in the case of Davis v. Beason, in 133 U. S. Rep., page 341, the supreme court of the United States sustained the validity of similar provisions of a bill enacted by the territorial legislature of Idaho, which had been introduced by Col. Enos Wall, now of Salt Lake City. Mr. Justice Field in the opinion delivered by him made the following comment:

"Bigamy and polygamy are crimes by the laws of all civilized and Christian countries. They are crimes by the laws of the United States, and they are crimes by the law of Idaho. They tend to destroy the purity of the marriage relation, to disturb the peace of families, to degrade women and debase man. Few crimes are more pernicious to the best interests of society and receive more general or more deserved punishment. To extend exemption from punishment for such crimes would be to shock the moral judgment of the community. To call their advocacy a tenet of religion is to offend the common sense of mankind. If they are crimes, then to teach, advise, and counsel their practice is to aid in their commission, and such teachings and counseling are themselves criminal and proper subjects of punishment, as aiding and abetting crimes are in all other cases."

Not only, then, was the bill valid, but its introduction was justified and rendered necessary because the previous stringent acts of Congress which had been passed to correct the evil conditions then existing in Utah had failed to accomplish their purpose; though notwithstanding their validity, and that they had in every instance been sustained by the highest court of the country, the hierarchy of the Mormon church was still recalcitrant and retained its absolute control of territorial political affairs. This control it abused by not only establishing and maintaining an anti-American, pernicious system and defeating the execution, especially of the laws punishing polygamy, and of a particular class of assassination prevalent in the Territory. The purpose of the bill was to wrest from the hands of the priesthood the political power which it had so long wrongfully usurped and shamefully abused.

After a full discussion of the bill before the House Committee on Territories, when Governor West and myself had spoken in favor of its passage, and John T. Caine, Franklin S. Richards and Jeremiah M. Wilson had spoken in opposition, the committee made a report to the House in favor of its passage. After a like discussion of the bill before the Senate Committee on Territories, and the committee had decided to make a report to the Senate favoring its passage, I was informed by Senator Cullom that he had been assured by a delegation of prominent Mormons, that if further action on the bill was delayed for a reasonable time, the practice of polygamy would be prohibited by the Mormon church, and that the delegation had requested that further action on the bill be temporarily delayed. The same assurance was given to Mr. Struble, and the request for delay was granted, but with the express understanding that if polygamy was not prohibited within a reasonable time vigorous steps would be taken to procure the passage of the bill.

Whitney's history, Vol. III, page 743, contains in substance the following:

"Among those who went to Washington to work against the Cullom-Struble bill was Hon. Geo. Q. Cannon, Bishop

Clawson, Col. Isaac Trumbo and Frank J. Cannon, the latter of whom, having applied in vain to Senator Edmunds and other stalwart Republicans, called upon James G. Blaine, and his powerful hand was interposed with the understanding that something would be done by the Mormons to meet the exigency of the situation."

Evidently he had been informed that the church authorities contemplated prohibiting polygamy.

The following are statements of Frank J. Cannon, contained in Chapter III, of his articles published in Everybody's Magazine:

"When the progress of the Cullom-Struble bill began to make its threatening advance, my father went secretly to Washington, and a short time afterward word came to me in Ogden, through the Presidency, that he wished me to arrange my business affairs for a long absence from Utah, and follow him to the Capital. I found him there in the office of Delegate John T. Caine. The Cullom-Struble bill had been favorably considered by the Committee on Territories, and the disfranchisement of all the Mormons in Utah seemed imminent. Every argument, political, and legal, had been used against the measure in vain."

After having stated that he had interviewed Mr. Blaine and a member of the Committee on Territories, he further said:

"I went to other members of the committee, privately, and told them that the Mormon church was about to make a concession concerning the doctrine of polygamy. I told them so in confidence, pointing out the necessity of secrecy, since to make public the news of such a proceeding in advance would be to prevent the church from authorizing it. * * * It remained to make our safety permanent, and I took train for Utah, on my father's counsel, to see President Woodruff. I had given my word that 'something was to be done.' I went to plead that it should be done, and done speedily. I told him (Woodruff) in detail of the events in Washington, and of the men who had helped us in them. I warned him that the passage of the measure of disfranchisement had been no more than retarded. I pointed out the fatal consequences for the community if the bill should ever become a law; the fatal conseqences for the leaders of the church if the non-polygamist Mormons, deprived of their votes, were ever left unable to control the administration of local government. I repeated the promises that my father had authorized me to carry to the senators and congressmen who still had the Cullom-Struble bill in hand; and I emphasized the fact that because of this promise the bill had been held back with the certainty that it would never become a law if we met the nation half way. To this statement he (Woodruff) said sadly: 'I had hoped we wouldn't have to meet this trouble this way. You know what it means to our people. Did your father tell you,' he asked, 'that I had been seeking the mind of the Lord?' I replied that he had."

Woodruff, as president of the Mormon church, issued a manifesto advising the Latter-day Saints to refrain from contracting any marriages forbidden by the law of the land. The Cullom-Struble bill was not passed, but its pendency was the "last straw which broke the camel's back." Evidently its pendency forced the issuance of the manifesto.

# CHAPTER XVI.

## The Effort for the Admission of Utah That Failed.

To extricate the high officers of the Mormon church from the dilemma they were in on account of the passage and vigorous and effective execution of the Edmunds act of 1882, and after most of them had for years been in hiding to avoid arrest, a vigorous effort was made by the Mormons previous to the announcement of the Woodruff manifesto to procure statehood for Utah. In 1888, an application having been made to Congress for the admission of Utah, I was requested by a committee of Gentiles to go to Washington and oppose its admission, which I did. Franklin S. Richards, John T. Caine, Jeremiah M. Wilson, a distinguished attorney, and Joseph M. McDonald of Indiana, appeared before the Senate Committee on Territories and spoke in favor of admission. Senator Dubois and myself appeared and spoke in opposition. The following quotation from the published proceedings before the committee shows the ground of my opposition:

"Mr. Baskin of Utah Territory, on behalf of the Gentiles of that Territory, addressed the committee as follows:

" 'While the theocratic tenet of the Mormon church is as great if not a greater evil than polygamy, and as much opposed to our American institutions, polygamy is the feature most antagonistic to the sentiment of the nation, and against which the laws of Congress relating to the Mormon problem have been more directly aimed. The political power of Utah Territory, by the grace of Congress placed and kept in the hands of the Mormon hierarchy, has been and still is the main prop and shield of the Mormon system. This power has been its greatest protection, has stimulated its growth, and still preserves its existence. Without the possession of this power by the Mormons, polygamy could never have reached its present status, or Mormonism ever have become a difficult national problem.

" 'The perpetuity of the objectionable features of the Mormon system is dependent upon the perpetuation of the political power of the church. The elimination of polygamy and theocratic rule would leave nothing vital in the system obnoxious to American sentiment. The Mormon church, fully realizing the great importance of the political power practically, though not in form, placed in its hands by the Organic Act of the Territory, with a zeal worthy of a better cause has stubbornly fought every measure introduced into Congress for the punishment of polygamy, or tending to curtail the power of the Mormon hierarchy, and as far as it was practicable used the power of the Territory to defeat the execution of all laws of the government abridging Mormon power or punishing Mormon practices. In 1862 Congress began to remove the safeguard which the Mormon legislature had thrown around the peculiar institutions and practices of the church, and protected by which safeguards the hierarchy had become confident, bold and arrogant. Congress continued to advance by very slow approaches in the same direction, and by the passage of what is known as the Poland law of 1874, the Edmunds law of 1882, and the Edmunds-Tucker law of 1887, placed the Mormons in a position of great distress. The leaders at last began to realize that the government of the United States was more powerful than the government of the Mormon church. The heads of this hostile government within the national government fled to places of concealment to escape punishment, and have remained concealed for nearly four years. The discussions in Congress, and the comments of the press of the country on the passage of the measures before referred to, revealed the fact, alarming to the Mormons, that there is a growing public sentiment in the country in favor of the passage of a law by Congress taking the political power of Utah out of the hands of those who have wrongfully used it to build up and protect a system diametrically opposed to American institutions. The dilemma of the leaders and the growing public sentiment threatening its very life (political power) has forced upon the Mormon church the necessity of the departure which has been taken in the matter of the recent application for statehood, under a constitution—ostensibly, but not in reality—prohibiting the practice of that feature of the Mormon system, the prohibition and authority to punish which in a constitution framed and adopted by members of the church it was thought would do most to appease public sentiment, and turn it in favor of the scheme of statehood. The departure is artfully strategic, is intended to deceive, and is well calculated to accomplish that purpose. The ends really sought to be attained by the admission of Utah is the perpetuation of the theocratic power of the church, the rescue of the system of celestial or plural marriage, as taught and practiced, from threatened destruction, the rescue of its leaders and other polygamists from arrest and punishment, and the securement of amenity to polygamy. The admittance of Utah under the constitution presented to Congress would successfully accomplish these ends. The admission of Utah at any time in the future while the church holds dominant political control in the Territory will accomplish the same end, whatever may be the provisions of the constitution under which the Territory shall be admitted. In proof of the fact that this movement is not made in good faith, and that its success would accomplish the ends above indicated, the following facts are submitted:

" 'On the 17th day of June last, without any agitation of the question of statehood among the masses, or any previous notice to the public of such a movement, on behalf of the central committee of the People's party—an organization within the church for the purposes of the church, composed exclusively of Mormons—the following communication was addressed to the chairman of the Democratic central committee of Utah:

"The territorial committee of the People's party, considering that the time is propitious for an application for admission into the Union of the Territory of Utah, has called mass conventions to be held in the several counties, June 25th, to nominate delegates to a constitutional convention to be held in this city June 30th, 1887. It is desired that the movement be made as general as possible, and that all classes of the people of the Territory shall participate in it. We therefore solicit the co-operation of the Democratic party of Utah, and through you as its chairman, we respectfully invite your committee and your party to take an active part in the mass convention, and to assist in the nomination of delegates to the constitutional convention, with the understanding that if you accept the invitation your party shall be accorded a thorough representation in the convention.

"By order of the People's Territorial Central Committee.

"(Signed) J. R. WINDER, Chairman."

" 'A similar communication was addressed to the chairman of the Republican committee. In thirteen days from the date of these communications a constitutional convention convened in Salt Lake City composed almost exclusively of Mormons, adopted the constitution which at the last general election, without any authority of law, in an irregular manner, was ratified by the mass of the Mormons at the polls. As the Gentiles of the Territory did not deem the time auspicious for the admission of Utah, they did not vote upon the question of the adoption of the constitution. Under this constitution, application for the admission of Utah Territory has been made and is being urged upon Congress. Article XV, section 12, of this constitution contains the following clause:

"Bigamy and polygamy being considered incompatible with a republican form of government, each of them is hereby forbidden and declared a misdemeanor."

" 'It is a pregnant fact that should be noted, that this clause does not state what acts shall constitute the crimes of bigamy and polygamy, and that the cohabitation clause of the Edmunds law, the only provision punishing polygamic practices that has ever been effective, was not inserted. Bigamy and polygamy, in general terms, are the only crimes prohibited. Celestial marriage is not mentioned. Yet celestial marriage is the system which the Mormons claim was revealed to the church, and is the only system of plural marriage practiced by them or accepted as a tenet to the Mormon church. They claim, further, that celestial marriage is entirely different from either bigamy or polygamy, and deny that they practice the last named crimes, or that either is permitted or tolerated in the church. What follows, shows their views upon this subject. The Deseret News, which is the official organ of the church, on May 20, 1886, contains the following:

"Polygamy, in the ordinary Asiatic sense of the term, never was, and is not now, a tenet of the Latter-day Saints. We have repeatedly shown that the Mormon system of plural marriage is not bigamy, and it does not contain the essential elements of that offense. We have also indicated that, properly speaking, it is not polygamy. In reviewing the message of President Arthur, we refuted the statement made by him that polygamy is the cornerstone of the Mormon church and said polygamy, speaking properly, is not now, and has never been, even a tenet of the Mormon faith. In that statement we made no attempt to deny the doctrine of celestial marriage, which is an essential part of the creed of the Latter-day Saints. What we claim is that the Mormon system of marriage is, properly speaking, neither polygamy nor bigamy."

" 'Article XVI, section 1, of that constitution provided that Article XV, section 12—which prohibits the practice of polygamy—shall not be amended or revised in any way except by the approval of Congress.

" 'The constitution of the United States provides that new States may be admitted into the Union. The time at which this power shall be exercised, and the precedent conditions which may be required by Congress, is entirely left to its discretion. In the exercise of this discretion Congress may, if it chooses, dictate to the applicants any or all of the provisions of their constitution. But whatever may be the character of the provision so imposed by Congress as a prerequisite for admission, the moment the State is in the Union it is vested by the express provision of the constitution of the United States with all of the rights, privileges and powers possessed by the other States, and the constitution at once applies to such State with the same force and effect it applies to the other States. It therefore follows, that any precedent conditions for admission imposed by Congress which abridges the rights of the new State in such a manner as to deprive it, when in the Union, of the rights which the other States enjoy, under the provisions of that constitution destroys the uniform operation of that instrument, and is null and void. The other States possess the right to amend their constitutions.

" 'This question, however, is of no practical importance in this case, because the Mormons will never disturb Article XII of the constitution which they have adopted, because it does not apply to their system of marriage, according to the distinction which they make between bigamy and polygamy and celestial marriage, and even if it applied, with the powers of a State in their hands it would be more harmless to them than the law of 1862 against polygamy has been. Is it likely that any member of the church would ever be prosecuted for the violation of Article XII of the constitution, with the administration of the criminal law of the State in the hands of judges, jurors, and prosecuting officers who belong to the church and believe that the practice of plural marriage by the Saints has the authority of divine revelation?' "

After a full discussion of the matter before the committee Senator Cullom reported the following resolution:

"Resolved, that it is the sense of the Senate Committee that new States should be admitted into the Union only upon a basis of equality with the existing States, and that Congress ought not to exercise any supervision over the provisions of the constitution of any such State further than is necessary to guarantee to every State in this Union a republican form of government. That the proposed constitution of the State of Utah submitted to Congress with the memorial praying for the admission of the Territory of Utah into the Union as a State, contains provisions which would deprive such proposed State, if admitted into the Union, of that equality which should exist among the different States. Resolved, further, that it is the sense of the Senate that the Territory of Utah ought not to be admitted into the Union as a State until it is certain beyond doubt that the practice of plural marriage, bigamy, or polygamy has been entirely abandoned by the inhabitants of said Territory, and until it is likewise certain that the civil affairs of the Territory are not controlled by the priesthood of the Mormon church."

The last of these resolutions expressed the general sentiment of the nation, and it was not until after the manifesto was issued, and the heads of the Mormon church had given a pledge that polygamy would not be renewed and the church would not in the future control the civil affairs of the State, that the Territory was admitted into the Union. Without such a pledge, statehood could not have been obtained.

From the following incident, I have not the least doubt that such a pledge was made to the members of Congress, pending the Enabling Act under which Utah was admitted: There was an act of Congress which prohibited incorporated cities of the territories from issuing bonds beyond a certain percentage of the amount of taxes annually assessed. Salt Lake City had issued bonds up to the limit, and as it was necessary to issue more bonds in order to complete certain necessary public improvements which had been commenced, I, as mayor of that city, went to Washington to procure a special act authorizing the issuance of a million dollars of extra bonds. While there I met, in the lobby of the Arlington hotel, Geo. Q. Cannon, who was one of the counselors of Wilford Woodruff, president of the Mormon church, Bishop Clawson and Isaac K. Trumbo, who were in Washington to aid in procuring the passage of the Enabling Act which was then pending. Mr. Trumbo asked me if I had come to again oppose the admission of Utah. Upon replying that I had not, he requested me to aid in the passage of that act, to which I replied, "The president of the Mormon church has the power in Utah to defeat or elect any party ticket or candidate for office whenever he desires to do so, and while that power exists, I cannot favor statehood for the Territory." Mr. Cannon then said that the ruling church authorities had made a solemn pledge that the church would take no part in political affairs, and that polygamy would not be renewed. I replied, "While I have no doubt that both you and President Woodruff will favor keeping that pledge, the successor of President Woodruff might disregard it; and while I will not act a hypocritical part by favoring statehood, I will not take any active steps in opposition to the passage of the pending Enabling Act, as most of the influential members of the Liberal party, to which I belong, favor the admission of the Territory."

# CHAPTER XVII.

## A Reference to the Mormon Battalion.

The masses of the people in Utah were formerly taught, and yet believe, that the government made a demand on the Mormons for a battalion of five hundred men to participate in the war with Mexico, and that the demand was made for the purpose of oppressing the Mormons.

In September, 1857, Brigham Young, in an address delivered in Salt Lake City and found in Vol. V, Journal of Discourses, used the following language:

"There cannot be a more damnable, dastardly order than was issued by the Administration to this people while they were in an Indian country in 1846. Before we left Nauvoo, no less than two United States senators came to receive a pledge from us that we would leave the United States, and then while we were doing our best to leave their borders, the poor, low, degraded curses sent a requisition for five hundred of our men to go and fight their battles. That was President Polk, and he is now weltering in hell with old Zachariah Taylor, where the present administrators will soon be if they do not repent. * * * Liars have reported that this people have committed treason, and upon their lies the President has ordered troops to aid in officering this Territory, and if those officers are like many who have previously been sent here, and we have reason to believe that they are, or they would not come when they know that they are not wanted; they are poor, miserable, blacklegs, broken-down political hacks, robbers and whore-mongers—men that are not for civilized society, so they dragoon them upon us for officers. I feel that I won't bear such cussed treatment, and that is enough to say, for we are just as free as the mountain air. * * * There is high treason in Washington, and if the law was carried out, it would hang up many of them, and the very act of James K. Polk, in having five hundred of our men, while we were making our way out of the country, under an agreement forced upon us, would have hung him between the heavens and the earth if the laws had been faithfully carried out. And now, if they can send a force against this people, we have every constitutional and legal right to send them to hell, and we calculate to send them there. * * * Our enemies had better count the cost, for if they continue the job they will want to let it out to subcontractors before they get half through with it. If they persist in sending troops here, I want the people of the West and the East to understand that it will not be safe for them to cross the plains."

Wilford Woodruff, in his address at the gathering of the pioneers on the 24th of July, 1880, said:

"Our government called upon us to raise a battalion of five hundred men to go to Mexico to fight the battles of our country. This draft was ten times greater, according to the population of the Mormon camp, than was made upon any portion of our nation. Whether our government expected we would comply with the request or not is not for me to say. But I think I am safe in saying that a plan was laid by certain parties for our destruction if we did not comply."

Both Brigham Young and Wilford Woodruff knew that the enlistment of the Mormon Battalion was requested by Colonel Little, who represented the Mormon church, and that President Polk granted the request for the purpose of assisting the Mormons on their journey to the West, and not to oppress or injure them. As an earnest of this I refer to the evidence following: Captain Allen was sent to the Mormon camps for the purpose of enlisting that Battalion, and he issued the following circular to the Mormons, which explains the object of that enlistment:

"I have come among you instructed by Col. S. F. Kearney of the U. S. Army, now commanding the Army of the West, to visit the Mormon camp and accept the service for twelve months of four or five companies of Mormon men who may be willing to serve their country for that period in our present war with Mexico; this force to unite with the Army of the West at Santa Fe, and be marched thence to California where they will be discharged. They will receive pay and rations, and other allowances such as other volunteers or regular soldiers receive, from the day they shall be mustered into the service, and will be entitled to all comforts and benefits of regular soldiers of the army, and when discharged as contemplated at California, they will be given, gratis, their arms and accoutrements with which they will be fully equipped at Fort Leavenworth. This is offered to the Mormon people now. This year an opportunity of sending a portion of their young and intelligent men to the ultimate destination of their whole people, and entirely at the expense of the United States, and this advance party can thus pave the way and look out land for their brethren who come after them. Those of the Mormons who are desirous of serving their country on the conditions here enumerated are requested to meet me without delay at their principal camp at Council Bluffs, where I am going to consult with their principal men, and to receive and organize the force contemplated to be raised. I will receive all healthy, able-bodied men of from eighteen to forty-five years of age.

"(Signed) J. ALLEN,<br>
"Capt. First Dragoons."

The following is a quotation from an article published in the Deseret News, and relates to an address delivered by B. H. Roberts on the 4th of July, 1911:

"* * * The calling of the Mormon Battalion, and the fact that this event was not intended by the general government to harm the Mormon people, but that it was for their welfare and the direct results of a request by the church leaders, was forcibly brought out, and that Col. Jesse C. Little, the eastern representative of the Mormon church, had asked President Polk to assist the people in their enforced western march, and that President Brigham Young stated that it was what he had wanted, was shown from letters and journals of many of the early church leaders, among them being the journal of John Taylor. The government intended to help the people in their western march, and the Mormon people were thus given a glorious opportunity to prove their patriotism to their country.

"The journal of President Taylor states that President Young said, 'We are pleased to show our patriotism for the country we expect to have for our future home. I think President Polk has done us a great favor in calling us.'

"Similar facts were read from the biography of President Wilford Woodruff and others. The exodus of the pioneers, and their arduous journey and their final entrance into the valley of Salt Lake were beautifully pictured, and numerous interesting events connected with that occasion were told."

The following is an extract from the testimony given in the naturalization case hereinbefore referred to by Henry W. Lawrence, a gentleman of the highest standing and whose veracity is beyond question, and who at present is a member of the governing commission of Salt Lake City:

"In 1847, during the Mexican war, when the Mormons were on the frontier, all in their camps, going out to Salt Lake—or west somewhere, there was a battalion called for from the Mormons to go and fight the battles in Mexico. I always supposed, from the teachings of the Mormon leaders, that it was a requisition, and I have heard over and over

the government handled roughly—denounced for calling upon
the Mormon people for 500 of their best men, to cripple them
right there on the banks of the Missouri, in the most trying
time.  The people were taught that the government had called
for these men so that we would not be prepared to protect
ourselves against even the Indians.  It was so represented by
our 'leaders.  I used often to think that that was a most
damnable thing.  That was preached in sermons by Brigham
Young, by George A. Smith and the other leading men of
the church, time and time again.  The true condition of the
thing was, we afterwards found out, and it was one of the
things that turned me against the system, that it was on the
solicitation of the agents of this church that that battalion
was asked for.  Jesse S. Little was one of them.  The government, out of kindness to the people, and on the solicitations
of the agents of this church, asked for that battalion.  They
paid them one or two months' wages in advance, and that
money was used to help buy teams and assistance for the
people, and helped them to come out here to Salt Lake.  Instead of the truth being told, they were told that it was done
in order to cripple them in the face of the Indians.  This was
one of the things they taught the people to prejudice them
against the government of the United States.

"From 1862 to 1865 the most radical talk was indulged
in; since that time they have been a little more careful in their
expressions.  This talk was indulged in, not only by Brigham
Young, H. C. Kimball, Geo. A. Smith and the twelve apostles,
but by other leading men of the Mormon church.  We were
told that the government had allowed us to be driven from
our homes, deprived of our property, the saints to be murdered,
the prophets to be murdered, and that they had deprived us
of all our rights as American citizens, and that by that means
we were alienated from the government.  Had it not been for
the teachings that were given to them by the leaders, there
is no reason why the people should not have been friendly to
the government of the United States.  If they felt that they
were free from the obligations of the church, they would be
a good, loyal people."

The following extracts are from prayers which were made
at the dedication of the St. George temple on January 1, 1877,
and published in the Deseret News of January 13, 1877.
Prayer of Wilford Woodruff, who afterwards issued the
manifesto:

"And we pray Thee our Father in Heaven, in the name of
Jesus Christ, if it be consistent with Thy will, that Thy servant
Brigham may stand in the flesh to behold the nation which
now occupies the land upon which Thou, Lord, hast said the

PORTER ROCKWELL.

Zion of God shall stand in the latter days; that nation which shed the blood of the saints and prophets which cry unto God day and night for vengeance; the nation which is making war with God and Christ; that nation whose sins, wickedness and abominations are ascending up before God and the Heavenly Host which causes all eternity to be pained, and the Heavens to weep like falling rain; Yea, O Lord, that he may live to see that nation, if it will not repent, broken in pieces like a potter's vessel and swept from the earth with a besom of destruction as were the Jaredites and Nephites, that the land of Zion may cease to groan under the wickedness and abomination of men."

Prayer of Apostle Lorenzo Snow, afterwards president of the church:

"We, thy servants and people, stretch forth our hands unto Thee, Father, our Lord Jesus Christ, and in His name we beseech Thee to hear the prayer of Thy servant Wilford Woodruff, which has been offered up in the first room of this house, and answereth it for this house and people."

From prayer of Apostle Brigham Young, Jr.:

"Hear and answer the prayer offered up by Thy apostles Wilford Woodruff and Lorenzo Snow, that they may penetrate the ears of the Lord of Sabaoth."

The foregoing remarks of Brigham Young on the subject of the Mormon Battalion is one among the many instances which show his flagrant duplicity; and the prayers of Woodruff, Snow and Brigham Young, Jr., are among the many instances which show the animus of the priesthood against the general government, and are of the same general character referred to by Mr. Lawrence in his testimony.

Whitney has studiously avoided mentioning in his history such occurrences as the preceding ones, or referring to any of the anomalous sermons from which I have made quotations. In the light of what I have shown respecting the Mormon Battalion, his treatment of the same in his history is as reprehensible as the way he treats the subject of the Mountain Meadows massacre.

# CHAPTER XVIII.

## Securing Free Schools for Utah.

Previous to the passage by the Legislature of the Free Public School Law of 1890, there were no free schools in the Territory of Utah. The prevalent school system before that year and the school houses and school facilities were disgraceful. The means resorted to by members of the Liberal party to procure the passage of the free school law of 1890, is stated in the following communication of Mr. C. E. Allen:

"Dec. 6th, 1911.
"Hon. R. N. Baskin, City.

"Dear Sir: In response to your request for a statement from me regarding public school legislation in the legislature of which I was a member, I submit the following:

"The so-called Edmunds-Tucker law was passed by the Congress of the United States sometime in February or March, 1887. Under this law the affairs pertaining to schools were taken out of the hands of the Territory so far as the appointment of a territorial superintendent of education was concerned, and this appointment was vested in the territorial court of Utah, as I recall it. I have not the law at hand.

"Also by this law the districting of the Territory for the election of members of the territorial legislature was placed in the hands of the so-called Utah Commission.

"In the summer of 1887 the Territory was redistricted, and the mining districts of Tintic, Bingham, and Stockton and Ophir, together with some farming districts, were made a legislative district.

"I was nominated for the lower house of the legislature by the so-called Liberal party of this legislative district, and was elected in August, 1887.

"In the fall of 1887 certain friends of mine in Salt Lake. (I was then living in Bingham Canyon) wrote to me asking if I would accept the appointment of territorial superintendent of schools. I answered my friends that I did not think I could give suitable attention to these matters while living in Bingham; that I did not care to leave my work there and come to the city to devote myself entirely to educational matters, and that I thought it best to appoint someone in the city who could be in more direct touch with the teachers and other persons connected with school affairs.

"Mr Parley L. Williams, a prominent attorney of this city then and now, was appointed, by the supreme court, territorial superintendent of schools.

"Before the meeting of the legislature, which occurred about the 10th of January, 1888, Mr. Williams drew up a bill which did not purport to change materially the law as then existing, except that the schools were made absolutely free under its provisions. This bill he placed in the hands of Judge Enos D. Hoge, who also was a member with me in the lower house of the legislature.

"When I came to Salt Lake in January to enter upon my duties as a member of the Twenty-eighth session of the Utah legislature, Judge Hoge placed this bill in my hands and asked me to look after it, saying that I would be better able to handle it since I had had considerable experience in school matters.

"In this legislature, of which W. W. Riter of Salt Lake was the speaker, I was appointed a member of the committee on education. The chairman of this committee was Hon. James H. Moyle. The names of the other members I do not recall. I introduced the bill prepared by Mr. Williams and it was sent to the committee on education in the lower house. We worked over it, as I recall the facts, about half the session, and finally the committee was induced to report it back to the house for passage.

"This bill was defeated in the house, as I recall the vote, by all the votes of the house except five. Three of these were elected by the so-called Liberal party and two were members of the People's party. They were Philo T. Farnsworth, now residing in Salt Lake City, and a Mr. Held, as I recall the name, who was a member from the southern part of Salt Lake county. After this bill failed in the house, the council [senate] took up educational matters. There a bill was introduced. This bill was presented to certain members of the council by Heber J. Grant, now and then an apostle in the Mormon church. It was commonly supposed to be the result of the wisdom of that organization, and Heber J. Grant openly fathered it.

"This bill proposed not to make the schools of Utah free, but to divert the school moneys to any church organization which was carrying on schools in the State of Utah in proportion to the number of pupils that such organization had in such schools. If this had been done the schools instead of becoming free would all have been under the domination of the various churches of the Territory. This bill was vetoed by Governor West.

"In the summer of 1889 I was again a candidate for election to the legislature from a Salt Lake district, having moved my residence from Bingham Canyon to the fifth municipal ward of this city. I was re-elected to the legislature at the election held in August.

"Between the time of my re-election and the assembling of the legislature I devoted considerable time to the study of the school laws of this Territory, the States of Kansas and South Dakota and the city of Buffalo. The laws which I found at these various localities seemed to afford me a better groundwork for the proposed laws for Utah than any other that I could find. I drafted two bills; one, if it should become a law, to apply in general to the Territory, the other to apply to cities.

"Just before Congress was to assemble in December of that year I called a meeting of four gentlemen besides myself, only two of whose names I now recall and those two were the only ones who attended the meeting. Governor Arthur L. Thomas and Hon. Parley L. Williams and myself met in response to this call to consider these bills. I presented to them the bills which I had drafted and told them of the difficulties I had had in the previous legislature, and said that I desired to have these laws passed either in Utah or in Washington, and asked Gov. Thomas to take them to Washington and present them to Senator Edmunds of Vermont and to ask him to introduce them in the Senate of the United States if the action of the territorial legislature should indicate that there was doubt concerning their passage here. Mr. Thomas and Mr. Williams both agreed with this plan, and Mr. Thomas took the bills and gave them to Senator Edmunds and requested him to introduce them into the Senate of the United States, provided there seemed to be a disposition here not to do anything in this matter.

"In the territorial Assembly of 1890 there were six Liberal members in the lower house. We had a meeting to decide upon the officers that we would present for election in the lower house and also to decide upon what positions upon committees we would ask for. I gave my reasons to the Liberal members and they unanimously agreed that I should seek a position on the committee of education. At this time the People's party in the legislature was divided into two factions; one was led by Hon. Samuel Thurman of Provo and one by Charles C. Richards of Ogden. These factions seemed to arise through the desire of the Ogden faction to prevent suitable appropriations being made to the insane asylum at Provo. I had shown considerable interest in the affairs of the insane asylum in the legislature of 1888, and had become quite friendly with Mr. Samuel Thurman through this. At the opening of the legislature in 1890, I went to Mr. Thurman and told him that I desired to be chairman of the committee on education. He thought it was considerable for the minority to ask for a chairmanship in the lower house. I replied that we had six solid votes which were agreed to be cast in any way that I should desire in order to further what we believed to be the interests of good education in this Territory; that if he desired these votes he could have them; if he did not, we would try to use them elsewhere. The result was that I was appointed by the Hon. James Sharp, speaker of the house, chairman of the committee on education.

"The two bills which I had prepared were introduced by me as Bills No. 1 and No. 2 of the session. They were immediately referred, of course, to the committee on education. Within a short time the committee on education had considered the bills and they had been reported back to the house and passed by the house; one unanimously, the other with only one negative vote.

"Then these bills went to the council and appeared to have died. Nothing could be heard of them; no one could tell when they would be reported. One morning an item appeared in the Salt Lake papers saying that, the day before, Senator Edmunds had introduced into the Senate of the United States a bill providing for free education in the Territory of Utah. Senator Edmunds had combined the two bills which I had prepared into one and presented them as one bill in the Senate of the United States.

"When I entered the Assembly hall that morning, one of the members belonging to the majority met me and said: 'Mr. Allen, what is the meaning of the introduction of a bill on education for the Territory of Utah by Senator Edmunds?' I replied: 'The bill which has been introduced by Senator Edmunds is the same as the two bills which were introduced by me here, which have passed this house and which have been held up in the council. I spent the whole session two years ago trying to get something done here on this question. Nothing could be accomplished. I do not propose to spend this whole winter here without results. If your party does not care to pass these bills, or something similar to them, and have the credit for doing so, you can take the same legislation from the hands of the United States."

"All at once the committee on education in the council became very active. My two bills were combined into one, essentially without change, and named the Collett bill, from Mr. Collett, who was chairman of the committee on education in the council, as I recall the facts, and the so-called Collett bill was passed by the council. This bill came down to the house. Some minor changes had been made in the original bills and several amendments which seemed to me to detract from the efficiency of the bill had been inserted, but the original bills with these exceptions were practically unchanged. The bill as sent down to the house from the council was passed by the house after certain amendments thereto had been made.

"The bill as passed was put into operation throughout the Territory during the year 1890, and with the changes which time has suggested, which changes have particularly been made with reference to the schools of cities, the law then put upon the statute books has been in force up to the present time.

"The above are the main facts concerning the passage of the free school laws in 1890. The minor details, of course, I do not readily recall.

"I hope they may be of use to you and you may feel free to use them in whatever way you choose.     Very truly,
"C. E. ALLEN."

Governor West, in his message vetoing the school act passed by the legislature in 1888, referred to in the letter of Mr. Allen, said:

"There are many grounds of objection to the enactment of such a law, which it is unnecessary to enumerate, as there is one which is insufferable—that is, the provision that private or denominational schools shall share in the public school fund.

"I can no more give my assent to such a provision than approve an appropriation from the public treasury for the benefit of any other private interest or individual. I regard such a provision as a blow at the public school system which prevails in every other section of our country.

"Under the proposed law, denominational schools may have the aid of the civil power by means of taxation to advance the tenets of the church. It seems a surprising fact that such a system should be proposed at this time. None of the reasons which can be urged in support of the general education of the youths of the Territory at the public expense can, in my judgment, justify such legislation."

Governor Thomas, in one of his messages to the legislature on the subject of free public schools, said:

"I can present no subject for your consideration of greater importance than the condition of public schools throughout the Territory. It is the bounden duty of the Territory to give to every child the opportunity of receiving a free public education. This is denied by existing school laws. I earnestly recommend that you enact such legislation as will lay the foundation of a system of education that will progress until the highest standard is reached. You will serve your Territory well by so doing."

In 1892 the committee on education of the upper house of the territorial legislature of which Mr. John D. Peters, a Liberal Mormon was chairman and I was a member, reported a free public school bill and recommended its passage. This bill retained all the vital provisions of the act of 1890, and strengthened it by additional requirements. The bill so reported was enacted and approved by the governor. Other provisions were afterwards added until now Utah's free school system is such as any civilized community might well be proud of, and is the boast of the generality of the inhabitants of this State.

The foundation of that efficient system was laid by the Act of 1890, which having been originated and drafted by Mr. Allen and its passage procured by his sagacity, he is entitled to the gratitude of the people of this State, and especially to the gratitude of the rising generation, for that act contained a section which made the education of the children of the Territory compulsory and also provided adequate methods for its enforcement. He is also justly entitled to the appellation, the "Father of Utah's Free

Schools." The Act of 1890 also authorized the boards of education of the respective cities to submit the question of issuing bonds for school purposes to the qualified electors.

In 1890 the board of education of Salt Lake City submitted to the electors of that city the question of issuing bonds to the amount of eight hundred and fifty thousand dollars, for the purpose of purchasing sites and erecting thereon school houses. The Liberal party at that time had a decided majority of electors in the city and as it was the policy of that party to improve the inadequate school facilities then existing, the electors of that party generally recognized the pressing necessity of substituting modern and commodious school houses in place of the miserable buildings in which the schools at that time were being held, and voted in favor of said bonds; consequently their issuance was authorized by a decisive majority of the votes cast. The board of education which submitted the issuance of said bonds to the vote of the electors was composed of six members of the Liberal party and four of the People's party, the latter being the name given to the Mormon church party.

Col. William Nelson, who was formerly United States marshal of the Territory, and acted in that capacity at the execution of John D. Lee on the scene of the Mountain Meadows massacre, and for years, until his death in November, 1913, the editor of the Salt Lake Tribune, was elected by the Liberal party a member of that board and afterwards was chosen by the board as its president. He held that position for several years and was most active, persistent and efficient in promoting the interests of the public schools of the city. During his incumbency thirteen modern school houses were, in pursuance of the policy of the Liberal party, erected in the city. Their perfect adaptation for school purposes and their superior appointments are not surpassed anywhere, and they are justly the pride of the city.

Until after the passage of the Edmunds-Tucker Act in 1887, no Gentiles were ever elected to the territorial legislature. From the organization of the Territory in 1850 until 1890, a period of forty years, no free school law was enacted by the legislature and even at that late date it was impelled to act, as shown by the letter previously referred to, by the assurance that failure to pass the free school bills introduced by Mr. Allen would impel action by Congress.

# CHAPTER XIX.

## The Mormon Business System.

If there ever was any spirituality in the Mormon church, it was destroyed under the leadership of Brigham Young, who made of the church a money-making institution. Under the monetary system established by him, if the church increases in membership at the same ratio as it has heretofore done it will in time acquire inordinate wealth, the possession of which will vest it with temporal power in the State. This a church should not possess, especially one which engages, generally, in monetary business affairs, and the capital of which is largely increased each year by tithing, and under a tenet of which its adherents, by oath-bound covenants, are pledged to obey its priesthood in temporal affairs. It is so manifestly against public policy for a corporation, especially a church corporation, to engage in general business, that the right to do so should never be granted or the practice tolerated anywhere.

Joseph F. Smith was chosen President of the Mormon church on November 10, 1901. At that date he was not a capitalist, yet in the investigation in the Smoot case before the Senate Committee in March, 1904, he testified that he was President of the State Bank of Utah, Consolidated Wagon and Machinery Company, Salt Lake & Los Angeles Railway Company, Saltair Beach Company (a bathing resort); president and director of the Utah Light and Power Company, Idaho Sugar Company, Inland Crystal Salt Company, Salt Lake Dramatic Association and Salt Lake Knitting Company, also a director of the Union Pacific Railroad Company, Zion's Cooperative Mercantile Institution (which is the largest one in Salt Lake City), and the Deseret News, owned by the Mormon church, and also vice president of the Bullion Beck and Champion Mining Company. (See printed report of the Smoot case, Vol. I, et seq.)

The Mormon church is largely interested in most, if not all, of these companies; also in the new Utah Hotel, the sugar plants in Utah, and many other business enterprises, and its investments therein were made by the various presidents of the church as "trustees in trust."

The practical working of the Mormon church's financial system is forcibly stated in the speech of Senator Thomas Kearns of Utah in the Smoot case, reported in the Congressional Record of February 28, 1905, in which he said:

"Whatever may have been its origin or excuse, the business power of the president of the church and of the select class which he admits into business relations with him is now a practical monopoly, or is rapidly becoming a monopoly, of everything that he touches. I want to call your attention to the extraordinary list of worldly concerns in which this spiritual leader holds official positions. The situation is more amazing when you are advised that this man came to his presidency purely by accident, namely, the death of his seniors in rank; that he had never shown any business ability, and that he comes to the presidency and the directorship of the various corporations solely because he is president of the church. He is already reputed to be a wealthy man, and his statements would seem to indicate that he has large holdings in the various corporations with which he is associated, although previous to his accession to the presidency of the church he made a kind of proud boast among his people of his poverty.

"He conducts railways, street-car lines, power and light companies, coal mines, salt works, sugar factories, shoe factories, mercantile houses, drug stores, newspapers, magazines, theatres, and almost every conceivable kind of business, and in all of these, inasmuch as he is the dominant factor by virtue of his being the Prophet of God, he asserts indisputable sway. It is considered an evidence of deference to him, and good standing in the church, for his hundreds of thousands of followers to patronize exclusively the institutions which he controls.

"And this fact alone, without any business ability on his part, but with capable subordinate guidance for his enterprises, insures their success—and danger and possible ruin for every competitive enterprise. Independent of the business concerns, he is in receipt of an income like unto that which a royal family derives from a national treasury. One-tenth of all the annual earnings of all the Mormons in the world flows to him. These funds amount to the sum of $1,600,000 annually, or five per cent upon $32,000,000, which is one-quarter of the entire taxable wealth of the State of Utah. It is the same as if he owned individually, in addition to all his visible enterprises, one quarter of all the wealth of the State and derived from it five per cent of income without taxation and without discount. The hopelessness of contending in a business way with this autocrat must be perfectly apparent to your minds. The original purpose of this vast tithe, as often stated by speakers for the church, was the maintenance of the poor, the building of meeting houses, etc. Today the tithes are transmuted in the localities where they are paid, into cash, and they flow into the treasury of the head of the church. No account is made, or ever has been made of these tithes.  The president expends them according to his own will and pleasure, and with no examination of his accounts except by those few men whom he selects for that purpose and whom he rewards for their zeal and secrecy.  Shortly after the settlement of the Mormon church property question with the United States, the church issued a series of bonds amounting approximately to $1,000,000, which was taken by financial institutions. This was probably to wipe out a debt which had accumulated during a long period of controversy with the nation.  But since, and including the year 1897, which was about the time of the issue of the bonds, approximately $9,000,000 have been paid in as tithes. If any of the bonds are still outstanding it is manifestly because the president of the church desires for reasons of his own to have an existing indebtedness.

"It will astound you to know that every dollar of United States money paid to any servant of the government who is a Mormon is tithed for the benefit of this monarch.  Out of every $1,000 thus paid he gets $100 to swell his grandeur.  This is also true of money paid out of the public treasury of the State of Utah to Mormon officials.  But what is worst of all, the monarch dips into the sacred school fund and extracts from every Mormon teacher one-tenth of his or her earnings and uses it for his unaccounted purposes; and by means of these purposes and the power which they constitute, he defies the laws of his State, the sentiment of his country, and is waging a war of nullification on the public school system, so dear to the American people.  No right-thinking man will oppose any person as a servant of the nation or the State, or as a teacher in the public schools on account of religious faith.  As I have before remarked, this is no war upon the religion of the Mormons; and I am only calling attention to the monstrous manner in which this monarch invades all the provinces or human life and endeavors to secure his rapacious ends.

"In all this there is no thought on my part of opposition to voluntary gifts by individuals for religious purposes or matters connected legitimately with religion.  My comment and criticism are against a tyranny which misuses a sacred name to extract from individuals the money which they ought not to spare from family needs, and which they do not wish to spare; my comment and criticism relate to the power of a monarch whose tyranny is so effective as that not even the moneys paid by the government are considered the property of the government's servants until after this monarch shall have seized his arbitrary tribute, with or without the willing assent of the victim, so that the monarch may engage the more extensively in commercial affairs, which are not a part of either religion or charity.

"With an income of five per cent upon one-quarter of the entire assessed valuation of the State of Utah today, how long will it take this monarch, with his constantly increasing demands for revenue, to so absorb the productive power that he will be receiving an income of five per cent upon one-half of the property, and then upon all of the property of the State? This is worse than the farming of taxes under the old French kings. Will Congress allow this awful calamity to continue?

"The view which the people of the United States entertained on this subject forty years ago was shown by the act of Congress in 1862, in which a provision, directed particularly against the Mormon church, declared that no church in a Territory of the United States should have in excess of $50,000 of wealth, outside of the property used for purposes of worship. It is evident that as early as that time the pernicious effects of a system which used the name of God and the authority of religion to dominate in commerce and finance were fully recognized.

"This immense tithing fund is gathered directly from Mormons, but the burden falls in some degree upon Gentiles also. Gentiles are in business and suffer by competition with tithe-supported business enterprises. Gentiles are large employers of Mormon labor, and as that labor must pay one-tenth of its earnings to support competitive concerns the Gentile employer must pay, indirectly at least, the tithe which may be utilized to compete, and even ruin him in business.

"And in return it should be noted that Mormon institutions do not employ Gentiles, except in rare cases of necessity. The reason is obvious: Gentiles do not take as kindly to the tithing system as do the Mormons.

"The Mormon citizen of Utah has additional disadvantages. After paying one-tenth of all his earnings as a tithe offering, he is called upon to erect and maintain the meeting houses and other edifices of the church; he is called upon to donate to the poor fund of his ward, through his local bishop; he is called upon to sustain the women's relief society, whose purpose is to care for the poor and minister to the sick; he is called upon to pay his share of the expenses for the 2,500 missionaries of the church, who are constantly kept in the field without drawing upon the general funds of the church. When all this is done, it is found that, in defiance of the old and deserved boast of the predecessors of the present president, there are some Mormons in the poorhouses in Utah, and these are sustained by the public taxes derived from the Gentiles and Mormons alike. * * * * * *

"Mr. President, I must not burden you with too many details, but in order for you to see how complete is the business power of this man, I will cite you to one case. The Great Salt Lake is estimated to contain 14,000,000,000 tons of salt. Probably salt can be made cheaper on the shores of this lake than anywhere else in the world. Nearly all its shore line is adaptable for salt gardens. The president of the church is interested in a large salt monopoly which has gathered in the various smaller enterprises. He is president of a railroad which runs from the salt gardens to Salt Lake City, connecting there with trunk lines. It costs to manufacture the salt, and place it on board the cars, 75 cts. per ton. He receives for it $5 and $6 per ton. His company and its subsidiary corporation are probably capitalized at three-quarters of a million dollars.

"Is there menace in this system? To me it seems like a great danger to all the people who are now affected, and therefore of great danger to the people of the United States, because the power of this monarchy within the Republic is constantly extending? If it be an evil, every apostle is in part responsible for this tyrannical course. He helped to elect the president: he does the president's bidding and shares in the advantages of that tyranny.

"I did not call the social system a violation of the pledges to the country, but I do affirm that the business tyranny of Mormon leaders is an express violation of the covenant made, for they do not leave their followers free in secular affairs. They tyrannize over them, and their tyranny spreads even to the Gentiles. In all this I charge that every apostle is a party to the wrong and to the violation. Although I speak of the president of the church as the leader—the monarch in fact— every apostle is one of his ministers, one of his creators, and also one of his creatures, and possibly his successor; and the whole system depends upon the manner in which the apostles and the other leaders shall support the chief leader. As no apostle has ever protested against this system, but has, by every means in his power, encouraged it, he cannot escape his share of the responsibility for it. It is an evil; they aid it. It is in violation of the pledge upon which statehood was granted; they profit by it."

Upon the admission of Utah as a State, the Congress of the United States lost its authority to correct the indefensible practice of the church in engaging in general business affairs, and this can only be done now by an enactment of the legislature of the State; that it possesses authority to prohibit a practice so manifestly against public policy as that in which the church, as I have shown engages, is clear. There is no hope however that a legislature can ever be elected in Utah which will do so, as long as the priesthood retains the political and financial power and influence which it now possesses.

# CHAPTER XX.

## C. S. Varian's Statement.

Hon. Robert M. Baskin, Salt Lake City, Utah:

My Dear Sir: Pursuant to your request for a statement from me, reviewing in part the erroneous and misleading accounts by Mr. Orson F. Whitney in his "History of Utah," of the proceedings and prosecutions under the act of Congress of March 22, 1882, while I was assistant United States attorney, during the incumbency of that office by my partner, William H. Dickson, I submit the following:

In order to have a clear understanding of the matter in hand it will be necessary to first ascertain the questions at issue between the government of the United States and the Mormon people at the time when prosecutions were begun to enforce the laws in Utah.

By the act of Congress approved July 8, 1862, polygamy was prohibited in the territories of the United States, and penalties prescribed for a violation of the law, and by the same act it was made unlawful for any corporation or association, for religious or charitable purposes, to acquire or hold real estate in the territories of greater value than $50,000, and providing for a forfeiture and escheat of all such property held in violation of the law, saving existing vested rights.

By the act of Congress of March 22, 1882, generally known as the "Edmunds law," bigamy and unlawful cohabitation were defined as offenses against the United States in the territories, and it was provided that it should be sufficient cause of challenge to any person drawn or summoned as a juryman or talesman, first, that he is or has been living in the practice of bigamy, polygamy, or unlawful cohabitation with more than one woman; or second, that he believes it right for a man to have more than one living and undivorced wife at 'the same time, or to live in the practice of cohabiting with more than one woman; that any person appearing as a juror or talesman may be challenged on either of the said grounds, or may be questioned on his oath as to the existence of such cause, and that other evidence may be introduced bearing upon the question which was to be tried by the court; but it was also provided that as to the first ground of challenge the person challenged should not be bound to answer if he should say under oath that his answer might tend to criminate him, and he declined on that ground; that if he did answer, his answer should not be given in evidence in any criminal prosecution against him for any such offense, but if. he declined to answer, he should be rejected as incompetent.

By act of Congress approved March 3, 1887, known as the "Edmunds-Tucker law," it was provided that in any prosecution for bigamy, polygamy, or unlawful cohabitation, under any statute of the United States "the lawful husband or wife of the person accused shall be a competent witness, and may be called, but shall not be compelled to testify in such proceeding, examination, or prosecution without the consent of the husband or wife, as the case may be; and such witness shall not be permitted to testify to any statement or communication made by either husband or wife to each other, during the existence of the marriage relation, deemed confidential at common law."

It also provided that in such prosecution an attachment might issue for any witness without previous subpoena, compelling his or her immediate attendance upon certain prescribed procedure, with the further provision that such person might be released upon bond, etc. It also provided that "every ceremony of marriage, or in the nature of a marriage ceremony, of any kind, in any of the territories of the United States, whether either or both or more of the parties to such ceremony be lawfully competent to be the subjects of such marriage or ceremony or not, shall be certified by a certificate stating the fact and nature of such ceremony, the full names of each of the parties concerned, and the full name of every officer, priest and person taking part in the performance of such ceremony, which certificate shall be drawn up and signed by the parties, and by every officer, priest and person taking part in such ceremony, and filed in the office of the probate court," etc.

The certificate or the record thereof was made prima facie evidence of the facts required to be stated therein, and penalties were imposed for violation of the law.

From the beginning, and from the time of the several enactments aforesaid, the members of the Mormon church had contemptuously ignored and refused to obey the foregoing provisions of law in the territories occupied in whole or in part by the Mormon people. This fact was so well understood and acknowledged in the United States that nationwide calls for obedience to the law were made at least twice in the platforms of national conventions of two of the great political parties.

The attitude of the Mormon church towards the government during the times here referred to is well expressed by Mr. Justice Bradley in delivering the solemn judgment of the supreme court of the United States in the case of the Mormon church against the United States, as follows:

"But it is also stated in the findings of fact, and is a matter of public notoriety, that the religious and charitable uses intended to be subserved and promoted are the inculcation and spread of the doctrines and usages of the Mormon church, or Church of Latter-day Saints, one of the distinguishing features of which is the practice of polygamy, a crime against the laws, and abhorrent to the sentiments and feelings of the civilized world. Notwithstanding the stringent laws which have been passed by Congress, notwithstanding all the efforts made to suppress this barbarous practice, the sect or community composing the Church of Jesus Christ of Latter-day Saints perseveres, in defiance of law, in preaching, upholding and defending it. It is a matter of public notoriety that its emissaries are engaged in many countries in propagating this nefarious doctrine, and urging its converts to join the community in Utah. The existence of such a propaganda is a blot on our civilization. * * * It is unnecessary here to refer to the past history of the sect, to their defiance of the government authorities, to their attempt to establish an independent community, to their efforts to drive from the territory all who were not connected with them in communion and sympathy. The tale is one of patience on the part of the American government and people, and of contempt of authority and resistance to the law on the part of the Mormons. Whatever persecutions they may have suffered in the early part of their history in Missouri and Illinois, they have no excuse for their persistent defiance of law under the government of the United States." (136 U. S. 48-49.)

There being no public record made of marriages solemnized in the temples, and, of course, none of polygamous marriages, the difficulty of ascertaining and punishing polygamists was almost insuperable, until Congress intervened with necessary legislation.

This preliminary statement is necessary for a proper estimate and just understanding of the conduct and motives of the judges and officers who undertook to enforce obedience to the laws of the United States in Utah.

Early in March of 1882, Mr. Dickson and I opened a law office in the City of Salt Lake, Utah, and Mr. Dickson at once took charge of the office. I remained in Nevada for a time for the purpose of settling up my affairs, but came to Salt Lake City in the summer, and also in the autumn, of that year, and during the following year was engaged in professional business here. Both of us were resident citizens of the Territory when District Attorney Van Zile resigned, and Mr. Dickson did not receive his appointment until two years after our beginning the practice of law in Utah, to wit, on March 4, 1884. We were not adventurers, political or otherwise, in any sense, but permanent residents of Utah.

The case of Rudger Clawson was stated by Mr. Whitney to be "the virtual opening, on the part of the courts, of the great anti-polygamy crusade." It will be noted that in this statement the historian truly expresses the thought of the Mormon people that all effort on the part of the government or its officers to enforce obedience to the anti-polygamy laws was a **crusade**—that is, a war against a religious faith. The opposition to the enforcement of such laws is termed in the "history"—"the general cause," meaning thereby the undertaking, in defiance of the laws, in which all the Mormon people were interested and allied. It is further stated that circumstances had made Clawson the champion of this cause. I may properly, therefore, begin this review with his case.

Admitting that Clawson was guilty of the charge made in the indictment against him, the historian devotes some pages to a criticism of the rulings by the court upon challenges to grand jurors made by the United States attorney and to the ruling supporting the motion for an open venire for grand jurors. As to the first motion, the whole matter hinged upon the construction of the language employed in section five of the Edmunds law. The defendant's counsel, upon motion to quash the indictment, insisted that the provision in that section authorizing challenges for cause upon the ground of belief, as hereinbefore set out, only applied to petit jurors and not to grand jurors. It would seem to all fair-minded persons that the judgment of the supreme court of the United States in that case sustaining the construction of the act advanced by the government attorneys, and accepted by Judge Zane, would be a sufficient acquittance of all improper conduct or motive. (114 U. S., 484.)

Indeed, without the express provision of the statute authorizing challenges upon the ground of belief that it was right to have more than one living and undivorced wife at one time, and to live in the practice of unlawful cohabitation with more than one woman, it should be plain to the most ordinary understanding that such belief would authorize a challenge to the favor, as at common law, since it would be idle to attempt to indict and prosecute men for crimes of polygamy and unlawful cohabitation, with grand and petit jurors who believed that the accused had a right to commit such offenses.

In the "history" is said that Mr. Dickson and I, as new men, were anxious to distinguish ourselves in an assault upon the system which had proved the rock upon which so many federal officials had gone to pieces; and pages are devoted to a discussion of the question presented by the motion made by the government in this case for an open venire to bring in additional jurors in order that the panel might be completed and the trial had. The jury-list for the year had been exhausted, and no names remained in the jury box. I assume full responsibility for moving the court to issue an open venire. I see no connection between my act in that behalf with any assumed desire to oppress the people. I had been the district attorney for the United States for the State of Nevada for a number of years during the administrations of three Presidents, and was reasonably familiar with the laws of the United States and the procedure of its courts. It is not true that I "expressed doubts" as to the power of the court to grant the motion, because I never had any question in the premises. In this matter, as in the matter of the challenges, the order of Judge Zane was approved and the case affirmed in the supreme court of the United States. (114

213

U. S., 477.) The brief for the United States, submitted upon the hearing of the case in the supreme court of the Territory, was called for by Solicitor-General Phillips, who approved the same in a personal letter to me.

Criticism is made of the foreman of the grand jury who, it is said, was an apostate Mormon, and it was asked, "Who can hate like an apostate?" I do not remember that, at any time in any case, any inquiry was ever made by the church attorneys upon the examination of jurors summoned for the grand or petit juries, as to any feeling or prejudice entertained against the Mormon people; and with all the denunciation and complaint of the time, which is in part crystallized and expressed by the historian, I have yet to learn of one person who was convicted of an offense against the laws of the United States who was innocent. Upon conviction in this case, the plaintiff asked to be admitted to bail pending his appeal, which was denied, and defendant sued out a writ of habeas corpus in the territorial court, and from the adverse judgment therein, appealed to the supreme court of the United States. That court, in accordance with the express provision of the territorial law (which was the law relied upon), held that the bail was not a matter of right after conviction and sentence, but was one of discretion with the court.

The case of the United States against Evans is considered, in the "history," as one affording an easy victory for the prosecution, the defendant's plural wife, Harriet Parry, and her mother, Elizabeth Parry, being "willing witnesses, bent upon his conviction." The historian proceeds to say that Mr. Dickson "was so confident of the result that he improved the interim after the jury retired, and before they had returned their verdict, by moving that the prisoner, pending judgment, be remanded to the custody of the marshal, and that, thereupon, counsel proceeded to argue the motion." This statement is, of course, not true. Mr. Dickson never made such a motion at such a time, and if inquiry had been made by the writer of the "history" of persons qualified to speak, he would have been informed that no court would have entertained such a motion. It is next asserted that the prosecuting officers had proceeded to great extremities in the matter of the trials above referred to, and thereafter deemed it advisable that they should know how far and to what extent they could rely upon the court of last resort to sustain them in their acts, but that they, as crusaders, were "in the meantime not idle." As further evidence of the justice and impartial attitude of this writer of history, one excerpt from Vol. III, page 326, is instructive. He there says:

"One thought seemed to pervade the minds of most of our federal officials at that period—the overthrow of Mormonism, or at all events, the suppression of polgamy and the annihilation of the political power of the Mormons. Murder, seduction, robbery, and other crimes were, to all appearances, less heinous to their eyes than plural marriage and the union of the Church and State that was alleged to exist in Utah. Against these twin objects of their aversion, every legal, judicial and executive battering-ram was mainly directed."

The records of the courts will show that during the period under consideration, at every term of the court, indictments were presented for all kinds of crimes, and the calendars were made up of cases wherein the Territory as well as the United States was the plaintiff. And here this writer of the "history" gives free play to his fancy, and from his imagination evolves the charge that—

"Whether innocent or guilty, presidents, apostles, bishops, and other elders of influence, must be made to feel, to some extent, the thumbscrew and the rack, for the purpose of extorting from the head of the church a declaration of the church's surrender."

In this connection, it is truly stated that the requirement of the Mormon leaders was: "Come within the law and advise your people to likewise"—Why not? Subsequently, by doing so or promising and professing to do so, those leaders brought peace to the people. Notwithstanding the open admission that no innocent person was convicted, charges are made of hirelings entering the bedchambers of women and sick rooms; of breaking into houses by deputies armed with axes; of driving women at night in vehicles filled with profane and half-drunken men; of more than one woman perishing from the effects of the brutal treatment received; of fugitives being shot at, and, in one instance, a reputable citizen being slain without provocation by an over-zealous marshal. The historian gives no particulars—and it is certain that he would have given names, dates, and details, if he were able to do so. Such conduct on the part of government officers would have

215

been generally denounced to the courts and at Washington, and promptly punished—had there been occasion. The entire statement is false. Nor was any person slain by a deputy marshal other than the man Dalton, whose case will be considered further on. In the recital of his indictments against the government and its officers in Utah, the writer takes up the cases of some persons convicted in Arizona who were sentenced to the Detroit House of Correction. He proceeds to quote from the supposed speech of one Bean, a delegate to Congress from Arizona, made before the Committee on Territories, of the House, in which he said that they had convicted three Mormon bishops for unlawful cohabitation, and then sentenced them, under the law for polygamy, for three years. This sort of stuff must be made for consumption in the rural districts of Utah, where the plain farmers are not familiar with the procedure or the practice of courts. If the writer had consulted some of the church lawyers before incorporating this matter in his "history," he would have learned that such a judgment could have been reached by even a writ of habeas corpus, to say nothing of an appeal, and that the places for confinement of federal prisoners were designated by the Department of Justice, and not by the courts. That the Mormon church was determined that its followers should not agree to or obey the laws of the United States, prohibiting polygamy, etc., is candidly admitted by the historian in his reference to the case of Orson P. Arnold, who pleaded guilty to the charge of unlawful cohabitation and promised to obey the law. It is said therein that most of the Mormon people gazed upon the incident (?) with astonishment and grief; "that his example was followed by several of his brethren, and probably would have been by many more but for the firm stand taken by the [Deseret] News, and the no less stalwart position of the Church leaders, whose views that paper enunciated."

The fact of the matter is, that practically an entire people were in open hostility and rebellion against the government of the United States. They were not in arms, it is true, but they denied the authority of Congress to enact laws and prescribe offenses, and the authority of courts to interpret those laws and the constitution; and they denounced officers who had taken oaths to enforce the laws of the government, because they had refused to close their eyes to violations of laws and stay their hands from

216

executing them. They only admitted the authority of the courts when the decisions were in accord with their views, and from adverse decisions, appeal was always made to a "higher law than the constitution."

It is not strange, therefore, that the authorities, most of them being polygamists, as is admitted, should strenuously object to any one of the people pleading guilty to a charge of polygamy or unlawful cohabitation. Arnold's example was followed later by a number of polygamists. Bishop Sharp, "one of the foremost characters in the community," as stated by the historian, pleaded guilty to the charge of unlawful cohabitation and promised to obey the laws as interpreted by the courts. I cannot say, of my own knowledge, that Bishop Sharp was deprived of his bishopric because of this action, since no Gentile can speak as to the reasons moving the church authorities in such a case; but it was currently reported and stated by persons said to have knowledge, that the bishop was deposed, and for that reason.

A serious question as to the construction of the act of Congress defining the crime of unlawful cohabitation was made in the case of Angus M. Cannon. On behalf of the government, it was contended that the Edmunds law was directed against the status which fixed the habit and practice of living under the guise of marriage with two or more women—holding them out to the world as his wives—and not against the sexual offenses defined by the statute, and that the question of sexual intercourse between them was immaterial. This contention was strenuously opposed by the church attorneys, but was sustained by the territorial supreme court, and finally by the supreme court of the United States. (116 U. S., p. 55).

About this time, at a meeting in the tabernacle called for the purpose, "a declaration of grievances and protests" was made, directed to the President and people of the United States, in which, among other things, it was said:

"We protest against the partial administration of the Edmunds law—punishment of one class for practicing their religion and exempting from prosecution the votaries of lust and crime."

"The United States attorney and assistant attorney and commissioner, in pursuance of an invitation extended by the chairman of the meeting, attended and took their places in the gallery at the northeast end. The body of the house was largely filled

217

with women, and as the United States officers arose in their seats to pass down and out from the gallery, the entire audience in the body of the house arose to their feet and hissed, pointing their fingers at them. This action was but the natural result of the false and misleading claim made by and on behalf of the church authorities as to the true interpretation of the laws, and the bitter and continuous public and private denunciation of the officers by the church authorities and press, whereby the people were taught to look upon the officers as monsters of vice and corruption.

A noticeable event of the period was the flight from Utah of President George Q. Cannon, who was under indictment, and for whom a reward was offered by the United States marshal. Cannon was arrested in Humboldt county, Nevada, by Frank Fellows, sheriff of that county, who subsequently told me that Mr. Cannon was in disguise, and on a railroad train going west, at the time of his arrest. While in the custody of a deputy marshal upon his return trip to Utah, he jumped from the train at or near Promontory, and the officer, upon learning of his absence, did the same, and after some hours he was finally recaptured and brought into the city and placed under heavy bonds upon three charges— $25,000 in one, and $10,000 upon each of the other two. When called for trial Mr. Cannon did not appear, and these bonds were forfeited. The sureties on the $25,000 bond promptly paid the amount, but those for the $20,000 bond becoming recalcitrant, suit was brought by the government and judgment was given against them in the territorial supreme court. Although the case was appealed, Congress in the meantime intervened and remitted the penalty, and so it was never heard in the supreme court of the United States. In this connection Mr. Whitney ventures to again depart from the field of historical truth, and inspired by his feelings doubtless, charges the government officers with being much chagrined and disappointed at this ending of the Cannon case, for which the forfeiture of the bond was no adequate compensation. This conclusion was erroneous. Mr. Cannon, as a fugitive from justice presented a more striking and persuasive object-lesson to his followers than his presence as a prisoner in the penitentiary could possibly have done. And the flight of the president and his counselors, and that of others high in authority in the church, evidencing as it did a disinclination on the part of the leaders to accept the prescription prescribed for their followers—of going to prison for conscience-sake—did much to open the eyes of a deluded people as to the unnecessary folly of continuing a hopeless resistance to the enforcement of the law.

There were three celebrated cases which are dealt with by Mr. Whitney and require notice, to wit, those of Thompson, McMurrin and Hampton. William Thompson, Jr., was a deputy marshal residing at Beaver and in charge of that district, early in the year 1885. An indictment was found in that district against Edward M. Dalton for unlawful cohabitation. A warrant was issued and he was arrested, but made his escape from custody and continued at large for a period of about one year, and until he was killed as hereinafter related. In the meantime he was reindicted, and there were two warrants for his arrest in the hands of Deputy Marshal Thompson. In the spring of 1886, pursuant to information received, Thompson went to Parowan for the purpose of rearresting Dalton. The facts as disclosed before the grand and trial juries, were substantially these: Thompson was at a friend's house, which was situated a little back from the road which intersected a crossroad at right angles about one hundred yards or such a matter from the house; Dalton was driving some stock and came around the corner from the crossroad, down in front of the house. Thompson stepped out from the gateway of the lot and called upon Dalton to surrender, stating (which Dalton already knew) that he had a warrant, or warrants, for him. Dalton was riding a superior animal, and without a moment's hesitation swung his horse around and put him on the run toward the cross-road. Just as he was turning the corner the marshal shot him, and Dalton died from the wound. Thompson was indicted by the grand jury for manslaughter, and I prosecuted for the government, Thompson being defended by Mr. P. L. Williams. It was the duty of the United States attorney to state the law governing the case to the court and jury as he understood it, and it was the duty of the trial judge to direct the jury as to the law as he found it to be. In my address to the court, which I now have, transcribed from the reporter's notes, I reviewed the acts of Congress on the subject of crimes from the foundation of the government, with the conclusion that there was no federal statute defining felonies or misdemeanors, and that the distinction observed by the common law was not applicable and could not be made effective under our system. For instance, all felonies at common law were punishable with death, and, until modified by English statutes, accompanied by corruption of blood and forfeiture of estate. Under the barbarous criminal laws of England, which were enforced at and even later than the time of the American Revolution, the most trivial offenses were declared to be crimes and punishable with death, and in subsequent years by transportation for life—such as stealing a six-penny handkerchief from a linen-draper's shop, or a loaf of bread from a baker's counter. Upon an examination of the acts of Congress it appeared that the terms, "felony" and "misdemeanor," were applied indiscriminately to offenses where the punishment was imprisonment in penitentiaries, and that in many instances, crimes which carried long terms of imprisonment in such places were designated misdemeanors, and where the offense was declared to be a felony, there was no difference in the penalties imposed from those attached to other offenses. In a large majority of cases the offenses declared were not designated either as felonies or misdemeanors. Indeed, the word "misdemeanor," as used at times in the English law and found in the constitution of the United States, is classed with high crimes like treason—offenses of magnitude—and not restricted to petty offenses. In the very law under which Dalton was indicted, Congress, in defining the offenses of polygamy and unlawful cohabitation, designated the latter offense as a misdemeanor, but as to polygamy, made no classification. Both were made punishable in the same way, the only difference being in the extent of the punishment.

I further contended that the territorial law relative to arrests was not applicable, and was not the rule by which the acts of government officers, executing the process of the United States courts, were to be tested. The contention of the church paper and the historian, as shown in the "history", was that under no circumstances could a marshal of the United States, with a warrant for the arrest of a man for unlawful cohabitation, employ force to arrest the offender, unless he could lay hands upon him and restrain him by superior strength. He must not use arms to make the arrest, because the territorial law only permitted such use of force in the case of felons. Upon this theory and conception of the law, if an indicted man was on horseback or in a carriage drawn by a fast team, and the marshal was on foot, he would fully perform his duty by politely requesting the accused person to dismount from his horse or alight from his carriage and submit to arrest, and if the man refused and rode or drove away, that was the end of it. I repudiated this theory in my argument to the court, and contended that, if it should be found by the jury that Dalton had been indicted and had escaped, or knew that a warrant was out for him and had been called upon to surrender, the further and only question for the jury to determine was whether it was necessary to shoot in order to prevent his escape; that the government of the United States had not the power, through its officers, to employ all means necessary to arrest and bring to the judgment of its courts offenders who had been indicted for violation of its laws, was a new and inadmissable theory. The presiding judge so charged the jury, and the jury presumably found the facts as hereinbefore stated, and acquitted Thompson. Of course the acquittal was denounced by the church authorities and press, since from the beginning they had recognized no authority above that of their seers and prophets, and had denounced all law which did not conform to their ideas of right and justice. There was a full report of the trial, including the argument and the charge of the court, which was printed in pamphlet form and sent to Washington. The church lawyers and representatives complained at the Department of Justice, and to senators and representatives of Congress, basing their complaints upon the law alleged to be set out in the "history," but nothing came of it. The startling and strange conception that the government of the United States was powerless to make arrests through its officers of persons charged with violations of its laws by using force if necessary, received no recognition at Washington. On the contrary, the law as asserted by the district attorney, and announced by the court, was recognized and approved. Nevertheless, in the church press and from the church pulpits, the killing of Dalton was denounced as a cold-blooded murder, and Deputy Thompson and I were charged as murderers. Upon the conclusion of the trial the Deseret News in a frenzy of ferocious rage, with a wealth of invective and denunciation seldom equaled and never surpassed, pictured the officers as assassins who henceforth were to be denied mercy through all eternity. The historian has seen fit to print in his veracious book a part of this despicable and vicious libel. It was time that something was done to instruct the Deseret News in the law of libel, and particularly that "liberty of the press" did not mean license. I brought suit for Thompson, but did not "press the issue," as there was no necessity for so doing. A compromise was proposed (by the attorney for the News), and $1,000 paid and accepted in satisfaction of the claim. No action was brought by or on behalf of myself or the others included in the libel. The only intention was to impress upon the church press, in the only available way, the necessity of observing the law of libel.

Although Mr. Whitney reproduced in the "history" a part of the libel, thus preserving it in permanent form for the benefit of the large number of his co-religionists who have access to the book, his own statement of the case clearly shows the errors of his conclusions. Is it fair to suggest, that in dealing with men not of his faith, the historian deems himself relieved from the restraints of the moral law, and free to say of any one of such,—

"Thou art stained
With every crime 'gainst which the Decalogue
Thunders with all its thunder"—?

I would not go so far. I am inclined to the opinion that he did not intend so much, nor realize the enormity of his act in republishing a confessed libel.

\*    \*    \*    \*    \*    \*    \*    \*    \*    \*    \*    \*

The next case, that of Joseph W. McMurrin, is dealt with by Mr. Whitney in a very peculiar way. Whether intentionally or not, the most important facts are eliminated in his recounting, and the case is presented in the usual way, with the inferences against the government and U. S. deputy marshal. Collin lived within and toward the center of the block which was entered from State street through Social Hall alley. The alley was not lighted, and upon the evening in question—stated in the "history" to be that of November 28th—Collin was going to his home and encountered four persons who made an attack upon him in the alley. He testified before the grand jury that the men making the assault were armed with clubs, and in the darkness he could not see their faces, and had no knowledge of who they were. McMurrin, it seems, admits that he struck at Collin in the alleyway. Naturally Collin defended himself, and in such defense he shot McMurrin. Collin surrendered to the marshal, who immediately informed me of the occurrence. I directed him to hold Collin, and made complaint

before the United States commissioner, and had a warrant issued. Subsequently the police authorities made a demand
upon the marshal, and then upon me, for the prisoner, and I
refused to permit him to be delivered to the police. I had no
intention of permitting the deputy to be placed in the hands
of the city police, as I had a very vivid recollection of what
happened to the insane negro who killed Marshal Burt some
years before when the police brought him to the station. Mc-
Murrin was indicted (Mr. Whitney is mistaken in his statement that no indictment was found), and for a week or more
while waiting for him to be able to appear to plead to the
indictment, his attending physician came every morning to
the clerk's office and filed his professional statement that Mc-
Murrin was unable physically to attend the court. On the
very day when he went into hiding or left the Territory, this
physician, in my presence, wrote his usual report and it was
filed. Some hours after we learned that McMurrin had gone.
As I am informed, he went to Europe, was connected in some
way with foreign missions, and did not return for several
years. When he did return, an application was made to me
by his friends, and I think he came to see me personally, resulting in my dismissing the indictment against him. I cannot remember whether this dismissal occurred during the
time Mr. Dickson was United States attorney and I assistant,
or whether it happened during my administration as United
States attorney, beginning in 1889. There is no doubt that
Collin was attacked because of his zeal and efficiency as a
deputy marshal, and the silly statement of McMurrin that he
had a difficulty with Collin, and having ran against him in the
dark alley, he struck at him, when Collin fired, is absurd. He
fails to account for the presence of the other men armed
with clubs, and gives no reason for his own presence at the
place.

\*    \*    \*    \*    \*    \*    \*    \*    \*    \*    \*    \*

The case of Hampton deserves more extended notice, since
it was made the subject of a sneering criticism by the historian, and moreover completely illustrates the disposition of
those who were arrayed against the government to—

"Compound for sins they are inclined to,
By damning those they have no mind to."

223

The thought seems to have been that if it should be ascertained that others of the non-Mormon population were found to be guilty of offenses against the law, it would be a sufficient answer to the prosecutions which were being brought by the government. In this view, certain prominent and influential Mormon citizens of Salt Lake City conceived the idea of opening houses of ill-fame in certain localities of the municipality for the purpose of enticing prominent government officials and others into the commission of offenses, in order that they might be detected and publicity be given to their crimes. A concise and complete statement of the matter is found in the report of the grand jury for the third judicial district of the Territory, made in December of the year 1885, and I quote therefrom as follows:

"Since the year A. D. 1876 there has been a statute of the Territory prohibiting the keeping of, residing in, or resorting to houses of ill-fame for the purpose of prostitution or lewdness. During a great part, if not all, of the period, ordinances of the municipality of Salt Lake City upon the same subject have been in existence. Under these ordinances a few weeks ago a number of prosecutions were instituted under circumstances which very generally attracted public attention. These proceedings were summarily brought to an end because of a ruling of this court, determining the questions of law immediately involved, adversely to the city. The attention of the grand jury, as well as the public, was, however, directed to certain matters connected with these prosecutions, and in the discharge of our duty, as understood by us, we have investigated the same as thoroughly as the means at our command would permit.

"Officers of the county and city government, together with private citizens, have appeared before us and been sworn and examined, and the present result of our inquiry is embodied in indictments herewith returned. We are not content, however, to pass the matter over without further and emphatic expression condemnatory of the methods and practices hereinafter mentioned. Sometime in April or May last, an officer of the city government not connected with the police, with others unknown at present to the grand jury, entered into a conspiracy to open houses of assignation and ill-fame within the city limits, for the avowed purpose of entrapping weak and vicious people into the commission of offenses against chastity and morality, in order that all such might be exposed and punished in the courts. This scheme involved the renting and fitting up of houses for the purpose, the employment

224

of public and private prostitutes, the conversion of the police bureau into a nest of spotters and spies, and the expenditure of a large sum of money. For years there have been well-known houses of prostitution in Salt Lake which have been under police surveillance, and at stated periods have contributed materially to the revenues of the municipality. Several of these houses are situated on the main and prominent streets of the city, and with their keepers and proprietors have been, and are by reputation, generally known in the community.

"We do not understand that the scheme above mentioned contemplated the investigation of these places, nor the enforcement of the law against those who resided therein or resorted thereto for the purposes of prostitution or lewdness. On the contrary, as appears by the evidence before us, the plan was conceived and carried into effect without reference to the suppression of existing nuisances, but with a design of using the criminal law as a snare for the weak and immoral, and with the object in part, at least, of creating a great public scandal. In pursuance of this scheme, houses were rented and furnished on West Temple street, and women placed in possession thereof. These houses were so altered and arranged in their interior that persons could be placed to observe all that transpired within, and every member of the police force of Salt Lake City, with two honorable exceptions, John Y. Smith and William Calder, volunteered his services as a spy and informer in aid of the conspiracy. The women were hired to perform their parts, and their exertions stimulated by the promise of exorbitant sums for their success in entrapping high officials. One of these creatures was promised $1,000 in the event of her being able to draw the governor of the Territory into her toils.

"In the course of their operations, these women conveyed notes of invitation to many prominent officials and citizens, requesting interviews on business at the places designated. The following, leaving the names blank, is a sample of these notes, delivered by messenger boys:

"Salt Lake City, July 25, 1885.

"Dear Sir: "If convenient, I would be pleased to have you call to see me this afternoon or about dusk this evening. I want to see you on particular business. Please send answer by messenger boy when you will call.
Respectfully,
_____"

"We are informed by persons engaged in this infamous plot, that from their secret posts of observation they from time to time personally witnessed all that took place in apartments in these houses visited by men and women who were weak and depraved enough to respond to the opportunities presented to them. Their names were taken and the evidence noted for future reference and use.

"When the exposure of this conspiracy was at hand the houses were closed. One woman was sent to California upon a ticket furnished her. Another was driven to Francklyn by a police officer, who had previously purchased her a ticket, and then took the train for Denver under an assumed name. One of these women was paid by the city official above referred to, $300 or $400, and the other, $700 for her services. When the women were safe out of the Territory, complaints were filed, warrants issued and arrests made, and the community thrown into a state of excitement and alarm. The money employed in this scheme, we are told by its prime mover, was paid by one of the high officials of Salt Lake City. It is claimed that the money was raised by private subscription. We have been unable to ascertain that any part of it came from the public treasury. Neither the mayor, chief of police, nor other city official, except as herein stated, so far as we can learn, were advised of the proceeding until the plot was ripe. All of the police officers engaged in it, it is claimed, performed the services required when off duty. One of them states that his services were rendered 'for the good of the cause.' We have promptly indicted all persons connected with this unlawful and criminal undertaking against whom we could procure evidence, but we are not satisfied to rest here without publicly directing the attention of the municipal and county officers to the fact that a great crime has been perpetrated.

"We do not understand that the criminal law of the Territory was designed to aid scoundrelly spies, sneaks and informers in enticing and encouraging well-disposed persons to commit crime, nor to tempt weak and wicked persons to disobey the law. The law is humane and considerate, and has for its object the prevention of crime and the reformation as well as the punishment of offenders. It does not, we think, contemplate the commission of crimes in order that additional crimes may be committed, and the last offenders exposed and punished."

It is stated in the "history," that a very large number of arrests were made by the police for offenses charged to have been committed within the houses referred to in the grand jury report, and that upon their reaching the district court all of them were dismissed by the prosecuting officer, and a criticism is based thereon. Upon the motion to dismiss, made in the district court, I assumed full responsibility, as I do now, for the action taken by the United States attorney's office. In support of the motion, I made the argument rest upon the fact that there was an unlawful conspiracy to induce, and not to prevent or punish, crime; that the thought underlying this conspiracy was based upon a conception that if Gentiles and strangers to the Mormon people were guilty of offenses against law and morals, that such fact would be evidence of unfairness in prosecution for violation of the laws of the United States against polygamy and unlawful cohabitation. Such a conclusion was, of course, a non sequitur. Conviction for crime upon the evidence of persons engaged in inviting and tempting people to commit crime has always been abhorrent to civilized peoples. In the argument made at the time, as reported, it was said:

"Your Honor will recollect in English history a long line of cases where there was rebellion threatening the British throne, and where the interests of the hour and the demands of justice required that this class of persons should be used and employed in bringing to justice offenders against the law. I say your Honor will recollect, how the English and Irish people steadily set their faces against that class of testimony, and it took all the power of the British crown and the judges under it to enforce verdicts in the teeth and face of the public conscience. In this country it is believed that no prosecutions founded upon that kind of evidence can be maintained, for the reason that the public conscience is against it, and the public conscience as represented in the jury box, will not permit the law to be prostituted and dishonored in that way.

"Now, if that be true generally as to persons known as informers and spies, how much more true is it of persons who are not entitled to even take those elevated names? They are not raised to the dignity of informers and spies; they are not men engaged in ferreting out crime—they are men who are producing crime—who by their money, influence or efforts, are debauching the public mind and attempting to lead the young and old down the very path that it was designed to keep them from going. Men and women, old and young, were to be drawn into their toils in order that they may have the supreme happiness and satisfaction of scandalizing reputations and breaking hearts here and there, or something of that kind."

In the "history" none of the facts relative to the opening of houses and paying out of money to prostitutes and the providing of places of observation within the houses are mentioned, and the whole and entire discussion of the subject is so unjust and unfair that its perusal simply excites resentment and disgust. Hampton was one of the leading spirits in this deplorable enterprise, and himself produced the evidence which resulted in his indictment by the grand jury and his conviction by the trial jury.

The writer of the "history" states that Hampton was convicted on the same kind of evidence that the district attorney had pronounced unworthy. Here again he falls into error. If the historian was ignorant in fact in the premises, nevertheless, if he had desired to be fair in the matter, he could have easily ascertained that Hampton had voluntarily gone before the grand jury, and taken the stand as a witness before the trial jury; that he was warned by the prosecuting officer in each instance that he was not expected to testify, and that if he did so voluntarily, what he said would be and could be used against him. He replied in substance that he had nothing to conceal, and that he was ready to tell all that he knew about the matter under investigation. There never has been, under any sytem of law or in any court organized for the trial of criminals, any prohibition against convicting a man of crime upon his own confession or testimony. Hampton was convicted and sentenced to an imprisonment of one year in the penitentiary, and his case was appealed to the supreme court of the Territory.

I may well close the reference to this case with an excerpt from the illuminating opinion of the court in affirming the judgment, delivered by Judge Powers, as follows:

"A peculiar state of facts is shown by the record in this case. It would seem that lewd women were employed to open houses of ill-fame in the city of Salt Lake. It is claimed that men who had not sufficient self-respect or morality to resist such allurements were beguiled therein, and that the unholy practices with the women were watched from adjoining rooms through peep-holes by members of the police force. It is insisted that this was done in the interest of virtue and morality. The defendant, Brigham Y. Hampton, is a prominent member of the Church of Jesus Christ of Latter-day Saints, commonly known as the Mormon church, and this fact becomes material in considering the objection to the panel of jurors hereafter referred to. He has held many positions of trust in Salt Lake City, and at the time of his conviction he was the collector of license of that city, and was also a member of the police force. In the spring of 1885 he, or some one connected with him, conceived the idea of employing prostitutes to do what he in his testimony, terms 'detective work.' He states that he had observed there were a great many street-walkers in this city, and that many young girls were being led from the path of virtue. He seems to have consecrated himself to a great work. He proposed to put an end to houses of ill-fame and prostitution, and he went about this work by immediately opening more houses. He hired his own prostitutes, he opened his own houses, and from points of vantage he and his co-laborers began a study of the bestial practices that occurred within the dens of infamy which he had established. He does not appear to have been the only one concerned in this trans-action, but he and a man named Salmon seem to have been the moving spirits. We shall not deal with any more of the details than we are compelled to do in determining the case; but this does not and should not prevent us from expressing our disapproval of the conduct of the defendant, or from con-demning, as the highest court of this Territory, the wicked and disgraceful conspiracy disclosed." (4 Utah Reports, 259).

I have thus dealt with some of the most prominent features of the erroneous, misleading and unfair accounts and ac-companying criticism contained in the "History of Utah," not in any spirit of resentment, or with the inclination to revive any of the bitterness of the past, but because I deem it my duty to voice this protest against what has been heretofore regarded as **history,** when in fact it is but a garbled record of events made for the purpose of defending the indefensible.

C. S. VARIAN.

Salt Lake City, Utah, April, 1914.

---

In addition to the above, Mr. Varian could have added the following quotation from Whitney's history, Vol. III, page 413, which further illustrates its character:

"Between midnight and daybreak, on September 13, 1885, the residences of United States Attorney Dickson, Assistant United States Attorney Varian, and United States Commis-sioner McKay, were visited by certain individuals armed with improvised grenades—slop jars filled with filth (human ex-crement), which were thrown through the windows and shat-tered against the (inside) walls of their dwellings, alarming the sleeping inmates, damaging furniture and other property to some extent, but inflicting no personal injury. * * * As a matter of course, the affair created a sensation, and efforts were made to magnify it far beyond its due proportions. It was but natural that the three officials, knowing their unpopularity with the Mormons, should hold them responsible for the deed, and that they would be accused of it must have been foreseen by the perpetrators. It was precisely for this reason that the Mormons denounced the imputation of guilt on the part of any of their number. It was difficult for them to believe, after all the forbearance they had shown towards those whom they deemed their oppressors, that they had any one among them so unwise—to put it no stronger—as to gratify malice, personal or communical, under circumstances that could not fail to cast odium upon the whole people and injure instead of benefiting their cause. That they had something to lose and nothing to gain by the outrage must be admitted. As stated, its authors were never discovered. The police were unsuccessful in ferreting out their identity. The Associated Press agent, in his telegraphed account of the affair, said that parties of Mormons did the deed, but was careless enough to add—'No clue to the perpetrators.'"

In the quotation above Whitney, by intendment, implicates the Gentiles and acquits the members of his church, notwithstanding he well knew that the unpopularity of the officers who were the victims of that atrocious outrage was not caused by any wrongful act committed against the Mormons, but simply occurred because they had performed their official duties by a vigorous, faithful and efficient enforcement of the acts of Congress against polygamic crimes, and for so performing their official duties they were outraged—not by Gentiles striving to injure the Mormon cause—but by some vicious and fanatical members of the church.

The foregoing quotation is only imitative of the duplicity of Brigham Young in a sermon delivered in 1863, six years after the perpetration of the Mountain Meadows massacre wherein he said:

"When a company of emigrants were traveling on the southern route to California, nearly all of the company were destroyed by Indians. The unfortunate affair has been laid to the charge of the whites. * * * I told Governor Cummings that if he would take an unprejudiced judge into that district where that horrid affair occurred, I would pledge myself that every man in the region round about should be forthcoming, when called for, to be condemned or acquitted. * * * But to this day they have not touched the matter for fear the Mormons will be acquitted of the charge of having a hand in it, and our enemies would be deprived of a favorite topic to talk about when urging hostilities against us—'the

Mountain Meadows massacre! only to think of the Mountain Meadows massacre!' "

Respecting the murder of Doctor Robinson, he in substance, as before shown, stated that he hoped the murderers would be discovered, for it would show the wickedness of their own clique who planned the deed intending that it should be attributed to the Mormons, on account of the doctor having had difficulty with the Mormon authorities. Of the murder of Brassfield, in a sermon he said: " * * * Whether he was killed by some one who had made a catspaw of him in his ill-starred operations, or by some one of his acquaintances to settle a grudge, thinking of course it would be laid upon the Mormons, is yet to be learned."

## CONCLUSION.

In these pages I have shown some of the radical evils for the correction of which the Liberal party in Utah was organized; also the measures originated and supported by its members to accomplish that purpose. The exceptionally stringent acts of Congress were rendered necessary by the pugnacity with which the hierarchy of the Mormon church persisted in maintaining its obnoxious system, and in defeating the execution of the laws framed for punishment of polygamists and perpetrators of a certain class of homicides. Such acts, though seemingly very rigorous, were the only available means by which the evils existing in Utah could be eradicated. The priesthood, therefore, and not the Liberal party, is responsible for any hardships which its adherents may have suffered from those radical measures. The Gentiles in the Territory would have shown themselves unworthy of American citizenship had they failed to organize and make a united effort to Americanize Utah. The purpose in organizing the Liberal party was to free the masses of the Mormon people from the arbitrary control by the priesthood of temporal and political affairs, and not to persecute or injure them.

Through the persistent efforts of that party, the change which occurred upon the issuance of the Woodruff manifesto and the admission of the Territory into the Union as a State, under the pledge given by the authorities of the church, was brought about. This change was an unqualified blessing to the people. Since that time Mormons have ceased to be Ishmaelites, and we no longer hear the proverbial expression, "Those who are not for us are against us." Both social and business relations in the State have been greatly improved. There no longer exists such bitter antagonism as was prevalent in former days, and, if I may be pardoned the personal reference, I will say that my election as a member of the supreme court of the State is conclusive evidence that this is true.

I venture to say that no persons, except extremely fanatical ones, would today favor such a system as was established and maintained for many years in the Territory by the priesthood of the Mormon church. While the political power of the priest-hood is not so absolute in the State as it was in the Territory, it still has the power to elect or defeat any party ticket, or candidate for office, except in a few cities in which there is a majority of Gentile electors. In Idaho and in each of the other states where large Mormon settlements exist, there are enough Mormon electors whose votes are sufficient to secure the success of any one of the political parties in favor of which they may be cast at any general election. As those electors are pledged by their oath-bound church covenants to obey the priesthood in all matters, the political power of the first presidency of the Mormon church is as predominant over members of the Mormon church in those states as it is over the members of that church in Utah. That power can only be annulled in Utah as elsewhere by the increas-ing immigration of Gentiles, and the liberalization of the rising generation of the Mormons. I hope that in future the high of-ficials of the Mormon church will abstain from performing those acts which show the priesthood is still desirous of controlling elections. It was this policy which caused the organization of the American party. If this be done, then the unfortunate local is-sues existing in several cities of the State will terminate, and thereafter there will be no political party division among the people except on national party lines, "a consummation devoutly to be wished."

Beyond a question many plural marriages have occurred in the State since the promulgation of the manifesto, yet none of the guilty parties have been arrested by the civil authorities and only about six have been disciplined by the church authorities, who are undubitably aware of the guilt of the persons who have contracted such unlawful alliances. The members of the high priesthood could have procured the arrest and punishment of all the guilty parties had they so desired. Their failure to do so, or even to have them disciplined by the church, indicates in no un-certain degree a connivance on their part. In the majority report of the Senate committee on the Smoot case, Vol. IV, page 476, of the published report of the proceedings states:

"A sufficient number of specific instances of the taking of plural wives since the manifesto of 1890, so-called, have been shown by the evidence as having taken place among officers of the Mormon church to demonstrate the fact that the leaders of this church, the first presidency and the twelve apostles, connive at the practice of taking plural wives, and have done so ever since the manifesto was issued, and which purports to put an end to the practice."

The law against polygamy will not be enforced in Utah so long as the priesthood retains its present power, therefore Congress should be authorized by an amendment of the constitution of the United States to legislate upon the subject of polygamy.

While a notable improvement of the conditions in Utah has come about, the tenets of the Mormon church have not been changed. Its financial system is still a menace, and the alleged revelation of polygmay has not been annulled, nor has the practice of polygamy been positively prohibited. The Woodruff manifesto neither abolished that revelation nor forbade the practice of polygamy. In it, Woodruff only advises the Latter-day Saints to refrain from contracting plural marriages, as appears from the following quotation therefrom:

"To Whom It May Concern:   *  *  *   Inasmuch as laws have been enacted by Congress forbidding plural marriage, which laws have been pronounced constitutional by the court of last resort, I hereby declare my intention to submit to those laws and to use my influence with the members of the church over which I preside to have them do likewise.  *  *  * And I now publicly declare that my advice to the Latter-day Saints is to refrain from contracting any marriages forbidden by the laws of the land."

President Woodruff, Joseph F. Smith, now the president of the Mormon church, and other high officials of that church, stated under oath, at a hearing had before a master in chancery appointed by the supreme court of Utah, that the manifesto applied to unlawful cohabitation as well as to polygamy. (See Appendix.) Yet Joseph F. Smith, in his testimony before the Senate committee in the Smoot case, testified that he had wilfully violated the law against unlawful cohabitation. The following is a quotation from his testimony, Vol. I, page 133 of the printed report of the Smoot case:

"I have cohabited with my wives, not openly, that is—not in a manner that I thought would be offensive to my neighbors; they have borne me children since 1890. I have done it knowing I am amenable to the law."

He further stated that he had five wives who had borne him eleven children since 1890, each wife having given birth to one or two of those children. The law against unlawful cohabitation has not been and is not at present being obeyed, and as before shown, a large number of known plural marriages have been formed since the manifesto and the admission of Utah as a State. It is clear from the language of the manifesto that the laws which Woodruff advised the Latter-day Saints to obey were those passed by Congress relative to polygamy and unlawful cohabitation, and which were held by the United States supreme court to be constitutional. Upon the admission of Utah as a State, those laws of Congress ceased to have any force in the new State. Upon such admission there ceased to be any law in Utah to which the manifesto applied, and therefore it became nugatory. In view of that fact, the number of known plural marriages which have occurred since the manifesto and the admission of the Territory into the Union, the failure of the prosecuting officers of the State to apprehend the offenders, and the quiescence of the high priesthood respecting the guilty parties, the Congress of the United States should be authorized to legislate upon the subject of polygamy.

While it is inconsistent with American citizenship for members of the Mormon church to enter into oath-bound obligations to obey the Mormon priesthood in temporal affairs, yet there is no legal remedy for the evil; and it will continue to exist until there arises, among the members of that church, a general sentiment against the practice, or rather, condition of servitude.

Joseph F. Smith, in his examination in the Smoot case (see Vol. I, page 192, of the official report of that proceeding), testified as follows:

"Here is Aunt Bathsheba Smith, who received her endowments in Nauvoo **as they are now given in the temples.** She is a living witness, and, if necessary, she will tell us that she received those privileges under the direction of Joseph Smith. Opponents say that Brigham Young established the endowments, and also plural marriage, but here is a witness who knows better."

From the testimony of this person it would appear that the endowment ceremonies have not been changed, and it follows that the oath-bound penal covenants are still being entered into by those who receive their endowments.

In the naturalization case before mentioned, Henry W. Lawrence, at present one of the five Commissioners governing Salt Lake City, and whose standing is as high as that of any man in Utah, testified that those who received their endowment covenant to avenge the blood of the prophets, Joseph and Hyrum Smith (who have sealed their testimony with their blood), were commanded to perpetuate this grewsome horror by teaching this doctrine to their children and their children's children unto the third and fourth generation, and to obey the priesthood in all things.

\*　\*　\*　\*　\*　\*　\*　\*　\*　\*　\*　\*

In conclusion, it is indeed regrettable, and even humiliating, to all who have endeavored to advance the good name of Utah and to place her in a position of equality in the sisterhood of states, to record that the solemn pledges made to the federal government by the Mormon priesthood for the purpose of procuring general amnesty, the restoration of escheated church property and the admission of the Territory as a State, have not been fulfilled.

To the unprejudiced reader, the publication of these Reminiscences will, I trust, appear justifiable for the reasons stated in my preface. It is furthest from my purpose to herein reopen old sores, or to revive the old animosities which are happily fast dying out, but, in the absence of any authentic treatise on the true history of many important events in that "storm and stress" period of our State, I have deemed it my duty to the present as well as to future generations to relate the undeniable facts pertaining to those events, and thus to refute the calumnious slanders cast upon the names of men who, animated by purely disinterested motives, have striven to correct the evils existing when Utah was a Territory, some of which are herein disclosed.

An abridged history of Utah has been written by Whitney which I am informed has been adopted as a text-book in the schools outside of Salt Lake City. The same guile which characterizes Whitney's larger history of Utah is present in his abridgment. The use as a text-book of the latter in the public schools is well calculated to create wrong impressions in the minds of the pupils respecting past occurrences in Utah. The action of Whitney in making false statements, his failure to state facts which were indispensable in a true history, his imputation of improper motives to those who opposed the hierarchy of Utah and strove to correct prevalent abuses, "was as dishonest as it was despicable."

# APPENDIX

## HOW AMNESTY WAS OBTAINED.

Below is found the petition through which universal amnesty was obtained for offenders under the Edmunds law. It was signed by the first presidency of the Mormon church, and by all the apostles. Then it was submitted to Governor Thomas, Judge Zane, and other prominent men who had been pronounced in their insistence that the laws should be obeyed in Utah, and they in turn certified to the full belief that the petition was sincere, and that if amnesty should be granted there would be no violation of faith.

"To the President of the United States:

"We, the First Presidency and Apostles of the Church of Jesus Christ of Latter-day Saints, beg respectfully to represent to your Excellency the following facts:

"We formerly taught to our people that polygamy or celestial marriage, as commanded by God through Joseph Smith, was right; that it was a necessity to man's highest exaltation in the life to come.

"That doctrine was publicly promulgated by our president, the late Brigham Young, forty years ago and was steadily taught and impressed upon the Latter-day Saints up to September, 1890. Our people are devout and sincere, and they accepted the doctrine, and many personally embraced and practiced polygamy.

"When the Government sought to stamp the practice out, our people, almost without exception, remained firm, for they, while having no desire to oppose the Government in anything, still felt that their lives and their honor as men was pledged to a vindication of their creed, and that their duty to those whose lives were a part of their own was a paramount one, to fulfill which they had no right to count anything, not even their own lives, as standing in the way.

"Following this conviction, hundreds endured arrest, trial, fine and imprisonment, and the immeasurable suffering borne by the faithful people no language can describe. That suffering in abated form still continues.

"More, the Government added disfranchisement to its other punishments for those who clung to their faith and fulfilled its covenants.

"According to our creed, the head of our church received from time to time revelations for the religious guidance of his people. In September, 1890, the present head of the church in anguish and prayer cried to God for help for his flock, and received permission to advise the members of the Church of Jesus Christ of Latter-day Saints that the law commanding polygamy was henceforth suspended.

"At the great semi-annual Conference which was held a few days later this was submitted to the people—numbering many thousands and representing every community of the people in Utah—and was by them in the most solemn manner accepted as the future rule of their lives.

"They have been faithful to the covenant made that day.

"At the late October Conference, after a year had passed by, the matter was once more submitted to the thousands of people gathered together, and they again in the most potential manner ratified the solemn covenant.

"This being the true situation, and believing that the object of this Government was simply the vindication of its own authority and to compel obedience to the laws, and that it takes no pleasure in persecution, we respectfully pray that full amnesty may be extended to all who are under disabilities because of the operation of the so-called Edmunds-Tucker law.

"Our people are scattered; homes are made desolate; many are still imprisoned; others are banished or in hiding.

"Our hearts bleed for these. In the past they followed our counsels, and while they are thus afflicted our souls are in sackcloth and ashes.

"We believe there is nowhere in the Union a more loyal people than the Latter-day Saints. They know no other country except this; they expect to live and die on this soil.

"When the men of the South who were in rebellion against the government in 1865 threw down their arms and asked for recognition along the old lines of citizenship, the Government hastened to grant their prayer.

"To be at peace with the Government and in harmony with their fellow-citizens who are not of their faith, and to share in the confidence of the Government and people, our people have voluntarily put aside something which all their lives they have believed to be a sacred principle.

"Have they not the right to ask for such clemency as comes when the claims of both law and justice have been fully liquidated?

"As shepherds of a patient and suffering people, we ask amnesty for them, and pledge our faith and honor for their future.

"And your petitioners will ever pray.

"Salt Lake City, December, 1891."

# PRESIDENT HARRISON'S PROCLAMATION.

Washington, D. C., Jan. 4, 1893.

Whereas, Congress, by a statute approved March 22, 1882, and by statutes in furtherance and amendment thereto, defined the crimes of bigamy, polygamy, and unlawful cohabitation in the territories and other places within the exclusive jurisdiction of the United States, and prescribed a penalty for such crimes; and

Whereas, on or about the 6th day of October, 1890, the Church of Latter-day Saints, commonly known as the "Mormon" church, through its president, issued a manifesto proclaiming the purpose of said church no longer to sanction the practice of polygamous marriages and calling upon all members and adherents of said church to obey the laws of the United States in reference to said subject-matter; and

"Whereas, it is represented that since the date of said declaration the members and adherents of said church generally obeyed said laws and abstained from plural marriages and polygamous cohabitation; and

Whereas, by a petition dated December 19, 1891, the officials of said church, pledging the membership thereof to the faithful obeyance of the laws against plural marriages and unlawful cohabitation, applied to me to grant amnesty for past offenses against said laws, which request a very large number of influential non-Mormons resident of territories, also strongly urged; and

Whereas, the Utah Commissioners in their report bearing date of September 15, 1892, recommended that said petition be granted, and said amnesty proclaimed under the proper conditions as to the future observance of the law with a view to the encouragement of those now disposed to become law-abiding citizens; and

Whereas, during the past two years such amnesty has been granted individual applicants in a very large number of cases, conditioned upon the faithful observance of the laws of the United States against unlawful cohabitation, and there are now pending many more such applications;

Now, therefore, I, Benjamin Harrison, President of the United States, by virtue of the powers in me vested, do hereby declare and grant full amnesty and pardon to all persons liable to the penalties of said act, by reason of unlawful cohabitation under the color of polygamous or plural marriage, who since November 1, 1890, have abstained from such unlawful cohabitation, but upon the express condition that they shall in future obey the laws of the United States hereinbefore named, and not otherwise. Those who shall fail to avail themselves of the clemency hereby offered will be vigorously prosecuted.

BENJAMIN HARRISON.

By The President:

JOHN W. FOSTER, Secretary of State.

# PRESIDENT CLEVELAND'S PROCLAMATION.

Washington, D. C., September 25th, 1894.

Whereas, Congress, by statute approved March 22, 1882, and by statutes in furtherance and amendment thereof, defined the crimes of bigamy, polygamy, and unlawful cohabitation in the territories and other places within the exclusive jurisdiction of the United States, and prescribed the penalties for such crimes, and

Whereas, on or about the 6th day of October, 1890, the Church of the Latter-day Saints, commonly known as the "Mormon" church, through its president, issued a manifesto proclaiming the purposes of said church no longer to sanction the practice of polygamous marriages, and calling upon all members and adherents of said church to obey said laws of the United States in reference to said subject-matter; and

Whereas, on the 4th day of January, A. D. 1893, Benjamin Harrison, then President of the United States, did declare and grant full pardon and amnesty to certain offenders under said acts upon condition of future obedience to their requirements, as is fully set forth in said proclamation of amnesty and pardon, and

Whereas, upon the evidence now furnished me I am satisfied the members and adherents of said church generally abstain from plural marriages and polygamous cohabitation, and are now living in obedience to the laws, and the time has now arrived when the interests of public justice and morality will be promoted by the granting of amnesty and pardon to all such offenders as complied with the conditions of said proclamation including such of said offenders as have been convicted under the provisions of said act;

Now, therefore, I, Grover Cleveland, President of the United States, by virtue of the powers in me vested, do hereby declare and grant a full amnesty and pardon to all persons who have in violation of said acts committed either of the offenses of polygamy, adultery, or unlawful cohabitation, under the color of polygamous or plural marriage, and who, having been convicted of violation of said act, are now suffering deprivation of civil rights in consequence of the same, excepting persons as have not complied with the conditions contained in said executive proclamation of January 4, 1893.

GROVER CLEVELAND.

By the President:

RICHARD C. OLNEY, Secretary of State.

## CONDITION OF RESTORATION.

Congress gave back escheated property because practices in violation of laws were understood to be stopped.

When Congress, in 1893, gave back to the Mormon church the personal property and money held by Receiver Henry W. Lawrence, it was with the evident understanding that all polygamous practices in Utah had been abandoned. This is shown clearly by the joint resolution of Congress restoring the property, which follows:

"Joint Resolution No. 11, providing for the disposition of certain personal property and money now in the hands of a Receiver of the Church of Jesus Christ of Latter-day Saints, appointed by the Supreme Court of Utah, and authorizing its application to the charitable purposes of said church.

"Whereas, the Corporation of the Church of Jesus Christ of Latter-day Saints was dissolved by act of Congress of March 3, 1887, and

"Whereas, the personal property and money belonging to said corporation is now in the hands of a receiver appointed by the Supreme Court of the Territory of Utah; and

"Whereas, according to a decision of the Supreme Court of the United States, the said property, in absence of other disposition by act of Congress, is subject to be applied to such charitable uses, lawful in their nature, as may most nearly correspond to the purposes which said property was originally destined; and

"Whereas, said property is the result of contribution and donations made by members of said church, and was designed to be devoted to the charitable uses thereof under the direction and control of the First Presidency of said church; and

"Whereas, said church has discontinued the practice of polygamy, and no longer encourages or gives countenance in any manner to practices in violation of law, or contrary to good morals, or public policy; and if the said personal property is restored to the said church it will not be devoted to any such unlawful purpose; therefore

"Be it resolved, by the Senate and House of Representatives of the United States of America, in Congress assembled, that the said personal property and money now in the hands of such receiver, not arising from the sale or rents of real estate since March 3, 1887, be, and the same is hereby restored to the said Church of Jesus Christ of Latter-day Saints, to be applied under the direction and control of the First

Presidency of said church to the charitable purposes and uses thereof, that is to say: For the payment of the debts for which said church is legally or equitably liable, for the relief of the poor and distressed members of said church, for the education of the children of said members, and for the building and repair of houses of worship for the use of said church, but in which the rightfulness of the practice of polygamy shall not be inculcated. And the said receiver, after deducting the expenses of his receivership, under the Supreme Court of the Territory of Utah, is hereby required to deliver the said property and money to the persons now constituting the Presidency of said church, or to such person or persons as they may designate, to be held and applied generally to the charitable uses and purposes of said church as aforesaid.

"Approved October 25, 1893."

# THE ANTI-POLYGAMY MANIFESTO.

The following is the Manifesto of President Wilford Woodruff, of the Mormon church, relative to polygamy, issued September 24, 1890:

To Whom it May Concern: Press dispatches having been sent for political purposes from Salt Lake City, which have been widely published, to the effect that the Utah Commission in their recent report to the Secretary of the Interior, allege that plural marriages are still being solemnized, and that forty or more such marriages have been contracted in Utah since last June, or during the past year; also that in public discourses the leaders of the church have taught, encouraged and urged the continuance of the practice of polygamy;

"I therefore, as President of the Church of Jesus Christ of Latter-day Saints, do hereby, in the most solemn manner declare that these charges are false. We are not teaching polygamy, or plural marriage, nor permitting any person to enter into its practice, and I deny that either forty or any other number of plural marriages have during that period been solemnized in our temple, or in any other place in the Territory.

"One case has been reported in which the parties alleged that the marriage was performed in the Endowment House in Salt Lake City in the spring of 1889, but I have not been able to learn who performed the ceremony; whatever was done in this manner was without my knowledge. In consequence of this alleged occurrence, the Endowment House was by my instruction taken down without delay.

"Inasmuch as laws have been enacted by Congress forbidding plural marriage, which laws have been pronounced constitutional by the court of last resort, I hereby declare my intention to submit to those laws and to use my influence with the members of the church over which I preside to have them do likewise.

"There is nothing in my teachings to the church or in those of my associates, during the time specified, which can reasonably be construed to inculcate or encourage polygamy, and when any Elder of the church has used language which appeared to convey any such teaching he has been promptly reproved. And I now publicly declare that my advice to the Latter-day Saints is to refrain from contracting any marriage forbidden by the law of the land.

WILFORD WOODRUFF,

"President of the Church of Jesus Christ of Latter-day Saints.

The foregoing was read on October 4, 1890, to the Mormon Conference then in session, and Lorenzo Snow thereupon offered the following, which was sustained unanimously:

"I move that, recognizing Wilford Woodruff as the President of the Church of Jesus Christ of Latter-day Saints, and the only man on the earth at the present time who holds the keys of the sealing ordinances, we consider him fully authorized by virtue of his position to issue the Manifesto which has been read in our hearing and which is dated September 24, 1890, and that, as a church in General Conference assembled, we accept his declaration concerning plural marriage as authoritative and binding."

# WHAT THE CHURCH LEADERS PROMISED.

### They State Under Oath the the Manifesto was Meant to Stop Unlawful Cohabitation as well as Polygamous Marriages.

After the seizure by the United States government of the real estate and personal property belonging to the Mormon church in 1891, Judge C. F. Loofbourow of Salt Lake City was appointed a master in chancery by the supreme court of the Territory to take testimony and report as to the most advantageous disposition of the money then in the hands of Receiver Henry W. Lawrence. At the hearing, which was held before Master Loofbourow on October 19 and 20, 1891, a number of prominent church officials testified with respect to the sources from which the fund had been derived, as well as to the disposition which had theretofore been made of it. Among the witnesses who testified at this hearing were Presidents Wilford Woodruff, George Q. Cannon and Joseph F. Smith, Apostles Lorenzo Snow, Anthon H. Lund and others. During the examination, Presidents Woodruff, Cannon and Smith, and Apostles Snow and Lund were subjected to a searching cross-examination by United States Attorney C. S. Varian with respect to the exact meaning of President Woodruff's manifesto suspending polygamy, and particularly with respect to whether or not the manifesto referred to polygamous relations already formed with the same force that it referred to and controlled the entering into of polygamous relations thereafter.

As the witnesses were all under oath, and the examination was a most thorough one, the following extracts from the testimony as given by the gentlemen at that time, upon the scope of the manifesto and its real meaning, will be read with interest. The manifesto was issued the year before.

The government was represented upon the hearing by United States Attorney Varian and Joseph L. Rawlins, the receiver by John A. Marshall, and the church by Franklin S. Richards, W. H. Dickson and Le Grand Young.

# PRESIDENT WOODRUFF'S TESTIMONY.

By C. S. Varian:

Q. Did you intend to confine this declaration (the manifesto) solely to the forming of new relations by entering into new marriages? A. I don't know that I understand the question.

Q. Did you intend to confine your declaration and advice to the church solely to the question of forming new marriages, without reference to those that were existing—plural marriages? A. The intention of the proclamation was to obey the law myself—all the laws of the land on that subject, and expecting the church would do the same.

Q. Let me read the language, and you will understand me, perhaps, better: "Inasmuch as laws have been enacted by Congress forbidding plural marriages, I hereby declare," etc. Did you intend by that general statement of intention to make the application to existing conditions where the plural marriages already existed? A. Yes, sir.

Q. As to the living in the state of plural marriage? A. Yes, sir; that is, to the obeying of the law.

Q. In the concluding portion of your statement you say: "I now publicly declare that my advice to the Latter-day Saints is to refrain from contracting any marriage forbidden by the law of the land." Do you understand that that language was to be expanded and to include the further statement of living or associating in plural marriage by those already in the status? A. Yes, sir; I intended the proclamation to cover the ground—to keep the laws—to obey the law myself and expected the people to obey the law.

By Mr. Dickson, of counsel for the church:

Q. Your attention was called to the fact that nothing was said in that manifesto about the dissolution of existing polygamous relations. I want to ask you, President Woodruff, whether in your advice to the church officials, and the people of the church, you have advised them that your intention was, and that the requirement of the church was, that the polygamous relations already formed before that should not be continued; that is, there should be no association with plural wives; in other words, that unlawful cohabitation as it is named and spoken of should also stop, as well as future polygamous marriages? A. Yes, sir; that has been the intention.

Q. And that has been your view and explanation of it? A. Yes, sir, that has been my view.

## APOSTLE LORENZO SNOW'S TESTIMONY.

Q. Do you believe that the association in plural marriage by those who are already in it is forbidden by this manifesto? A. Well, I cannot say what was in the mind of President Woodruff when he issued that manifesto touching that matter, but I believe from the general scope of the manifesto that it certainly embraced the plural marriage, because it is clearly an intention, as indicated in that manifesto of President Woodruff, that the law should be observed touching matters in relation to plural marriage.

Q. You mean, now, the law of the land? A. Yes, sir.

Q. Do you understand now that the manifesto conveys that prohibition—the prohibition against the association in plural marriage between those who have already entered into it at the time the manifesto was given as well as a prohibition against the contracting of future plural marriage relations? A. Well, I do; I thought I had explained that; perhaps I might be unhappy in my expression, but, as I said, the intention and scope of that manifesto was expressing President Woodruff's mind in regard to himself and every member of the church, and that was, that the law should be observed in all matters concerning plural marriage, embracing the present conditions of those that had previously entered into marriage. Is that a plain answer?

---

## APOSTLE LUND'S EVIDENCE.

Q. How is it as to the people who have already formed those relations—is it right for them to continue to associate in plural marriage with their wives? A. The manifesto does not expressly state it, but the President of the church has said it was not.

Q. Was that the first time you understand that it was included? A. I understood his advice for the church from the presidency was to obey the law of the land.

---

## PRESIDENT JOSEPH F. SMITH'S TESTIMONY.

By Franklin S. Richards:

Q. Do you understand that the manifesto applies to the cohabitation of men and women in plural marriage where it had already existed? A. I cannot say whether it does or not.

Q. It does not in terms say so, does it? A. No; I think, however, the effect of it is so; I don't see how the effect of it can be otherwise.

247

# INDEX

9

# Reply to Certain Statements
## by O. F. Whitney

The following reproduction of
*Reply to Certain Statements by O. F. Whitney*, published
in 1916, is textually unaltered but was re-typeset for the sake
of legibility. Typographical errors and other anomalies
have been preserved as in the original.

# REPLY

BY

R. N. BASKIN

TO

## Certain Statements

BY

O. F. WHITNEY

IN HIS

## HISTORY OF UTAH

PUBLISHED IN 1916

PORTER ROCKWELL

# CONTENTS.

# REVIEW OF WHITNEY'S RECENT HISTORY.

The following is an excerpt from Whitney's recent history of Utah, published in 1916.

"The slain emigrants at (Mountain Meadow) cannot, of course, speak for themselves, either in denial or admission of the truth of these charges. But there have always been proxies who were more than willing to assert that the travelers conducted themselves with strict propriety, neither committing the deeds nor uttering the threats attributed to them. Anti-'Mormon' writers upon the theme have almost invariably taken this ground, in their eagerness to depict the crime in its most hideous aspects. As if it were not sufficiently atrocious to suit their purpose, they have painted it blacker still, hoping thereby to injure, not the guilty perpetrators, but those whom they hate far more—the leaders, dead and living, of the 'Mormon' Church.*

The note there referred to is as follows   *The laterst attempt of this kind is by R. N. Baskin of Salt Lake City. As late as the year 1914—practically the present hour—when the ancient bitterness between "Mormons" and "Gentiles" has so far abated that they can affiliate socially, politically, and in business, as never before, this Bourbon of the dead past, who "learns nothing" and "forgets nothing," drags from the grave and holds up to public's view the skeletons of the old blood-curdling sensations which all good citizens desire to have buried in oblivion. In the face of all the evidence to the contrary, he tries to make it appear that the "Mormon" Church and its leading men were responsible for the Mountain Meadows Massacre. That crime was committed in 1857; Mr. Baskin, according to his own account, came to Utah in 1865. All he knows about the massacre he learned from others after his arrival here; and the same is true of more of his so-called "Reminiscences." They are largely a rehash of stale anti-"Mormon" stories, based upon the testimony of apostates, jail-birds, and self confessed murderers. He complains of inaccuracies in other writings, while his own book fairly bristles with them. It abounds in coarse abuse and venomous vituperation. Under pretense of correcting alleged mistatements of history, he vents his personal spleen, and pours the vitriol of his implacable hatred upon "Mormons" and "Mormonism" in general. A special feature is the revival of the musty Munchausenism respecting "Danites" or blood-avengers who, according to Baskin, once made a business of killing apostates and enemies of the "Mormon" Church. It does not seem to have dawned upon his comprehension that if the extravagant tales he re-

3

peats and his frenetic "opinions" founded thereon were even half way true, he would never have lived to write any reminiscences. Had there been any "Danites" they would have disposed of him long ago. The mere fact that this inveterate "Mormon" hater is alive and well ought to be accepted as conclusive proof of the non-existence of such an organization, past or present. He has lived here fifty years, not only unmolested, but treated with kindness and consideration, which he now repays by endeavoring to injure the people who made it possible for him to append to his signature as a private citizen. "Ex-Chief Justice of the Supreme Bench of Utah."

That diatribe is indicative of Whitney's chagrin, caused by the exposure in my Reminiscences of Utah, of his duplicity and falsification of history, and impels me to answer each of his groundless aspersions.

Before doing so, however, I shall review his recent history in connection with his larger one, and further expose him.

---

## THE MORMON BATTALION.

The following is an excerpt from Whitney's recent history of Utah: "An agent of the Lattery-day Saints, acting under instructions from Brigham Young, who had succeeded Joseph Smith at the head of the 'Mormon' community, went to the City of Washington to solicit government aid for his people. No gift of money or of other means was asked—only employment in freighting provisions and naval stores to Oregon or other points on the Pacific. That agent, Jesse C. Little, represented in his petition—presented after the exodus began—that many of his co-religionists had already left Illinois for California, and that thousands of others, in the United States and in the British Isles, would go there as soon as they were able. President Polk received Mr. Little kindly, and promised to do what he could do for the homeless people."

It is stated in his larger history, Vol. 1, P. 125, that, "Jesse C. Little, after his first interview with President Polk addressed to him a petition from which the following is quoted: 'We are true-hearted Americans, true to our native country, true to its glorious institutions, and we have a desire to go under outstretched wings of the American eagle. We would disdain to receive assistance from a foreign Power, although it should be proffered, unless, our government shall turn us off in this great crisis and compel us to be foreigners. If you will assist in this crisis, I hereby pledge my honor, as a representative of this people, that the whole body will stand ready at your call, and act as one man in the land to which we are going, and

4

should our territory be invaded we will hold ourselves ready to enter the field of battle.'"

I have only had access to excerpts from that petition. It is clear, however, from the one just quoted, soldiers were asked for and not, as alleged by whitney, "a force of teamsters, with wagons, to freight stores and supplies." This also appears from what afterwards occurred. Whitney states in his large history that "about the middle of June, Elder Little left Washington for the West, and was accompanied by Colonel Thomas L. Kane, who had been commanded by the President to carry special dispatches to General Kearney at Fort Leavenworth, relative to the 'Mormon Battalion.' Upon the receipt of those dispatches General Kearney detailed Captain Allen to confer with the 'Mormons' at their camp in Iowa. Upon arriving there he delivered to the leaders the circular which is hereinafter set out. What had previously transpired and that circular conclusively show that by the efforts of Mr. Little President Polk was induced to grant to the 'Mormons' the privilege of forming a battalion, for the purpose, and subject to the conditions contained in that circular, which is as follows. "I have come among you, instructed by Col. S. F. Kearney, of the U. S. Army, now commanding the Army of the West, to visit the Mormon Camp, and to accept the services for twelve months of four or five companies of Mormon men who may be willing to serve their country for that period in our present war with Mexico; this force to unite with the Army of the West at Santa Fe, and be marched thence to California, where they will be discharged.

"They will receive pay and rations and other allowances, such as other volunteers or regular soldiers receive, from the day they shall be mustered into srvice, and will be entitled to all comforts and benefits of regular soldiers of the Army, and when discharged, as contemplated, at California, they will be given gratis their arms and accoutrements, with which they will be fully equipped at Fort Leavenworth. This is offered to the Mormon people now—this year—an opportunity of sending a portion of their young intelligent men to the ultimate destination of their whole people, and entirely at the expense of the United States, and this advance party can thus pave the way and look out the land for their brethren to come after them. Those of the Mormons who are desirous of serving their country on the conditions here enumerated, are requested to meet me without delay at their principal camp at the Council Bluffs, whither I am going to consult with their principal men, and to receive and organize the force contemplated to be raised. I will receive all healthy, able bodied men, of from eighteen to forty-five years of age."

No coercion was intended. It was optional with the Mormons to raise or decline to raise a battalion. Certainly one would not have been formed, if Brigham Young had deemed it injurious. It was what he wanted, and his followers were grateful for the privilege granted them. This is shown by an address delivered by B. H. Roberts hereinafter referred to and the following excerpt from the daily journal of Wilford Woodruff. (See his Biography, P. 254.)

"There was a meeting with Colonel Kane, and in it the adoption of certain resolutions of respect and gratitude, to President Polk for the steps taken by him in arming five hundred men, and furnishing them an opportunity to reach the valleys of the Rocky Mountains."

Brigham Young, Wilford Woodruff, Heber C. Kimball, and Willard Richards were present at that meeting. Subsequently the masses of the Mormons in Utah, bitterly denounced the general government because they were taught by their ecclesiastical oracles and believed that President Polk made a requisition for the Mormon Battalion for the purpose of weakening to such an extent the main body of the Mormons on their journey westward, that they might be destroyed by the savage, and war-like Indians, in habiting the regions through which they were to pass. The address of B. H. Roberts which was delivered on July Fourth, 1911, is referred to by the Deseret News in an article as follows. "The calling of the Mormon Battalion, and the fact that this event was not intended by the general government to harm the Mormon people, but that it was for their welfare and the direct results of a request by the church leaders, was forcibly brought out, and that Col. Jesse C. Little, the eastern representative of the Mormon church, had asked President Polk to assist the people in their enforced western march, and that President Brigham Young stated that it was what he had wanted, was shown from letters and journals of many of the early church leaders, among them being the journal of John Taylor. The government intended to help the people in their western march, and the Mormon people were thus given glorious opportunity to prove their patriotism to their country.

"The journal of President Taylor states that President Young said, 'We are pleased to show our patriotism for the country we expect to have for our future home. I think President Polk has done us a great favor in calling us.' Similar facts were read from the biography of President Wilford Woodruff and others."

In September, 1857, Brigham Young, in an address delivered in Salt Lake City, and found in Vol. 5, Journal of Discourses, used the following language:

"There cannot be a more damnable, dastardly order than was issued by the Administration to this people while they were in an Indian country in 1846. Before we left Nauvoo, no less than two United States Senators came to receive a pledge from us that we would leave the United States, and then while we were doing our best to leave their borders, the poor, low, degraded cusses sent a requisition for five hundred of our men to go and fight their battles. That was President Polk, and he is now weltering in hell with old Zachariah Taylor, where the present administrators will soon be, if they do not repent. * * * There is high treason in Washington, and if the law was carried out, it would hang up many of them, and the very act of James K. Polk in having five hundred of our men, while we were making our way out of the country, under an agreement forced upon us, would have hung him betweeen the heavens and the earth if the laws had been faithfully carried out."

The Government to assist the balance of the Mormon emigrants to purchase and equip trains, paid the Battalion three months advanced wages which was turned over to Brigham Young to be used for that purpose. Whitney fails to mention that fact, although I stated it on indisputable authority in my Reminiscenes. His purpose in failing to do so is apparent.

The following is an excerpt from a sermon of Brigham Young contained in the Journal of Discourses, Vol. 2, P. 173. "While fleeing from our enemies another test of our fidelity was contrived by them for our destruction * * * acquiesced in by the government, consisting of a requisition from the War Department, to furnish a battalion of five hundred to fight for them in the war with Mexico. I ask again, could we refrain from considering both the people and the government our deadly foes * * * We were required to turn out of our traveling camps, five hundred of our most efficient men, and leave the old, the young, the women upon the hands of the residue to take care of and support, and in case we refused to comply with so unreasonable a requirement, we were to be deemed enemies of the Government, and fit for slaughter."

Those scandalous sermons and numerous others of like import and many more in which the government in other respects was bitterly censured, delivered by Brigham Young, and many of the apostles, bishops and elders of the Mormon church, and also the prayers offered up at the dedication of the St. George Temple on the 1st of January, 1877, show how malevolenty opposed, the priesthood was to the general government, and explains why a large majority of the laymen of the Mormon church were unfriendly to it until conditions changed.. The following are extracts from prayers offered up at that dedication.

By Woodruff:

"We pray thee Our Father in Heaven, in the name of Jesus Christ, if it be consistent with Thy will, that Thy servant Brigham may stand in the flesh to behold the nation which now occupies the land upon which Thou, Lord, has said the Zion of God shall stand in the latter days; that nation which shed the blood of the saints and prophets which cry unto God day and night for vengance; the nation which is making war with God and Christ; that nation whose sins, wickedness and abominations are ascending up before God and the Heavenly Hosts which causes all eternity to be pained, and the Heavens to weep like falling rain; Yea, O Lord, that he may live to see that nation, if it will not repent, broken in pieces like a potter's vessel and swept from the earth with a beson of destruction as were the Jaredites and Nephites, that the land of Zion may cease to groan under the wickedness and abomination of men."

By Apostle Lorenzo Snow, afterward President of the church:

"We, thy servants and people, stretch forth our hands unto Thee, Father, our Lord Jesus Christ, and in his name we beseech Thee to hear the prayer of thy servant Wilford Woodruff, which has been offered up in the first room of this house, and answereth it for this house and people."

By Apostle Brigham Young, Jr.:

"Hear and answer the prayers offered by thy apostles, Wilford Woodruff and Lorenzo Snow, that they may penetrate the ears of the Lord of Sabaoth."

Whitney, in his history, after garbling the facts by stating only such as suited his purpose of falsifying, asserts that "Such was the origin of the call for the Mormon Battalion—five hundred able bodied men, to assist the United States in its war with Mexico, coming at such a time, and embodying a proposition so different from the one submitted by Agent Little at Washington, it created at first some consternation. A force of teamsters, with wagons, to freight stores and supplies was one thing; a battalion of five hundred fighting men, quite another. In the midst of an exodus rife with dangers and hardships, the services of that number of men could ill be spared."

Whitney here insinuates that the privilege of raising the battalion was not granted to assist, but to injure the Mormons. Whitney when writing his histories was not ignorant of the facts pertaining to the battalion, and if he had been an honest and impartial historian, instead of such an insinuation, he would have frankly admitted that the President intended to assist, and not to injure the Mormons. He further asserts that "The extreme view that the call of this Battalion was a hostile move on the part of the General Government, having as its object the weakening of the 'Mormon' community, and its probable dispersion or destruction by Indians beyond the frontier, finds few if any supporters at the present time."

Whitney knows that the view above mentioned is false, and was caused by the untruthful and outrageous sermons before mentioned, and was generally held by the Mormon people, until its falsity was exposed by B. H. Roberts in his address and by my Reminiscences of Early Utah. Since then it has not been so prevalent, but yet many persons who are not aware of that exposure, still believe that the outrage above indicated, by that extreme view, was perpetrated by the General Government. The facts which I have stated constitute an essential part of the history of Utah. Yet Whitney has studiously avoided stating the facts which show

8

the hostility of the priesthood to the General Government. That hostility was intensified by the untruthful and outrageous sermons before mentioned, and the irrepressible conflict which began in the early days of Utah, continued until the salutary change, which was brought about, mainly by the efforts of the Liberal Party, occurred. The fairness of Mr. Roberts is shown by his address, and the guile of Whitney by his version of the battalion.

---

## CAUSE OF THE FACTIONAL STRIFE.

Whitney in his recent history asserts that "Responsibility for the factional strife that tore Utah almost from the hour of her creation, rests largely upon the essentially un-American system of sending strangers to rule over communities with which they have little or nothing in common."

The organic act of Utah is the same as the acts by which the numerous other Territories, in the United States, were organized. In none of them did such a conflict, as the one in Utah, occur, but would have arisen in all of them had the Mormon Priesthood dominated their local affairs as was done by it in Utah..

Whitney knew what caused the conflict in the Territory of Utah, and if he had been an impartial historian, he would have stated it in his histories. He failed to do so because he would have exposed the infamous un-American system inaugurated and maintained by the Mormon Priesthood until the salutary change occurred.

The attempt of the priesthood as stated in the opinion of the Supreme Court of the United States hereafter quoted: "To drive from the Territory all who were not connected with them (the Mormon sect) in communion and sympathy;" the pernicious acts passed by the Mormon Legislature for the purpose of securing immunity to polygamy and other heinious crimes like the Mountain Meadow massacre, and rendering impossible the execution of any law which interfered with the efforts of the Mormon Priesthood to maintain the theocratic rule which prevailed, until the pernicious acts above mentioned was disapproved by Congress, and the priesthood was forced by the stringent acts passed by Congress and their enforcement to abandon theocratic rule and polygamy, was the sole cause of the strife in the Territory.

Because it is easy for Whitney and others of his class to discredit among the masses of the Mormon people, this statement, by simply denying that it is true the following indisputable evidence upon which it is based and proves its correctness, is stated at much greater length than, otherwise, would not have been done.

9

## FROM PRESIDENT BUCHANAN'S ANNUAL MESSAGE.

"Brigham Young was appointed the first Governor    *    *    *
"While he has been both Governor and Superintendent of Indian Affairs, he has been at the same time, the head of the church.    *    *    His power has been absolute over both church and State. The people of Utah almost exclusively belongs to the church, and believing with a fanatical spirit that he is Governor of the Territory by Divine Appointment, they obey his commands as if they were direct revelations from Heaven."

----

## FROM PRESIDENT GRANT'S THIRD ANNUAL MESSAGE.

"In Utah remains a remnant of barbarism repugnant to civilization—to dcency, and to the laws of the United States. Neither polygamy nor any other violation of existing statutes will be permitted within the Territory of the United States. It is not with the religion of the self-styled saints that we are now dealing, but with their practices.

"They will be protected in the worship of God according to the dictates of their consciences, but they will not be permitted to violate the laws under the cloak of religion."

----

## FROM PRESIDENT GRANT'S SPECIAL MESSAGE OF FEBRUARY 14, 1873.

"Evidently it was never intended to vest the Territorial legislature with power which would enable it, by creating judicatures of its own or increasing the jurisdiction of Courts appointed by Territorial authority,    *    *    *    to take the administration of the law out of the hands of judges appointed by the President or to interfere with their action. After several years of unhappy experience it is apparent that in both of these respects the Territory of Utah requires special lgislation by Congress.

"Public sentiment in that territory, produced by circumstances too notorious to require further notice, makes it necessary, in my opinion, in order to prevent the miscarriage of justice and maintain the supremacy of the laws of the United States and the Federal Government, to provide that the selection of grand and petit jurors for the district courts, if not under the

10

control of Federal officers, shall be placed in the hands of persons entirely independent of those who are determined not to enforce any act of Congress obnoxious to them, and also to pass some act which shall deprive the probate courts, or any court created by the Territorial legislature of any power to interfere with or impede the action of the court by the United States judges.

"I am convinced that so long as Congress leaves the selection of jurors to local authorities it will be futile to make any effort to enforce laws not acceptable to a majority of the people of the Territory, or which interfere with local prejudices or provide for the punishment of polygamy or any of its affiliated vices or crimes."

---

## FROM THE ANNUAL MESSAGE OF PRESIDENT HAYES.

"The Mormon sectarian organization which upholds polygamy, has the whole power of making and executing the local legislation of the Territory. By its control of the grand and petit juries, it possesses large influence over the administration of justice. Exercising, as the heads of this sect do, the local political power of the Territory, they are able to make effective their hostility to the law of Congress on the subject of polygamy, and, in fact, do prevent its enforcements. Polygamy will not be abolished if the enforcement of the law depends on those who practice and uphold the crime. It can only be suppressed by taking away the political power of the sect which encourages and sustains it.

"Religious liberty and the separation of church and state, are among elementary ideas of free institutions. To re-establish the interests and principles which polygamy and Mormonism have imperiled, and to fully re-open to the intelligent and virtuous of all creeds, that part of our domain which has been in a great degree closed to general immigration by intolerant and immoral institutions, it is recommended that the Government of the Territory of Utah be re-organized. I recommend that Congress provide   *   *   *   a government analogous to the provisional government established for the territory northwest of the Ohio, by the ordinance of 1787. If, however, it is deemed best to continue the existing form of local government, I recommend that the right to vote, hold office, or sit on juries in the Territory of Utah, be confined to those who neither practice, nor uphold polygamy.

"If thorough measures are adopted, it is believed that within a few years the evils which now afflict Utah will be eradicated, and the Territory will in good time become one of the most prosperous and attractive of the new states of the Union."

11

(Thorough measures were adopted and the State has become very prosperous. Had they not been adopted, the evils which retarded progress and caused the lamentable conflict in the Territory would not have been eradicated and the present salutary conditions would not have occurred.)

---

## FROM PRESIDENT CLEVELAND'S ANNUAL MESSAGE.

"There is no feature of this practice (polygamy) or the system (Theocracy) that sustains it, which is not opposed to all that is of value in our institutions. There should be no relaxation in the firm, but just execution of the law now in operation, and I should be glad to approve such other discreet legislation as will rid the country of this blot upon its fair fame."

In the case of the church vs. the United States, 136 U. S. Rep. P. 49, in the opinion, it is said that "It is unnecessary here to refer to the past history of the sect—to their defiances of the government's authority, to their attempt to establish an independent community, to their efforts to drive from the Territory all who were not connected with them in communion and sympathy. The tale is one of patience on the part of the American government and people, and of contempt of authority and resistance to law on the part of the Mormons."

In Miles vs. the United States, 103 U. S. Rep., it is said:

"It is made clear by the record that polygamous marriages are so celebrated in Utah as to make the proof of polygamy very difficult. They are conducted in secret, and the persons by whom they are solemnized are under such obligations of secrecy that it is almost impossible to extract the facts from them when placed upon the witness stand. If both wives are excluded from testifying to the first marriage, as we think they should be under the existing rules of evidence, testimony sufficient to convict in a prosecution for polygamy in the Territory of Utah is hardly attainable. But this is not a consideration by which we can be influenced. We must administer the law as we find it. The remedy is with Congress, by enacting such a change in the law of evidence in the Territory of Utah as to make both wives witnesses on indictments for bigamy.

Brigham Young, in the Journal of Discourses, vol. 4, Page 77, said: "The kingdom is established. It is upon the earth. The kingdom we are talking about, preaching about and trying to build up, is the kingdom of God on earth, not in the starry heavens, nor in the sun; we are trying to establish the kingdom of God on the earth, to which really and properly everything pertaining to men, their feelings, their faith, their convictions, their desires, and every act of their lives belong, that they may be sealed by

12

it spiritually and temporally. We are called upon to establish the Kingdom of God literally, just as much as spiritually.

"There is no man on the earth who can receive the kingdom of God in his heart and be governed according to the laws of that kingdom without being governed and controlled in all temporal matters."

In Vol. 6, page 23, of said Journal, he further said:

"The kingdom of God circumscribes the municipal law of the people in their outward government."

Orson Pratt, one of the twelve apostles, and the most celebrated scholar of the Mormon church, published in Liverpool, England, a series of essays from which the following is an extract: "The Kingdom of God is an order of government established by divine authority. It is the only legal government that can exist in any part of the universe. All other governments are illegal and unauthorized.   *   *   *   Any people attempting to govern themselves by laws of their own notion, and by officers of their own appointment are in direct rebellion against the Kingdom of God."

The following is an extract from a sermon of John Taylor, one of the twelve apostles, and afterwards the successor of Brigham Young, found in the Journal of Discourses, Vol. 5, page 149: "Some people ask, What is Priesthood? It is the legitimate rule of God, whether in Heaven or on the earth, and it is the only legitimate power that has a right to rule upon the earth.   *   *   *   Who owns the gold and silver and the cattle on a thousand hills? God. Who then has a right to appoint rulers? None but Him, or the man he appoints." I could add a large number of other quotations of like import from Mormon sermons and publications.

The supreme court of the Territory, in the case of the United States vs. the Church (15 Pac. 467), uses this language in the opinion delivered by Chief Justice Zane:   *   *   *   *   "The people who comprise this organization claim to be directed and led by the inspiration that is above all human wisdom and subject to a power above all municipal government, above all man-made laws These facts belong to history, therefore we have taken notice of them."

Governor West, in a message to the territorial legislature, said: "These many voices of the past, replete with anguish, ask us why—of all the people in our land of nearly every nationality, of no religion, and all religions, with beliefs and creeds as various and numerous almost, as the different nations of men—should this people stand singular and alone in its woeful history? Can anyone doubt who approaches with unprejudiced mind the considerations of the question that the cause is founded in the theocracy established and maintained here, in the education of the people to believe that God has chosen this people to take possession of the earth and dominate and control all other peoples? That through his priesthood God governs them immediately, not alone in faith and morals, but in all the affairs and relations of life, and that the council of the priesthood is the supreme voice of God, and must be obeyed without question.

"It necessarily follows that perfect and complete unity has and does exist among the Mormon people; and absolute oneness, without division and dissent. The unity in the State which comes from a fair discussion of public questions, securing by merit conviction of the mind and triumph of the right, is desirable and commendable. The unity that is obtained by recognizing the supremacy of one man, or set of men, the attributing to him or them a knowledge and power not granted to others—derived from a superhuman and supreme source, and therefore not to be questioned, but must be obeyed—is the establishment of complete absolutism in those holding power, and the most abject and servile slavery on those submitting. The submission to a government by God through his priesthood, and the unity it enforces, brought this people to accept, sustain, and uphold polygamy whether practicing it or not, regardless of the sentiment of the Christian world, and in defiance to the laws of the land."

After I had been convinced by investigation that the deplorable conditions which I have conclusively shown existed in the Territory of Utah, could be corrected only by stringent legislation of Congress, I drafted the Cullom Bill in 1869, and submitted it to Shelby M. Cullom, who was then the chairman of the Territorial committee of the Lower House of Congress.

He introduced the bill and it was passed by the Lower House, but was not acted upon by the Senate. It contained all of the recommendations of the Presidents herein before mentioned and which was afterward enacted by Congress, and were potent facts in causing the chang of conditions in Utah.

---

## LOCAL SELF GOVERNMENT.

Whitney further states that "Local self-government—that basic principal of all true Democracy—would doubtless have solved many of the problems that vexed our Territorial history." Pish!

In the light of the past history of the Territory, does any sane person believe that if unlimited, instead of restricted self-government had been granted by the act organizing the Territory and left in force that the evil conditions which formerly vexed it, would have been changed, or that the Territory would have been admitted into the Union, or that the Mormon Priesthood would have relinquinshed its theocratic control, or that the Liberal Party, which was organized for the sole purpose of eradicating those evil conditions, would have disbanded?

14

JOHN D. LEE

# MOUNTAIN MEADOW MASSACRE

Whitney in his large history, asserted that the Arkansas emigrants, "During their entire journey through the Territory they appear to have conducted themselves in the most offensive manner. They swaggered through the town declaring their intention, as soon as they should have conveyed their women and children to a place of safety, to return with military force sufficient to complete such destruction of the Mormons as the United States soldiery might leave unfinished.

"They averred that the murdered leaders of the Church had received their tardy deserts, and gave the impression, if they did not positively boast, that in their company, were hands which had been reddened with the Prophet's blood. Nor were their offenses confined to harrowing and insulting words. They acted like a band of marauders, preying upon the possessions of those through whose country they traveled and committed petty indignities upon person and property. Still greater crimes were charged to them by the Indians. They were said to have not only wantonly shot some of the braves, but were known to have poisoned beef where the savages would likely get it. Several deaths attributed to this cause occurred among the Indians near Filmore, and numbers of their animals perished through drinking water from springs poisoned by the emigrants when about breaking camp. * * * Against this company, as stated, was laid the fearful charge of injecting poison into the carcass of one of their oxen, first having learned that the Indians would be likely to eat the meat, and of throwing packages of poison into the springs. In other ways they contrived to render themselves obnoxious to the settlers and hateful to the natives."

That is an infamous libel, and in my Reminiscences, having shown it to be such, Whitney in his recent history modifies it in some respects. His modification, however, is almost, if not quite as libelous, as his former accusations of the murdered emigrants. He admits that the Arkansas company was mainly made up of respectable and well to do people, but asserts "That along with them went a rough and reckless set of men calling themselves 'Missouri Wild Cats.' The latter were a boisterous lot, and their conduct was probably one of the chief causes of the calamity that came upon them and their betters." His assertion that the Arkansas company, which was led by Captain Fancher was associated with the Wild Cat company, which was led by Captain Dukes, is refuted by the following quotation from his recent history. "The Duke company was delayed by trouble with the Indians, one of whom they shot and two of their number being wounded in return. This occurred near Beaver, a new settlement between Filmore and Parowan. (The Mountain Meadows is eighty miles south of

Beaver.) Attacked by the red men, these emigrants were compelled to corral their wagons and seek protection in a rifle pit. Through the intervention of Utah Militia officers—'Mormons'—the Indians were placated and the emigrants allowed to proceed. When beyond the last of the line of settlements, they were again attacked and again saved, the mediators being "Mormon" guides and interpreters, who pursuaded the Missourians to buy off the savages with their loose stock. These travelers reached the Pacific Coast in safety. Meanwhile the Arkansas company had met with a horrible fate. They numbered about thirty families, aggregating one hundred and thirty-seven persons, including the Wild Cat Missourians."

In Whitney's large history, Vol. 2, Page 819-820, it is stated that, "Lee had told the Militia that the emigrants were to be killed, and a good many of them objected, but did not dare to say anything to those in command."

Can there be stronger evidence than the foregoing quotations that the Militia participated in that horrible massacre, and that the Wild Cats were not with nor associated with the Arkansas company on their journey south? What a revolting spectacle those statements of Whitney present! Think of it! While the disorderly Wild Cats were being protected from the attacks of the Indians by "Mormon" Militia Officers, thirty families were slaughtered—the men by Utah Militiamen, and the women and all the children old enough to expose the fearful deed, by savage Indians placed in ambush for that purpose!

At the first trial of John D. Lee and after it was shown that Lee had, by his treacherous promise of protection, induced the Arkansas emigrants to surrender and give up their arms, it was further shown by the evidence that a number of Indians were placed in concealment in a clump of cedars and oaks, near the road, several hundred yards from the emigrant corral. The wounded men and seventeen little children, too young to expose the awful crime, were placed in wagons. The women and the other children were formed into a separate procession, the men were arranged in rank, and by the side of each was placed a Mormon assassin armed with a gun, ostensibly to protect the emigrants.

The wagons containing the wounded men and young children, under order moved ahead, the women and other children followed at some distance behind the wagons, and the men with their ostensible guards followed at a distance of about one hundred yards in the rear. When the women and other children reached the ambuscade of the Indians, the signal agreed upon was given by Bishop Higbee, who was a major in the Utah Militia, and each fiendish Mormon guard shot or cut the throat of the defenseless victim he was pretendedly guarding, and the Indians, not more merciless than the white skinned Mormons present, rushed from ambush and slaughtered the helpless women and innocent children, and the wounded men in the wagons were slain.

Whitney states in his large history that "The first reports that the Indians, several hundred in number, had attacked and slain some of the emigrants, and that men were needed to guard the remnant and bury the dead. It was upon this call to Colonel Haight that John M. Higbee, a major in one of the battalions of Militia, on Thursday the 8th, set out with a body of men and wagons for the Meadows.  *  *  *  *  They found an angry host of Indians, bent on blood-shed, and outnumbering ten to one of their own force. An attempt by the Militia to assist the emigrants would have transferred to themselves the Indian attack  *  *  *  The whites who were from Santa Clara County, believed as did Higbee's men, that they were summoned there on a mission of mercy to bury the dead and protect the survivors, but the fury of the Indians was uncontrollable."

Whitney makes the following statement in his recent history:

"In the opening slaughter, seven men were killed, and sixteen wounded. The survivors made a brave defense, and held the enemy at bay. At this time the only white man known to have been with the Indians was John D. Lee. Subsequently others came upon the scene, lured to the Meadows, as they claimed, by the reprsentation that their services were needed to bury the dead. Some of them participated in the butchery that followed."

What a marvelous and unnatural occurrence is here presented. For men belonging to a civilized and christian race, *lured* to the meadows, according to Whitney's absurd statement, to bury the emigrants who had been slain, to participate in the slaughter of their surviving comrades, is most revolting. No sensible person who may read the two foregoing statements will believe that Whitney believed—that any men were *lured* to the Meadows, or that "Higbee's men were summoned there on a mission of mercy to bury the dead and protect the survivors," or doubt that they were ordered out to assist in the massacre. Higbee was a Major in the Militia and gave the signal agreed upon, which started the slaughter.

At the second trial of John D. Lee the following was elicited in the examination of Jacob Hamblin by William Howard, United States attorney: Hamblin was Brigham Young's Indian interpreter.

Q. Tell what Lee told you.    A. Well, he spoke of many little incidents.

Q. Mention any of those incidents.    A. There were two young ladies brought out.

Q. By whom?    A. By an Indian chief at Cedar City, and he asked him (Lee) what he should do with them, and the Indian killed one and he killed the other.

Q. Tell the story he told you.    A. That is about it.

Q. Where were these young girls brought from; did he say?    A. From a thicket of oak brush where they were concealed.

17

Q. Tell just what he said about that.    A. The Indian killed one and he cut the other one's throat, is what he said.

Q. Who cut the other's throat?    A. Mr. Lee.

Q. Tell us all the details of the conversation and killing.    A. Well, he said they were all killed, as he supposed; that the chief of Cedar City then brought out the young ladies.

Q. What did he say the chief said to him?    A. Asked what should be done with them.

Q. What else did the chief say?    A. He said they didn't ought to be killed.

Q. Did the chief say to Lee why they should not be killed?    A. Well, he said they were pretty and he wanted to save them.

Q. What did he tell you that he said to the chief?    A. That according to the orders [the orders he had] they were too old and big to let live.

Q. What did he say he told the chief to do?    A. The chief shot one of them.

Q. Who killed the other?    A. He did, he said.

Q. How?    A. He threw her down and cut her throat.

Q. Did you ascertain in that conversation, or subsequently, where it was they were killed?    A. When I got home I asked my Indian boy and we went out to where this took place, and we saw two young ladies lying there with their throats cut.

Q. What was the condition of their bodies?    A. They were rather in a putrefied state; their throats were cut; I didn't look further than that.

Q. What were their ages?    A. Looked about fourteen or fifteen.

It was shown by the evidence in Lee's first trial that many of the other victims had their throats cut, but Whitney in treating of those trials avoided mentioning the phenomenal historical occurrences thus disclosed. Why he did so is *very apparent*. To have done so, would have too vividly brought to mind the *endowment cut throat penalties*.

In the Rocky Mountain Saints, it is stated that the "Wild Cats came as near to them (the Arkansas Company) in traveling as convenient for the grazing of cattle and the purpose of camp at night. Within sight of each other they formed their corrals, but while the one resounded with vulgar songs, boisterous roaring and tall swearing, *in the other there was the peace of domestic bliss and conscious rectitude.*

Whitney's reference to the foregoing is as follows:

"Impartial history paralleled the assertion that the emigrants conducted themselves properly, with the statement quoted by Mr. Stenhouse ( a non-'Mormon' when he wrote) that the camp of the 'Wild Cat' Missourians 'resounded with vulgar songs, boisterous roaring, and tall swearing.'"

To that garbled statement there is appended the following note:

"Readers of the Baskin 'Reminiscences' will look in vain therein for

18

any allusions to these incidents. While their author quotes copiously from the Stenhouse books, he is discreetly silent upon the subject of the 'Missouri Wild Cats' and their unseemly behavior. The reason is apparent. The mention of such things would have marred the picture he was painting, in which he desired to exhibit the emigrants in the best light possible, and the Mormons in the worst light possible."

His purpose in garbling Stenhouse's statement is apparent. If he had not done so, he would have shown the high character of the Arkansas emigrants, and furnished further evidence that there was no association between them and the "Wild Cats."

Of course I did not mention the Wild Cat Missourians, because the Arkansas company was a separate and distinct one, and wholly disconnected with the Wild Cats, as the quotation which I have made from Whitney's recent history respecting the attack of the Indians on the latter and the quotation from Stenhouse's Rocky Mountain Saints, conclusively show.

This being the case and as in my Reminiscences I was vindicating the inoffensive Arkansas emigrant against the infamous libel of Whitney, the character of the Wild Cats and anything that they may have done was irrelevant.

I had no other purpose than the refutation of his infamous libel, by showing the high character of the emigrants, and that in passing through the Territory to the Mountain Meadows, where they were foully betrayed, and brutally slaughtered, they acted with propriety.

Mr. Forney, superintendent of Indian affairs, who was sent by the Government to gather up thte little children who were not slain, and return them to the former homes of their murdered parents, made a close investigation into the details of the massacre, and in his official report dated at Salt Lake City, 1859, (See Senate Document, No. 42, 36th Congress, First session, Page 87-88), said: "Conflicting statements were made to me of the behavior of this emigrant company while traveling through the Territory. I have accordingly deemed it a matter of material importance to make a strict inquiry to obtain reliable information on this subject. Not that bad conduct on their part could in any degree palliate the enormity of the crime, or be regarded as any extenuation. My object was common justice to the surviving orphans. The result of my inquiries enables me to say that the company conducted themselves with propriety.  *  *  *

"That an emigrant company, as respectable as I believed this was, would carry along several pounds of arsenic and strychnine, apparently for no other purpose than to posion cattle and Indians, is too improbable to be true."

The high character and previous good conduct of a person charged with crime is admitted as material evidence by the courts. That the emigrants were God-fearing and highly respectable and exemplary, was so conclusively shown in my "Reminiscences," that Whitney was forced to admit in his recent history that the "Arkansas emigrants were mainly made up of respectable people."

James H. Berry, a United States Senator from Arkansas, in a speech made by him in the Smoot case, reported in the Congressional Record of Feb. 12th, 1907, said:     "In 1857, I lived in the County of Carroll, State of Arkansas.  In the spring of that year there left that county, and two adjoining counties, between a hundred and forty, and a hundred and fifty— including men, women and children—emigrants for California.  They consisted of the best citizens of that country  *  *  *  *  I was a boy, seventeen years old on that day when they (the little children saved) were brought to the village Court House.

"I saw them as they were lined upon th ebenches, and Colonel Mitchell told the people whose children they were, at least, whose he thought they were.  I have seen much of life since that day.  I have seen war along the lines of the border States in *all* its horror; but no scene in my life was ever impressed upon my mind as that which I saw there that day—presented by those little children, their fathers, mothers, brothers and sisters, dead on the far off plains of Utah, and they absolutely without means, with no human being to look too."

Those children were robbed by the fiends who massacred their parents, and their little brothers and sisters who were old enough to expose the horrible deed and Brigham Young, who at the time was governor of the Territory, and superintendent of Indian affairs made no attempt to prevent the outrage.

In the Rocky Mountain Saints it is stated:

"One of their number (the Arkansas emigrants) had been a Methodist preacher, and probably most of the adults were members of that denomination.  They were moral in language and conduct, and united regularly in morning and evening prayers.  On Sunday they did not travel ,but observed it as a day of sacred rest for man and beast.  At the appointed hour of service, this brother-preacher assembled his fellow travelers in a large tent, which served as a meeting house within their wagon circled camp, for the usual religious exercises."

Bancroft, in his history of Utah, page 550, states:

"It was Saturday evening when the Arkansas families encamped at the Mountain Meadows.  On the Sabbath day they rested, and at the usual hour, one of them conducted divine service in a large tent, as had been their custom through their journey."

It is clear that there was no conjunction of action of those companies and Whitney's futile attempt to show that there was, in order to bolster up his infamous slander of the Arkansas emigrants is a glaring outrage, and he has done it in a way that exposes his self stultification.

20

Whitney further states in his recent history that:

"According to the testimony of 'Mormons' and Non-'Mormons' alike (the Arkansas emigrants) were far from being the white souled saints that a certain writer would have the public believe. Those Wild Missourians were quite capable of making the blood thirsty threats attributed to them, and of carrying out those threats, as 'Mormon' history amply shows. And the spirit they manifested—they being the aggressive, dominant element in the company—would naturally be regarded by the settlers, however mistakenly as the spirit of the entire camp. It is quite conceivable, too, that some of the Arkansas emigrants were of the same mood, and that they joined with the Missourians in their tantalizing talk."

That a company made up of thirty families, as God-fearing, prayerful and highly respectable as I have shown the Arkansas Emigrants to have been, and in which there were many women, young girls in their teens and small children, were associated with such a disorderly company as the Wild Cats, and acted in concert with them in perpetrating the outrages charged by Whitney, is too extraordinary and improbable to admit of belief. And, most certainly will not be given credence on the uncorroborated statement of a historian as reckless and unscrupulous as Whitney has shown himself to be.

It is clear that there was no conjunction of action of those companies, and Whitney's futile attempt to show that there was, in order to bolster up his infamous slander of the Arkansas emigrants is as "dishonorable, as it is despicable."

Isaac C. Haight was president of the Parowan stake of Zion, within which were Cedar City and Mountain Meadows. He was also Colonel in the Territorial Militia of which Brigham Young was the commander-in-chief, and Daniel H. Wells, was Lieutenant General. John M. Higbee was first counselor to president Haight, and also Major in the Militia. Notwithstanding, Haight and Higbee, were among the prime movers of the massacre. Neither of them were court martialed or removed from the Militia. According to Whitney—Higbee and Lee, were not excommunicated from the church until thirteen years after the massacre. None of the other fifty-two Mormon participants were ever disciplined by the church. William H. Dame and Klingensmith, who were Mormon bishops and Haight and Higbee, and some others of less prominence, were indicted with Lee. They fled to places of concealment and all of them except Klingensmith, who gave himself up and testified in Lee's first trial, were shielded from arrest by the inhabitants in the extreme southern part of the Territory. After a lapse of considerable time the hidden retreat of John D. Lee, was disclosed to a deputy United States marshall, and he was arrested. The peace officers were unable to arrest any of the others who were indicted with Lee. They remained in concealment, and according to Whitney's statement died in exile. The Arkansas company must have had considerable money. What became of it has never been disclosed. The other property of the company was very valuable. Some of the cattle were branded with the church brand. Most of the other property was sold at auction in Cedar City, under the direction of President Haight. Much of that which was sold was paid for in grain, which was put in the church tithing house granary. Common humanity required that that property should have been sold by the civil officers of the Territory, and the proceeds which would have amounted to many thousands of dollars used for the nurture and education of the little children that were not slaughtered. Instead of this, they were robbed by the high Mormon official at Cedar City who planned the massacre and actively participated in the slaughter of the parents of those helpless children. That robbery is secondary in perfidy to the Massacre itself. Notwithstanding that unconscionable robbery is an important fact in the history of the crime, Whitney studiously avoids making any reference to it. His failure to do so is apparent. I have never, on account of the crime, denounced or held accountable any persons except those whom the evidence proved were either principal actors or accessories before or after the fact, in the commission of that horrible crime.

I have frequently been asked the question—What made the perpetration of such a crime by a civilized and Christion race possible? My answer was and is now—The cut throat sermons of Brigham Young and other high officials of the Mormon church, quoted in my Reminiscences, from the Mormon Journals of Discourses, preached a short time before the Massacre, and the covenants of unquestioned obedience to the priesthood, and avengement of the blood of the prophets entered into in the Mormon endowment house, under death penalties, engendered the fiendish and fanatical spirit displayed by the perpetrators of that crime and rendered its execution possible.

---

## THE REYNOLDS CASE.

Whitney in his large history asserts that William Carey, United States District Attorney, for the purpose of testing the constitutionality of the anti-polygamy law, "Stipulated that the defendant in the case should produce the evidence for his own indictment and conviction, and it was generally understood that the infliction of punishment in this instance would be waived. Only the first half of the arrangement was realized. The defendant in the test case, George Reynolds, supplied the evidence upon which he was convicted, but his action did not shield him from punishment."

There was not the slightest foundation for that statement. It was a malicious falsehood framed in Whitney's mind, which I apprehend is disordered. His purpose evidently was, as in many other cases, to discredit the Federal officers who were executing the law, and to make it appear that a glaring outrage had been perpetrated on George Reynolds.

To besmirch me, also, he wrongfully asserted that I was Carey's assistant in the trial. If any such arrangement had been made the severe sentence passed upon Reynolds would have been a glaring outrage upon him, and Mr. Carey's action in the matter would have been dishonorable in the extreme.

In Whitney's recent history, his version of that celebrated Reynolds case, shows that his former one was maliciously false. He is careful however, in that later version, to omit stating the glaring perjury which was committed by a high church official, one of the defendant's witnesses, and which is fully shown in my Reminiscences.

---

## ANOTHER OF WHITNEY'S MALICIOUS FALSEHOODS.

In his recent history, he asserts that, "As a result of the harsh enforcement of the law, the whole community was terrorized. Special government funds having been provided for the purpose, a large force of deputy marshals was employed and a system of espionage inaugurated. "Hunting cohabs" became a lucrative employment. Paid informers men and women, were set to work to ferret out offenses punishable under the recently enacted Congressional legislation. Some of these assumed the role of peddlers or of tramps, imposing upon the good feelings of those whom they sought to betray. Others passed themselves off as tourists intent upon gathering information respecting the country and its resources. Children going to, or returning from school were stopped by strangers upon the street and interrogated concerning the relations and acts of their parents. At night dark forms prowled around people's premises, peering ing into windows or watching for the opening of doors, to catch glimpses of persons supposed to be inside. More than one of the hirelings thrust themselves into sick rooms and women's bed chambers, rousing the sleepers, by pulling the bed clothes from off them. If admittance was refused, houses would be broken into. Delicate and refined women, about to become mothers, or with infants in arms, were awakened at unseemly hours and conveyed long distances through the night, to be arraigned before United States Commissioners. Male fugitives, if they did not immediately surrender when commanded, were fired upon. All these statements are susceptible of proof; many of them being referred to in public documents and newspapers of that period."

The same assertion was made in his large history, and is answered by Charles S. Varian, who at that time was assistant United States District Attorney. In a chapter written by him and attached to my Reminiscences is the following: "The historian gives no particulars—and it is certain that he would have given names, dates, and details, if he were able to do so. Such conduct on the part of Government officers would have been generally denounced and promptly punished—had there been occasion. The entire statement is false."

At that time Judge Zane was on the bench, and William H. Dickson was United States District Attorney, he and his deputy, Mr. Varian, were in charge of the prosecutions in the district courts of the Territory. Had any such outrages been perpretated, as Whitney alleges were "referred to in public documents and newspapers of that period," during the time they were being committed, they would have come to the knowledge of Judge Zane, the other District Judges, and those prosecuting officers, and would, as every unbiased person who is acquainted with the high characters of those Judges, and prosecuting officers, knows that, such outrages would have been immediately stopped, and the perpetrators punished. I was in Salt Lake City at that time, and was a close observer of the current events— especially of the efforts being made to execute the Edmunds law of 1882. If any such outrages had been committed and noticed in the Journals and newspapers I would have heard of them, but I never did! I am not as modest as Mr. Varian and *possitively assert* that that assertion of Whitney's is one of his numerous malicious falsehoods—framed in his own disordered brain, to discredit the federal officers who faithfully executed the Edmunds law, and also to make it appear, that at that time, the Mormons were being persecuted.

---

## ANSWER TO WHITNEY'S NOTE.

He censures me for stating in my Reminiscenes, historical facts which he asserts, "all good citizens desire to have buried in oblivion." I am vindicated by Whitney himself in the following excerpt from his recent book. "The narration of the unpleasant facts recorded in this volume is not intended to stir up bitter memories or perpetuate senseless feuds and differences. Such events could never happen again. No present day person or class is held responsible for them, and by gones, should be treated as bygones. Nevertheless, happen they did—the page of history condemns them—and no record of those times would be complete if they were omitted. This is the reason for the reproduction here."

My Reminiscences contain many historical facts which are very unpleasant to Whitney and his class, "but happen they did" and no record of
the times of their occurrence "would be compete if they were omitted." Because they *were* omitted by Whitney and for the further reasons stated in
the preface to my Reminiscenes which follows. I stated them: "The glaring
false statements in Whitney's history of Utah, respecting the nature and effect of certain occurrences which have in a great part gone to make up the
history of Utah, together with his malignment of the motives of myself and
other Gentiles who in the past opposed the peculiar theocratic and anti-
American system established and maintained in Utah, while it was a Territory by the high priesthood of the 'Mormon' church, are the reasons for
the writing of these Reminiscences of my connection with the conflict
waged for many years between Mormons and Gentile.s * * * After the
careful scrutiny of Whitney's history, I deemed it due the men, many of
whom were Federal officials and few of whom are yet living and who have
been so wantonly besmirched by him to correct, at least, some of his erroneous assertions and covert insinuations."

It is insinuated in that note that my statements respecting the massacre is not reliable, because I came to the Territory after that crime was
committed, and that all I know about it was learned from others. It is
true that before the first trial of Lee, at which I assisted the United States
District Attorney, all that I had previously learned was from the unsworn
statements of others, and printed reports, but at that trial I learned the
facts from the testimony of the witnesses examined, several of whom participated in the massacre and revealed the crime in all of its horrible
details.

In my Reminiscences and in this review, I have asserted that certain
atrocious statements by Whitney are "as dishonest as they are despicable"—a derogatory expression which he himself without the slightest justification applied in his large history to the action of Judge McKean and myself. In every instance that I used that, and other derogatory expressions,
the text upon which they were predicated, justify their use. Those justifiable expressions are what caused Whitney to assert in that note that my
Reminiscences "abound in coarse abuse and venomous vituperation.'

He also asserts that "a special feature (of my Reminiscences) is the a
revival of the musty Munchausenism respecting "Danites" and that had
there been any Danites they would have disposed of me long ago." The
fact that I escaped assassination does not disapprove the former existence
of such an organization, for the following reasons. The assassination of
Brassfield and Doctor Robinson aroused the indignation of the Nation
and was bitterly denounced by the news papers.

In 1866, General Sherman, then commander of the Department which
included Utah, telegraphed Brigham Young that "he hoped to hear of no

25

more murders; that he was bound to give protection to all citizens and that murderers must be punished; that the country was full of tried and experienced soldiers which would be pleased to avenge any wrong committed against any American citizen." It is a significant fact that since the reception of that telegram, and the indignation expressed throughout the country that no similar assassinations have occurred in the Territory.

Those significant occurrences evidently, were not misunderstood by Brigham Young, and they put a stop to the activities of the Danites. Besides this—I had done nothing to displease the priesthood before draughting the Cullom bill in the latter part of the winter of 1869, and procuring its introduction in Congress, and until the discovery of the celebrated Emma mine, and the Union Pacific Railroad which reached Ogden, in March 1869, had brought many gentiles to the Territory who had joined the Liberal Party which had been formed to ablish the despotic reign of the theocratic priesthood which prevailed in the Territory, and to establish democratic rule instead thereof. Many of the members of that party were as actively striving to bring about that result as myself. My assassination therefore would have strengthened the Liberal cause and intensified the conflict. I am sure that none of the early apostates now living think that my assertion that there formerly existed in the Territory the Danite organization is Munchauserin.

William S. Gobde, who had apostatized from the "Mormon" church, and started what is known as the Gobdeite movement, had a house to rent. As I was desirous of renting one, I went with him to look at it. His bedroom window on the ground floor was guarded with strong iron bars. When he noticed that they attracted my attention, he said, "Those bars should recommend this house to you!" I replied—"they express more forcibly than words can do, that you have jeopardized your life by apostacy and that you are guarding against murderous assaults by the Danites." "Yes," said he, "that is the reason why I barred that window."

Whitney further asserts that my Reminiscences "are largely a rehash of stale anti-Mormon stories, based upon the testimony of apostates, jail birds, and self-confessed murderers."

Apostacy from the Mormon church does not discredit the *apostate by a long shot*.

It is true I gained much important information from Bill Hickman and a number of witnesses who testified that they participated in the Mountain Meadows Massacre, but was forced to participate by their church leaders and Militia officers.

Hickman was one of the chief Danites, and at the time he and his associate Danites committed their crimes, they were members, in good standing, of the Mormon Church.

I have on more than one occasion seen Porter Rockwell, a notorious

BILL HICKMAN

Danite and drunkard partake of the Sacrament with other members of the Mormon church.

None of the fifty-two Mormons who participated in the Massacre, except President Haight, John D. Lee and Klingensmith, were excommunicated or disfellowshiped by the church.

The testimony of criminals is entitled to credence when corroborated by creditable witnesses and circumstances.

My Reminiscences contain no doubtful facts.

Any unbiased person who reads the evidence and the quotations from the sermons of Orson Hyde and Brigham Young contained in the chapter of my Reminiscences on the subject of the Danites will not doubt that *such* an organization existed and was active in the earlier days of the Territory.

Whitney accuses me of being an "inveterate Mormon hater." He has cast on me, in his large history many other groundless aspersions. If this *one* were true, (he knows that it is not), I would have few, if any, Mormon friends. I have, however, at the present time the friendship and respect of a host of "Mormons." I am now, and ever have been, a friend of the masses of the people of the Territory, as shown by my political career.

Soon after settling in Salt Lake City, in 1865, I became firmly convinced that the irrepressible conflict caused by the prevalence of polygamy and the immunity which had been given to it by Territorial legislation and the un-American system established by the theocratic priesthood, could only be ended by congressional legislation, and that the interests of both the Gentiles and Mormons demanded its termination. Until this was done, I knew that the peace of the Territory would continue to be disturbed and the existing bitterness would as the strife continued, become more intense. To assist in the accomplishment of that desirable and salutary end, in 1869, I drew and procured its introduction in Congress, the Cullom Bill. Some Gentiles thought its provisions were too severe and opposed it. The evils it sought to eradicate were so radical, deep seatd, and strongly protected by the measures of the Territorial Legislature, and the influence of the priesthood that no provisions less stringent than the Cullom Bill would have had much if any, effect. The lapse of time, their enactment by Congress, and their enforcement has shown the wisdom and neccessity of those provisions. When George Q. Cannon and I were opposing candidates for the office of Territorial delegate to Congress, because I was advocating the Cullom Bill, he charged me with being an enemy of the Mormon community. I replied to that false charge, "My alien antagonist (George Q. Cannon) has stated to the Mormon community that I am their worst enemy. I assure the Mormon people I am not their enemy, but their friend. I claim no rights or privileges for myself, as an American citizen, which I do not accord to my fellow citizens. In common with the Liberal party I desire the establishment of the supremacy of law, freedom of thought, freedom of speech and freedom of action in Utah, as it exists in other States and Territories of the Union; the enactment of an election law which will insure honest elections and enable every man, however poor or dependant he may be, to go to the polls and freely deposit his ballot for whomsoever he may choose, without the fear of the infliction of ecclesiastical penalties; to establish a system under which every one may freely and fully exercise his own individuality, choose his own business, politcal and social relations, without the consent of any bigoted apostle, bishop or teacher. A system under which every man will have an equal chance with every other man—an equal chance by personal worth or dint of honest effort to attain the highest social, political, and business advancement without having to lay his manhood down at the foot of the priesthood, or kiss the great toe of some pretended prophet. A system under which the people, and not the church, may frely choose their own rulers, and religious bigotry cease to be an essential requisite to the attainment of office or business patronage. A system which will put an end to monopolies and church artistocracy, restore the natural laws of trade and social intercourse, and allow without question every man to manage his own affairs, hold the title to his own property, and run the course of life without weight upon his shoulders."

As the Mormon priesthood after the stringent legislation by Congress continued to be recalcitrant, and after the act of the Idaho Territorial legislature, which was introduced by Col. Wall of this city, disfranchising all polygamists, and all who belonged to or contributed to the support of any organization which sanctioned polygamy etc., was held to be vailid by the Supreme Court of the United States, I drew a similar bill and procured its introduction in the United States Senate by Senator Cullom, and by Mr. Stuble in the House. It is known as (The Cullom Stuble Bill.)

After it had been discussed by Governor West and my self before the committee on Territories of which Mr. Strubble was chairman, and had been reported favorably to the House, Frank J. Cannon, was sent from Washington to Salt Lake City by his father, George Q. Cannon, to inform President Woodruff that unless something was speedily done by the priesthood to stop polygamy, that that bill would pass.

That information forced President Woodruff to issue the manifesto, in which he recommended his followers to obey the laws of the land. The masses of the Mormon people at an annual Conference of the church, by ratifying the Manifesto, promised to comply with President Woodruff's request. This was all that the Nation had demanded, and all that I, in common with the Liberal party, had striven for more than twenty years to bring about.

28

The manifesto, its ratification by the people, and the promise of the priesthood to relinquish theocratic control of political affairs ended the conflict and paved the way for admission of the Territory into the Union, and brought about the glorious conditions which now exist. The only thing that the Mormons did in the long contest between the Liberal, and the Mormon Party to bring about that salutary change, was to yield to the just demands of the Government and the Liberal party, to come within the law—and sustain a Republican system instead of a theocratic one.

In that long contest, I openly, and above board honestly and untiringly strove to Americanize theocratic Utah; because I knew that that was indispensably necessary to stop the lamentable conflict and establish peace in the distracted Territory. No one can be more highly gratified at the glorious results which have followed, than I am myself. Nor do I believe that any persons except some fanatical polygamists like Whitney, regards me as a former enemy or at present, "a Mormon hater." Whitney has made so many false statements and aspersions of honorable and faithful officials, and other individuals, and has omitted to state so many historical facts, that it would take more time to treat of them, than I can devote to the subject. I have, however, disclosed enough of them to show that his histories are not entitled to credence, nor their author to respect. It is stated in the Deseret News that his recent history was written for use in the public schools. Its use there would be a glaring outrage which I hope will not be permitted.

Whitney also asserts that "the real and avowed author of the Cullom Bill was Robert N. Baskin, of Salt Lake City, that human mainspring of nearly every anti-Mormon movement that Utah has known." Yes, that is true, and I am very proud of the fact, because what I did in that regard materially assisted in stopping the former bitter conflict and brought about conditions different from the evil ones which formerly existed in Utah when it was a Territory, and which, it was evident to me, the interest of the Mormons and Gentiles, alike, demanded, but could not, possibly, be attained except by the establishment of American Republic rule in place of the Theocratic rule of the Mormon Priesthood.

The change to new conditions brought about is an unqualified blessing, and I again assert that no one can be more highly gratified on account of its occurance than I am myself.

Though not a prophet, I have been profitable to the masses of the Mormon people.

29